The Political Unconscious

The Political Unconscious

NARRATIVE AS A
SOCIALLY SYMBOLIC ACT

FREDRIC JAMESON

Cornell University Press

ITHACA, NEW YORK

First published 1981 by Cornell University Press
First printing, Cornell Paperbacks, 1982

Printed in the United States of America

Library of Congress Cataloging in Publication Data

Jameson, Fredric.
    The political unconscious.

    1. Includes index.
    1. Criticism. 2. Hermeneutics. 3. Narration (Rhetoric) 4. Communism and literature. 5. Fiction—History and criticism I. Title
PN81.J29   801'.95   80-21459
ISBN (cloth) 0-8014-1233-1
ISBN (paper) 0-8014-9222-X

Paperback printing   10

O ma belle guerrière!

Early versions of Chapters 2, 3, and 4 appeared in *New Literary History, Sub-stance, Social Science Information,* and *Nineteenth Century Fiction.*

CONTENTS

To imagine a language means to imagine a form of life.
—WITTGENSTEIN

Since the world expressed by the total system of concepts is the world as society represents it to itself, only society can furnish the generalized notions according to which such a world must be represented. . . . Since the universe exists only insofar as it is thought, and since it can be thought totally only by society itself, it takes its place within society, becomes an element of its inner life, and society may thus be seen as that total genus beyond which nothing else exists. The very concept of totality is but the abstract form of the concept of society: that whole which includes all things, that supreme class under which all other classes must be subsumed.
—DURKHEIM

PREFACE

Always historicize! This slogan—the one absolute and we may even say "transhistorical" imperative of all dialectical thought—will unsurprisingly turn out to be the moral of *The Political Unconscious* as well. But, as the traditional dialectic teaches us, the historicizing operation can follow two distinct paths, which only ultimately meet in the same place: the path of the object and the path of the subject, the historical origins of the things themselves and that more intangible historicity of the concepts and categories by which we attempt to understand those things. In the area of culture, which is the central field of the present book, we are thus confronted with a choice between study of the nature of the "objective" structures of a given cultural text (the historicity of its forms and of its content, the historical moment of emergence of its linguistic possibilities, the situation-specific function of its aesthetic) and something rather different which would instead foreground the interpretive categories or codes through which we read and receive the text in question. For better or for worse, it is this second path we have chosen to follow here: *The Political Unconscious* accordingly turns on the dynamics of the act of interpretation and presupposes, as its organizational fiction, that we never really confront a text immediately, in all its freshness as a thing-in-itself. Rather, texts come before us as the always-already-read; we apprehend them through sedimented layers of previous interpretations, or—if the text is brand-new—through the sedimented reading habits and categories developed by those inherited interpretive traditions. This presupposition then dictates the use of a method (which I have elsewhere termed the "metacommentary") according to which our object of study is less the text itself than the interpretations through which we attempt to confront and to appropriate it. Interpretation is here construed as an essentially allegorical act, which consists in rewriting a given text in terms of a particular interpretive master code. The identification of the latter will then lead to an evaluation of such codes or, in other words, of the "methods" or approaches current in American literary and cultural study today. Their juxtaposition with a dialectical or totalizing, properly Marxist ideal of understanding will be used to demonstrate the structural limitations of the other interpretive codes, and in particular to show the "local" ways in which they construct their objects of study and the "strategies of containment" whereby they are able to project the illusion that their readings are somehow complete and self-sufficient.

The retrospective illusion of the metacommentary thus has the advantage of allowing us to measure the yield and density of a properly Marxist interpretive act against those of other interpretive methods—the ethical, the psychoanalytic, the myth-critical, the semiotic, the structural, and the theological—against which it must compete in the "pluralism" of the intellectual marketplace today. I will here argue the priority of a Marxian interpretive framework in terms of semantic richness. Marxism cannot today be defended as a mere substitute for such other methods, which would then triumphalistically be consigned to the ashcan of history; the authority of such methods springs from their faithful consonance with this or that local law of a fragmented social life, this or that subsystem of a complex and mushrooming cultural superstructure. In the spirit of a more authentic dialectical tradition, Marxism is here conceived as that "untranscendable horizon" that subsumes such apparently antagonistic or incommensurable critical operations, assigning them an undoubted sectoral validity within itself, and thus at once canceling and preserving them.

Because of the peculiar focus of this retrospective organization, however, it may be worth warning the reader what *The Political Unconscious* is not. The reader should not, in the first place, expect anything like that exploratory projection of what a vital and emergent political culture should be and do which Raymond Williams has rightly proposed as the most urgent task of a Marxist cultural criticism. There are, of course, good and objective historical reasons why contemporary Marxism has been slow in rising to this challenge: the sorry history of Zhdanovite prescription in the arts is one, the fascination with modernisms and "revolutions" in form and language is another, as well as the coming of a whole new political and economic "world system," to which the older Marxist cultural paradigms only imperfectly apply. A provisional conclusion to the present work will spell out some of the challenges Marxist interpretation must anticipate in conceiving those new forms of collective thinking and collective culture which lie beyond the boundaries of our own world. The reader will there find an empty chair reserved for some as yet unrealized, collective, and decentered cultural production of the future, beyond realism and modernism alike.

If this book, then, fails to propose a political or revolutionary aesthetic, it is equally little concerned to raise once again the traditional issues of philosophical aesthetics: the nature and function of art, the specificity of poetic language and of the aesthetic experience, the theory of the beautiful, and so forth. Yet the very absence of such issues may serve as an implicit commentary on them; I have tried to maintain an essentially historicist perspective, in which our readings of the past are vitally dependent on our experience of the present, and in particular on the structural peculiarities of what is sometimes called the *société de consommation* (or the "disaccumulative" moment of late monopoly or consumer or multinational capitalism), what Guy Debord calls the society of the image or of the spectacle. The point is that in such a society, saturated with messages and with "aesthetic" experiences of all kinds, the issues of an older philosophical aesthetics themselves need to be radically historicized, and can be expected to be transformed beyond recognition in the process.

Nor, although literary history is here everywhere implied, should *The Political Unconscious* be taken as paradigmatic work in this discursive form or genre, which is today in crisis. Traditional literary history was a subset of representational narrative, a kind of narrative "realism" become as problematic as its principal exemplars in the history of the novel. The second chapter of the present book, which is concerned with genre criticism, will raise the theoretical problem of the status and possibility of such literary-historical narratives, which in *Marxism and Form* I termed "diachronic constructs"; the subsequent readings of Balzac, Gissing, and

Conrad project a diachronic framework—the construction of the bourgeois subject in emergent capitalism and its schizophrenic disintegration in our own time—which is, however, here never fully worked out. Of literary history today we may observe that its task is at one with that proposed by Louis Althusser for historiography in general: not to elaborate some achieved and lifelike simulacrum of its supposed object, but rather to "produce" the latter's "concept." This is indeed what the greatest modern or modernizing literary histories—such as Erich Auerbach's *Mimesis*—have sought to do in their critical practice, if not in their theory.

Is it at least possible, then, that the present work might be taken as an outline or projection of a new kind of critical method? Indeed it would seem to me perfectly appropriate to recast many of its findings in the form of a methodological handbook, but such a manual would have as its object *ideological analysis,* which remains, I believe, the appropriate designation for the critical "method" specific to Marxism. For reasons indicated above, this book is not that manual, which would necessarily settle its accounts with rival "methods" in a far more polemic spirit. Yet the unavoidably Hegelian tone of the retrospective framework of *The Political Unconscious* should not be taken to imply that such polemic interventions are not of the highest priority for Marxist cultural criticism. On the contrary, the latter must necessarily also be what Althusser has demanded of the practice of Marxist philosophy proper, namely "class struggle within theory."

For the non-Marxist reader, however, who may well feel that this book is quite polemic enough, I will add what should be unnecessary and underline my debt to the great pioneers of narrative analysis. My theoretical dialogue with them in these pages is not merely to be taken as yet another specimen of the negative critique of "false consciousness" (although it is that too, and, indeed, in the Conclusion I will deal explicitly with the problem of the proper uses of such critical gestures as demystification and ideological unmasking). It should meanwhile be obvious that no work in the area of narrative analysis can afford to ignore the fundamental contributions of Northrop Frye, the codification by A. J. Greimas of the whole Formalist and semiotic traditions, the heritage of a certain Christian hermeneutics, and above all, the indispensable explorations by Freud of the logic of dreams, and by Claude Lévi-Strauss of the logic of "primitive" storytelling and *pensée sauvage,* not to speak of the flawed yet monumental achievements in this area of the greatest Marxist philosopher of modern times, Georg Lukács. These divergent and unequal bodies of work are here interrogated and evaluated from the perspective of the specific critical and interpretive task of the present volume, namely to restructure the problematics of ideology, of the unconscious and of desire, of representation, of history, and of cultural production, around the all-informing process of *narrative,* which I take to be (here using the shorthand of philosophical idealism) the central function or *instance* of the human mind. This perspective may be reformulated in terms of the traditional dialectical code as the study of *Darstellung:* that untranslatable designation in which the current problems of *representation* productively intersect with the quite different ones of *presentation,* or of the essentially narrative and rhetorical movement of language and writing through time.

Last but not least, the reader may well be puzzled as to why a book ostensibly concerned with the interpretive act should devote so little attention to issues of interpretive validity, and to the criteria by which a given interpretation may be faulted or accredited. I happen to feel that no interpretation can be effectively disqualified on its own terms by a simple enumeration of inaccuracies or omissions, or by a list of unanswered questions. Interpretation is not an isolated act, but takes place within a Homeric battlefield, on which a host of interpretive options are either openly or implicitly in conflict. If the positivistic conception of philological accuracy be the only alternative, then I would much prefer to endorse the current provocative celebration of strong misreadings over weak ones. As the Chinese proverb has it, you use one ax handle to hew another: in our context, only another, stronger interpretation can overthrow and practically refute an interpretation already in place.

I would therefore be content to have the theoretical sections of this book judged and tested against its interpretive practice. But this very antithesis marks out the double standard and the formal dilemma of all cultural study today, from which *The Political Unconscious* is scarcely exempt: an uneasy struggle for priority between models and history, between theoretical speculation and textual analysis, in which the former seeks to transform the latter into so many mere examples, adduced to support its abstract propositions, while the latter continues insistently to imply that the theory itself was just so much methodological scaffolding, which can readily be dismantled once the serious business of practical criticism is under way. These two tendencies—theory and literary history—have so often in Western academic thought been felt to be rigorously incompatible that it is worth reminding the reader, in conclusion, of the existence of a third position which transcends both. That position is, of course, Marxism, which, in the form of the dialectic, affirms a primacy of theory which is at one and the same time a recognition of the primacy of History itself.

FREDRIC JAMESON

Killingworth, Connecticut

The Political Unconscious

/ 1

ON INTERPRETATION:
Literature as a
Socially Symbolic Act

This book will argue the priority of the political interpretation of literary texts. It conceives of the political perspective not as some supplementary method, not as an optional auxiliary to other interpretive methods current today—the psychoanalytic or the myth-critical, the stylistic, the ethical, the structural—but rather as the absolute horizon of all reading and all interpretation.

This is evidently a much more extreme position than the modest claim, surely acceptable to everyone, that certain texts have social and historical—sometimes even political—resonance. Traditional literary history has, of course, never prohibited the investigation of such topics as the Florentine political background in Dante, Milton's relationship to the schismatics, or Irish historical allusions in Joyce. I would argue, however, that such information—even where it is not recontained, as it is in most instances, by an idealistic conception of the history of ideas—does not yield interpretation as such, but rather at best its (indispensable) preconditions.

Today this properly antiquarian relationship to the cultural past has a dialectical counterpart which is ultimately no more satisfactory; I mean the tendency of much contemporary theory to rewrite selected texts from the past in terms of its own aesthetic and, in particular, in terms of a modernist (or more properly post-modernist) conception of language. I have shown elsewhere[1] the ways in which

---

1. See "The Ideology of the Text," *Salmagundi*, No. 31–32 (Fall 1975/Winter 1976), pp. 204–246.

such "ideologies of the text" construct a straw man or inessential term—variously called the "readerly" or the "realistic" or the "referential" text—over against which the essential term—the "writerly" or modernist or "open" text, *écriture* or textual productivity—is defined and with which it is seen as a decisive break. But Croce's great dictum that "all history is contemporary history" does not mean that all history is *our* contemporary history; and the problems begin when your epistemological break begins to displace itself in time according to your own current interests, so that Balzac may stand for unenlightened representationality when you are concerned to bring out everything that is "textual" and modern in Flaubert, but turns into something else when, with Roland Barthes in *S/Z*, you have decided to rewrite Balzac as Philippe Sollers, as sheer text and *écriture*.

This unacceptable option, or ideological double bind, between antiquarianism and modernizing "relevance" or projection demonstrates that the old dilemmas of historicism—and in particular, the question of the claims of monuments from distant and even archaic moments of the cultural past on a culturally different present[2]—do not go away just because we choose to ignore them. Our presupposition, in the analyses that follow, will be that only a genuine philosophy of history is capable of respecting the specificity and radical difference of the social and cultural past while disclosing the solidarity of its polemics and passions, its forms, structures, experiences, and struggles, with those of the present day.

But genuine philosophies of history have never been numerous, and few survive in workable, usable form in the contemporary world of consumer capitalism and the multinational system. We will have enough occasion, in the pages that follow, to emphasize the methodological interest of Christian historicism and the theological origins of the first great hermeneutic system in the Western tradition, to be permitted the additional observation that the Christian philosophy of history which emerges full blown in Augustine's *City of God* (A.D. 413–426) can no longer be particularly binding on us. As for the philosophy of history of a heroic bourgeoisie, its two principal variants—the vision of progress that

---

2. This is to my mind the relevance of a theory of "modes of production" for literary and cultural criticism; see, for further reflections on this issue and a more explicit statement on the "historicist" tendencies of Marxism, my "Marxism and Historicism," *New Literary History*, 11 (Autumn, 1979), 41–73.

emerges from the ideological struggles of the French Enlightenment, and that organic populism or nationalism which articulated the rather different historicity of the central and Eastern European peoples and which is generally associated with the name of Herder—are neither of them extinct, certainly, but are at the very least both discredited under their hegemonic embodiments in positivism and classical liberalism, and in nationalism respectively.

My position here is that only Marxism offers a philosophically coherent and ideologically compelling resolution to the dilemma of historicism evoked above. Only Marxism can give us an adequate account of the essential *mystery* of the cultural past, which, like Tiresias drinking the blood, is momentarily returned to life and warmth and allowed once more to speak, and to deliver its long-forgotten message in surroundings utterly alien to it. This mystery can be reenacted only if the human adventure is one; only thus—and not through the hobbies of antiquarianism or the projections of the modernists—can we glimpse the vital claims upon us of such long-dead issues as the seasonal alternation of the economy of a primitive tribe, the passionate disputes about the nature of the Trinity, the conflicting models of the *polis* or the universal Empire, or, apparently closer to us in time, the dusty parliamentary and journalistic polemics of the nineteenth-century nation states. These matters can recover their original urgency for us only if they are retold within the unity of a single great collective story; only if, in however disguised and symbolic a form, they are seen as sharing a single fundamental theme—for Marxism, the collective struggle to wrest a realm of Freedom from a realm of Necessity[3]; only if they are

3. "The realm of freedom actually begins only where labor which is in fact determined by necessity and mundane considerations ceases; thus in the very nature of things it lies beyond the sphere of actual material production. Just as the savage must wrestle with Nature to satisfy his wants, to maintain and reproduce life, so must civilized man, and he must do so in all social formations and under all possible modes of production. With his development this realm of physical necessity expands as a result of his wants; but, at the same time, the forces of production which satisfy these wants also increase. Freedom in this field can only consist in socialized men, the associated producers, rationally regulating their interchange with Nature, bringing it under their common control, instead of being ruled by it as by the blind forces of Nature; and achieving this with the least expenditure of energy and under conditions most favorable to, and worthy of, their human nature. But it nonetheless still remains a realm of necessity. Beyond it begins that development of human energy which is an end in itself, the true realm of freedom, which, however, can blossom forth only with this realm of necessity as its basis." Karl Marx, *Capital* (New York: International Publishers, 1977), III, 820.

grasped as vital episodes in a single vast unfinished plot: "The history of all hitherto existing society is the history of class struggles: freeman and slave, patrician and plebeian, lord and serf, guild-master and journeyman—in a word, oppressor and oppressed—stood in constant opposition to one another, carried on an uninterrupted, now hidden, now open fight, a fight that each time ended, either in a revolutionary reconstitution of society at large or in the common ruin of the contending classes."[4] It is in detecting the traces of that uninterrupted narrative, in restoring to the surface of the text the repressed and buried reality of this fundamental history, that the doctrine of a political unconscious finds its function and its necessity.

From this perspective the convenient working distinction between cultural texts that are social and political and those that are not becomes something worse than an error: namely, a symptom and a reinforcement of the reification and privatization of contemporary life. Such a distinction reconfirms that structural, experiential, and conceptual gap between the public and the private, between the social and the psychological, or the political and the poetic, between history or society and the "individual," which—the tendential law of social life under capitalism—maims our existence as individual subjects and paralyzes our thinking about time and change just as surely as it alienates us from our speech itself. To imagine that, sheltered from the omnipresence of history and the implacable influence of the social, there already exists a realm of freedom—whether it be that of the microscopic experience of words in a text or the ecstasies and intensities of the various private religions—is only to strengthen the grip of Necessity over all such blind zones in which the individual subject seeks refuge, in pursuit of a purely individual, a merely psychological, project of salvation. The only effective liberation from such constraint begins with the recognition that there is nothing that is not social and historical—indeed, that everything is "in the last analysis" political.

The assertion of a political unconscious proposes that we undertake just such a final analysis and explore the multiple paths that lead to the unmasking of cultural artifacts as socially symbolic acts.

4. Karl Marx and Friedrich Engels, "The Communist Manifesto," in K. Marx, *On Revolution*, ed. and trans. S. K. Padover (New York: McGraw-Hill, 1971), p. 81.

It projects a rival hermeneutic to those already enumerated; but it does so, as we shall see, not so much by repudiating their findings as by arguing its ultimate philosophical and methodological priority over more specialized interpretive codes whose insights are strategically limited as much by their own situational origins as by the narrow or local ways in which they construe or construct their objects of study.

Still, to describe the readings and analyses contained in the present work as so many *interpretations,* to present them as so many exhibits in the construction of a new *hermeneutic,* is already to announce a whole polemic program, which must necessarily come to terms with a critical and theoretical climate variously hostile to these slogans.[5] It is, for instance, increasingly clear that hermeneutic or interpretive activity has become one of the basic polemic targets of contemporary post-structuralism in France, which—powerfully buttressed by the authority of Nietzsche—has tended to identify such operations with historicism, and in particular with the dialectic and its valorization of absence and the negative, its assertion of the necessity and priority of totalizing thought. I will agree with this identification, with this description of the ideological affinities and implications of the ideal of the interpretive or hermeneutic act; but I will argue that the critique is misplaced.

Indeed, one of the most dramatic of such recent attacks on interpretation—*The Anti-Oedipus,* by Gilles Deleuze and Félix Guattari—quite properly takes as its object not Marxian, but rather Freudian, interpretation, which is characterized as a reduction and

5. See Michel Foucault, "The Retreat and Return of the Origin," chap. 9, part 6, of *The Order of Things* (New York: Vintage, 1973), pp. 328–335; as well as the same author's *Archeology of Knowledge,* trans. A. M. Sheridan Smith (New York: Pantheon, 1972), in particular, the introduction and the chapter on the "history of ideas"; Jacques Derrida, "The Exorbitant. Question of Method," in *Of Grammatology,* trans. Gayatri Spivak (Baltimore: Johns Hopkins University Press, 1976), pp. 157–164; as well as his "Hors livre," in *La Dissémination* (Paris: Seuil, 1972), pp. 9–67; Jean Baudrillard, "Vers une critique de l'économie politique du signe," in *Pour une critique de l'économie politique du signe* (Paris: Gallimard, 1972); along with his *Mirror of Production,* trans. Mark Poster (St. Louis: Telos, 1975); Gilles Deleuze and Félix Guattari, *The Anti-Oedipus,* trans. Robert Hurley, Mark Seem, and Helen R. Lane (New York: Viking, 1977), pp. 25–28, 109–113, 305–308; Jean-François Lyotard, *Economie libidinale* (Paris: Minuit, 1974), especially "Le Désir nommé Marx," pp. 117–188; and last but not least, Louis Althusser, et al., *Reading Capital,* trans. Ben Brewster (London: New Left Books, 1970), especially "Marx's Immense Theoretical Revolution," pp. 182–193.

a rewriting of the whole rich and random multiple realities of concrete everyday experience into the contained, strategically prelimited terms of the family narrative—whether this be seen as myth, Greek tragedy, "family romance," or even the Lacanian structural version of the Oedipus complex. What is denounced is therefore a system of allegorical interpretation in which the data of one narrative line are radically impoverished by their rewriting according to the paradigm of another narrative, which is taken as the former's master code or Ur-narrative and proposed as the ultimate hidden or unconscious *meaning* of the first one. The thrust of the argument of the *Anti-Oedipus* is, to be sure, very much in the spirit of the present work, for the concern of its authors is to reassert the specificity of the political content of everyday life and of individual fantasy-experience and to reclaim it from that reduction to the merely subjective and to the status of psychological projection which is even more characteristic of American cultural and ideological life today than it is of a still politicized France. My point in mentioning this example is to observe that the repudiation of an older interpretive system—Freudian rewriting, overhastily assimilated to hermeneutics in general and as such—is in *The Anti-Oedipus* coupled with the projection of a whole new method for the reading of texts:

> The unconscious poses no problem of meaning, solely problems of use. The question posed by desire is not "What does it mean?" but rather "*How does it work?*" . . . [The unconscious] represents nothing, but it produces. It means nothing, but it works. Desire makes its entry with the general collapse of the question "What does it mean?" No one has been able to pose the problem of language except to the extent that linguists and logicians have first eliminated meaning; and the greatest force of language was only discovered once a *work* was viewed as a machine, producing certain effects, amenable to a certain use. Malcolm Lowry says of his work: it's anything you want it to be, so long as it works—"It works too, believe me, as I have found out"—a machinery. But on condition that meaning be nothing other than use, that it become a firm principle only if we have at our disposal *immanent criteria* capable of determining the legitimate uses, as opposed to the illegitimate ones that relate use instead to a hypothetical meaning and re-establish a kind of transcendence.[6]

6. Deleuze/Guattari, *Anti-Oedipus*, p. 109.

From our present standpoint, however, the ideal of an immanent analysis of the text, of a dismantling or deconstruction of its parts and a description of its functioning and malfunctioning, amounts less to a wholesale nullification of all interpretive activity than to a demand for the construction of some new and more adequate, immanent or antitranscendent hermeneutic model, which it will be the task of the following pages to propose.[7]

I

This Nietzschean and antiinterpretive current is, however, not without its equivalent in a certain contemporary Marxism: the enterprise of constructing a properly Marxist hermeneutic must necessarily confront the powerful objections to traditional models of interpretation raised by the influential school of so-called structural or Althusserian Marxism.[8] Althusser's own position on the subject is spelled out in his theory of the three historical forms of causality (or "effectivity"), in a document so significant for contemporary theory that it is worth quoting at some length:

> The epistemological problem posed by Marx's radical modification of Political Economy can be expressed as follows: by means of what concept is it possible to think the new type of determination which has just been identified as the determination of the phenomena of a given region by the structure of that region? ... In other words, how is it possible to define the concept of a structural causality? ...
> Very schematically, we can say that classical philosophy ... had

---

7. From the present perspective, in other words, Deleuze and Guattari's proposal for an *anti*interpretive method (which they call schizo-analysis) can equally well be grasped as a new hermeneutic in its own right. It is striking and noteworthy that most of the antiinterpretive positions enumerated in note 5 above have felt the need to project new "methods" of this kind: thus, the archeology of knowledge, but also, more recently, the "political technology of the body" (Foucault), "grammatology" and deconstruction (Derrida), "symbolic exchange" (Baudrillard), libidinal economy (Lyotard), and "sémanalyse" (Julia Kristeva).

8. The issues raised in this section, unavoidable ones for any serious discussion of the nature of interpretation, are also unavoidably technical, involving a terminology and a "problematic" which largely transcends literary criticism. As they will inevitably strike certain readers as scholastic exercises within the philosophically alien tradition of Marxism, such readers may be advised to pass at once to the next section (below, p. 58), in which we return to a discussion of the various current schools of literary criticism proper. It should be added that not all the writers described as "Althusserians," at the level of historical generality which is ours in the present section, would accept that characterization.

two and only two systems of concepts with which to think effectivity. The mechanistic system, Cartesian in origin, which reduced causality to a *transitive* and analytical effectivity, could not be made to think the effectivity of a whole on its elements, except at the cost of extraordinary distortions (such as those in Descartes' "psychology" and biology). But a second system was available, one conceived precisely in order to deal with the effectivity of a whole on its elements: the Leibnitzian concept of *expression*. This is the model that dominates all Hegel's thought. But it presupposes in principle that the whole in question be reducible to an *inner essence*, of which the elements of the whole are then no more than the phenomenal forms of expression, the inner principle of the essence being present at each point in the whole, such that at each moment it is possible to write the immediately adequate equation: such and such an element (economic, political, legal, literary, religious, etc., in Hegel) = the inner essence of the whole. Here was a model which made it possible to think the effectivity of the whole on each of its elements, but if this category—inner essence/outer phenomenon—was to be applicable everywhere and at every moment to each of the phenomena arising in the totality in question, it presupposed that the whole had a certain nature, precisely the nature of a "spiritual" whole in which each element was expressive of the entire totality as a "pars totalis". In other words, Leibnitz and Hegel did have a category for the effectivity of the whole on its elements or parts, but on the absolute condition that the whole was not a structure. . . .

[The third concept of effectivity, that of structural causality,] can be entirely summed up in the concept of "Darstellung", the key epistemological concept of the whole Marxist theory of value, the concept whose object is precisely to designate the mode of *presence* of the structure in its *effects*, and therefore to designate structural causality itself. . . . The structure is not an essence outside the economic phenomena which comes and alters their aspect, forms and relations and which is effective on them as an absent cause, absent because it is outside them. The absence of the cause in the structure's "metonymic causality" on its effects is not the fault of the exteriority of the structure with respect to the economic phenomena; on the contrary, it is the very form of the interiority of the structure, as a structure, in its effects. This implies therefore that the effects are not outside the structure, are not a pre-existing object, element or space in which the structure arrives to imprint its mark: on the contrary, it implies that the structure is immanent in its effects, a cause immanent in its effects in the Spinozist sense of the term, that the whole existence of the structure consists of its effects, in short, that the structure, which is merely a specific combination of its peculiar elements, is nothing outside its effects.[9]

Althusser's first type of effectivity, that of mechanistic or mechanical causality, exemplified in the billiard-ball model of cause and effect, has long been a familiar exhibit in the history of ideas and in particular in the history of science, where it is associated with the Galilean and Newtonian world-view, and is assumed to have been outmoded by the indeterminacy principle of modern physics. This type of causality is generally the target of the loose contemporary consensus on the "outmoded" character of the category of causality as such; yet even this type of causal analysis is by no means everywhere discredited in cultural studies today. Its continuing influence may be observed, for instance, in that technological determinism of which MacLuhanism remains the most interesting contemporary expression, but of which certain more properly Marxist studies like Walter Benjamin's ambiguous *Baudelaire* are also variants. Indeed, the Marxist tradition includes models which have so often been denounced as mechanical or mechanistic— most notably the familiar (or notorious) concept of "base" (infrastructure and "superstructure"— for it to have no small stake in the reexamination of this type of causality.

I would want to argue that the category of mechanical effectivity retains a purely local validity in cultural analysis where it can be shown that billiard-ball causality remains one of the (nonsynchronous) laws of our particular fallen social reality. It does little good, in other words, to banish "extrinsic" categories from our thinking, when the latter continue to have a hold on the objective realities about which we plan to think. There seems, for instance, to have been an unquestionable causal relationship between the admittedly extrinsic fact of the crisis in late nineteenth-century publishing, during which the dominant three-decker lending library novel was replaced by a cheaper one-volume format, and the modification of the "inner form" of the novel itself.[10] The resultant transformation of the novelistic production of a writer such as Gissing must thus necessarily be mystified by attempts of literary scholars to interpret

9. Althusser et al., *Reading Capital*, pp. 186–189.

10. Frank Kermode, "Buyers' Market," *New York Review of Books*, October 31, 1974, p. 3.

the new form in terms of personal evolution or of the internal dynamics of purely formal change. That a material and contingent "accident" should leave its trace as a formal "break" and "cause" modification in Gissing's narrative categories as well as in the very "structure of feeling" of his novels—this is no doubt a scandalous assertion. Yet what is scandalous is not this way of thinking about a given formal change, but rather the objective event itself, the very nature of cultural change in a world in which separation of use value from exchange value generates discontinuities of precisely this "scandalous" and extrinsic type, rifts and actions at distance which cannot ultimately be grasped "from the inside" or phenomenologically, but which must be reconstructed as symptoms whose cause is of another order of phenomenon from its effects. Mechanical causality is thus less a concept which might be evaluated on its own terms, than one of the various laws and subsystems of our peculiarly reified social and cultural life. Nor is its occasional experience without benefit for the cultural critic, for whom the scandal of the extrinsic comes as a salutary reminder of the ultimately material base of cultural production, and of the "determination of consciousness by social being."[11]

It must therefore be objected, to Althusser's ideological analysis of the "concept" of mechanical causality, that this unsatisfactory category is not merely a form of false consciousness or error, but also a symptom of objective contradictions that are still with us. This said, it is also clear that it is the second form of efficacity Althusser enumerates, so-called "expressive causality," which is the polemic heart of his argument as well as the more vital issue (and burning temptation) in cultural criticism today. The counter-slogan of "totalization" cannot be the immediate response to Althusser's critique of "expressive causality," if for no other reason that totalization is itself numbered among the approaches stigmatized by this term, which range from the various conceptions of the world-views or period styles of a given historical moment (Taine, Riegl, Spengler, Goldmann) all the way to contemporary structural or post-

11. The problem of mechanical causality imposes itself most vividly, perhaps, in film criticism, as a tension between the study of technological innovation and that of "intrinsically" filmic languages; but it can be expected to be an issue in most other areas of mass culture as well.

structural efforts at modeling the dominant episteme or sign-system of this or that historical period, as in Foucault, Deleuze-Guattari, Yurii Lotman, or the theorists of consumer society (most notably Jean Baudrillard). Such a catalogue suggests, not merely that Althusser's critique may be construed much more widely than the work of Hegel, which is its central exhibit (and may find application in thinkers who are expressly non- or anti-Hegelian), but also that what is at stake here would seem significantly related to problems of cultural periodization in general and to that of the category of a historical "period" in particular. However, the more properly Marxist models of "expressive causality" denounced by Althusser are strictured from a rather different perspective as involving the practice of mediation and as dramatizing still relatively idealistic conceptions of both individual and collective praxis: we will return to these two reproaches later in the present chapter.

As for periodization, its practice is clearly enveloped by that basic Althusserian conceptual target designated as "historicism";[12] and it can be admitted that any rewarding use of the notion of a historical or cultural period tends in spite of itself to give the impression of a facile totalization, a seamless web of phenomena each of which, in its own way, "expresses" some unified inner truth—a world-view or a period style or a set of structural categories which marks the whole length and breadth of the "period" in question. Yet such an impression is fatally reductive, in the sense in which we have seen Deleuze and Guattari denounce the unifying operation of the Freudian familial reduction. On its own terms, therefore, the Althusserian critique is quite unanswerable, which demonstrates the way in which the construction of a historical totality necessarily involves

12. Whatever the theoretical content of the debate on historicism, it should be understood that this term is *also* a political code word in the Althusserian corpus, and designates various Marxist theories of so-called "stages" in the transition to socialism: these range from Lenin's theory of imperialism and Stalin's distinctions between "socialism" and "communism" all the way to Kautsky and social democratic schemas of historical development. On this level, then, the polemic against "historicism" is part of the more general Althusserian offensive within the French Communist Party against Stalinism, and involves very real practical, political, and strategic consequences. (The classical structuralist and semiotic arguments against historicism are to be found in the concluding chapter ["History and Dialectic"] of Claude Lévi-Strauss's *The Savage Mind* (Chicago: University of Chicago Press, 1966), and A. J. Greimas, "Structure et histoire," in *Du sens* [Paris: Seuil, 1970]).

the isolation and the privileging of one of the elements *within* that totality (a kind of thought habit, a predilection for specific forms, a certain type of belief, a "characteristic" political structure or form of domination) such that the element in question becomes a master code or "inner essence" capable of explicating the other elements or features of the "whole" in question. Such a theme or "inner essence" can thus be seen as the implicit or explicit answer to the now impermissible interpretive question, "what does it mean?" (The practice of "mediation" is then, as we shall see, understood as a more seemingly dialectical but no less idealistic mechanism for moving or modulating from one level or feature of the whole to another: a mechanism which, however, as in bourgeois periodization, has no less the effect of unifying a whole social field around a theme or an idea.)

Above and beyond the problem of periodization and its categories, which are certainly in crisis today, but which would seem to be as indispensable as they are unsatisfactory for any kind of work in cultural study, the larger issue is that of the representation of History itself. There is in other words a synchronic version of the problem: that of the status of an individual "period" in which everything becomes so seamlessly interrelated that we confront either a total system or an idealistic "concept" of a period; and a diachronic one, in which history is seen in some "linear" way as the succession of such periods, stages, or moments. I believe that this second problem is the prior one, and that individual period formulations always secretly imply or project narratives or "stories"—narrative representations—of the historical sequence in which such individual periods take their place and from which they derive their significance.

The fullest form of what Althusser calls "expressive causality" (and of what he calls "historicism") will thus prove to be a vast interpretive allegory in which a sequence of historical events or texts and artifacts is rewritten in terms of some deeper, underlying, and more "fundamental" narrative, of a hidden master narrative which is the allegorical key or figural content of the first sequence of empirical materials. This kind of allegorical master narrative would then include providential histories (such as those of Hegel or Marx), catastrophic visions of history (such as that of Spengler), and cyclical or Viconian visions of history alike. I read the Althusserian dictum, "History is a process without a *telos* or a subject,"[13] in this spirit, as a repudiation of such master narratives and their twin categories of narrative closure (*telos*) and of character (subject of history). As such historical allegories are also often characterized as being "theological" and as we will have occasion shortly to return to that striking and elaborate hermeneutic which is the patristic and medieval system of the four levels of scripture, it may be useful to illustrate the structure of the master narrative with reference to that now archaic and cumbersome allegorical framework in which its operation is most clearly visible.

The medieval system may perhaps most conveniently be approached through its practical function in late antiquity, its ideological mission as a strategy for assimilating the Old Testament to the New, for rewriting the Jewish textual and cultural heritage in a form usable for Gentiles. The originality of the new allegorical system may be judged by its insistence on preserving the literality of the original texts: it is not here a matter of dissolving them into mere symbolism, as a rationalistic Hellenism did when, confronted with the archaic and polytheistic letter of the Homeric epic, it rewrote the latter in terms of the struggle of the physical elements with one another, or of the battle of vices and virtues.[14] On the contrary, the Old Testament is here taken as historical fact. At the same time, its availability as a system of figures, above and beyond this literal historical reference, is grounded in the conception of history itself as God's book, which we may study and gloss for signs and traces of the prophetic message the Author is supposed to have inscribed within it.

So it is that the life of Christ, the text of the New Testament, which comes as the fulfillment of the hidden prophecies and annunciatory signs of the Old, constitutes a second, properly allegorical level, in terms of which the latter may be rewritten. Allegory is here the opening up of the text to multiple meanings, to successive rewritings and overwritings which are generated as so many levels

13. *Réponse à John Lewis* (Paris: Maspéro, 1973), pp. 91–98.
14. I here draw heavily on Henri de Lubac, *Exégèse mediévale* (Paris: Aubier, 1959–1964, 4 vols.); for the distinction between a tripartite and a quadripartite system of levels, see in particular Vol. I, pp. 139–169, and also pp. 200–207.

and as so many supplementary interpretations. So the interpretation of a particular Old Testament passage in terms of the life of Christ—a familiar, even hackneyed, illustration is the rewriting of the bondage of the people of Israel in Egypt as the descent of Christ into hell after his death on the cross[15]—comes less as a technique for closing the text off and for repressing aleatory or aberrant readings and senses, than as a mechanism for preparing such a text for further ideological investment, if we take the term *ideology* here in Althusser's sense as a representational structure which allows the individual subject to conceive or imagine his or her lived relationship to transpersonal realities such as the social structure or the collective logic of History.

In the present instance, the movement is from a particular collective history—that of the people of Israel, or in other words a history culturally alien to the Mediterranean and Germanic clientele of early Christianity—to the destiny of a particular individual: the transindividual dimensions of the first narrative are then drastically "reduced" to the second, purely biographical narrative, the life of Christ, and such reduction is not without its analogies with that attributed by Deleuze and Guattari to the repressive simplification the Freudian family triangle brings to the lived richness of daily life. But the results are quite different: in the case of the four levels, it is precisely this reduction of the alien collective to the valorized individual biography which then permits the generation of two further interpretive levels, and it is precisely in these that the individual believer is able to "insert" himself or herself (to use the Althusserian formula), it is precisely by way of the *moral* and *anagogical* interpretations that the textual apparatus is transformed into a "libidinal apparatus," a machinery for ideological investment. On the third or moral level, for example, the literal and historical fact of the bondage of the people of Israel in Egypt can be rewritten as the thralldom of the believer-to-be to sin and to the preoccupations of this world ("the fleshpots of Egypt"): a bondage from which personal conversion will release him or her (an event figured doubly as the deliverance from Egypt and the resurrection of Christ). But this third level of the individual soul is clearly insufficient by itself, and

15. For further examples of such allegorical topoi, see Jean Daniélou, *From Shadows to Reality: Studies in the Biblical Typology of the Fathers*, trans. Wulston Hibberd (London: Burns & Oates, 1960).

at once generates the fourth or anagogical sense, in which the text undergoes its ultimate rewriting in terms of the destiny of the human race as a whole, Egypt then coming to prefigure that long purgatorial suffering of earthly history from which the second coming of Christ and the Last Judgment come as the final release. The historical or collective dimension is thus attained once again, by way of the detour of the sacrifice of Christ and the drama of the individual believer; but from the story of a particular earthly people it has been transformed into universal history and the destiny of humankind as a whole—precisely the functional and ideological transformation which the system of the four levels was designed to achieve in the first place:

Anagogical	political reading (collective "meaning" of history)
Moral	psychological reading (individual subject)
Allegorical	allegorical key or interpretive code
Literal	historical or textual referent

The system of the four levels or senses is particularly suggestive in the solution it provides for an interpretive dilemma which in a privatized world we must live far more intensely than did its Alexandrian and medieval recipients: namely that incommensurability referred to above between the private and the public, the psychological and the social, the poetic and the political. While the relationship the Christian scheme projects between anagogical and moral is not available to us today, the closure of the scheme as a whole is instructive, particularly in the ideological climate of a contemporary American "pluralism," with its unexamined valorization of the open ("freedom") versus its inevitable binary opposition, the closed ("totalitarianism"). Pluralism means one thing when it stands for the coexistence of methods and interpretations in the intellectual and academic marketplace, but quite another when it is taken as a proposition about the infinity of possible meanings and methods and their ultimate equivalence with and substitutability for one another. As a matter of practical criticism, it must be clear to anyone who has experimented with various approaches to a given text that the mind is not content until it puts some order in these findings and invents a hierarchical relationship among its various interpretations. I suspect, indeed, that there are only a finite number of interpretive possibilities in any given textual situation, and that the program to which the various contemporary ideologies of pluralism are most passionately attached is a largely negative one: namely to forestall that systematic articulation and totalization of interpretive results which can only lead to embarrassing questions about the relationship between them and in particular the place of history and the ultimate ground of narrative and textual production. At any rate, it was clear to the medieval theorists that their four levels constituted a methodological upper limit and a virtual exhaustion of interpretive possibilities.[16]

Taken at its most wide-ranging, then, the Althusserian critique of expressive causality may be seen to strike beyond its immediate target in so-called Hegelian idealism, at the implicit or explicit theodicy that must emerge from interpretations that assimilate levels to one another and affirm their ultimate identity. Yet Althusser's work cannot be properly evaluated unless it is understood that it has—like so many philosophical systems before it—an esoteric and an exoteric sense, and addresses two distinct publics at once. We will return later to the coding system by where an ostensibly abstract philosophical proposition includes a specific polemic position taken on issues within Marxism itself: in the present instance, the more general attack on allegorical master codes also implies a specific critique of the vulgar Marxist theory of levels, whose conception of base and superstructure, with the related notion of the "ultimately determining instance" of the economic, can be shown, when diagrammed in the following way, to have some deeper kinship with the allegorical systems described above:

	CULTURE
Superstructures	IDEOLOGY (philosophy, religion, etc.)
	THE LEGAL SYSTEM
	POLITICAL SUPERSTRUCTURES AND THE STATE

Base or infrastructure	THE ECONOMIC, OR MODE OF PRODUCTION	{ RELATIONS OF PRODUCTION (classes)
		FORCES OF PRODUCTION (technology, ecology, population)

16. Thus, even the mystically tempting alternative of *seven* levels of meaning was found in practice to reduce itself to mere variations on the original four: e.g., the interpretive identification of the people of Israel with the church—the allegorical rewriting of the Old Testament in terms of church history—was judged in practice to

That this orthodox schema is still essentially an allegorical one becomes clear whenever it is prolonged into interpretation. Here Lukács' essays on realism may serve as a central example of the way in which the cultural text is taken as an essentially allegorical model of society as a whole, its tokens and elements, such as the literary "character," being read as "typifications" of elements on other levels, and in particular as figures for the various social classes and class fractions. But in other kinds of analysis as well—the orthodox "ideological analyses" of philosophical positions or legal measures, or the demystification of the structure of the state in class terms—a movement of allegorical decipherment takes place in which the conception of class interest supplies the functional or link between a superstructural symptom or category and its "ultimately determining" reality in the base.

What our preceding discussion of the medieval levels suggests, however, is that this is by no means the whole story, and that to grasp the full degree to which this schema projects an essentially allegorical operation, we must enlarge its master code or allegorical key to the point at which the latter becomes a master narrative in its own right; and this point is reached when we become aware that any individual mode of production projects and implies a whole sequence of such modes of production—from primitive communism to capitalism and communism proper—which constitute the narrative of some properly Marxian "philosophy of history." Yet this is a paradoxical discovery: for the very work of the Althusserian school, which has so effectively discredited the Marxian versions of a properly teleological history, is also that which has done most, in our time, to restore the problematic of the mode of production as the central organizing category of Marxism.[17]

---

be a variant on the second or allegorical level, insofar as the life of Christ was also, secondarily, an allegory of the history of the church (De Lubac, Vol. II, pp. 501–502).

17. See in particular Etienne Balibar, "The Basic Concepts of Historical Materialism," in *Reading Capital*, pp. 199–308; Emmanuel Terray, *Marxism and "Primitive" Societies*, trans. Mary Klopper (New York: Monthly Review, 1972); and Barry Hindess and Paul Hirst, *Pre-capitalist Modes of Production* (London: Routledge & Kegan Paul, 1975). The classical Marxist discussions are to be found in Karl Marx, *Grundrisse*, trans. Martin Nicolaus (Harmondsworth: Penguin, 1973), pp. 471–514; and Friedrich Engels, *The Origin of the Family, Private Property, and the State* (Moscow: Progress, 1968). I discuss the relevance of the concept of mode of production for cultural study in my forthcoming *Poetics of Social Forms*.

The conception of the political unconscious outlined in this book is an attempt to cut through this particular dilemma by relocating it within the object. A minimal defense of the procedures of expressive causality will then take much the same form as did our previous discussion of mechanical causality: we can view both as local laws within our historical reality. The idea is, in other words, that if interpretation in terms of expressive causality or of allegorical master narratives remains a constant temptation, this is because such master narratives have inscribed themselves in the texts as well as in our thinking about them; such allegorical narrative signifieds are a persistent dimension of literary and cultural texts precisely because they reflect a fundamental dimension of our collective thinking and our collective fantasies about history and reality. To such a dimension correspond not only those cobwebs of topical allusion which the ahistorical and formalizing reader attempts desperately to brush away—that dry and intolerable chitinous murmur of footnotes reminding us of the implied references to long-dead contemporary events and political situations in Milton or Swift, in Spenser or Hawthorne; if the modern reader is bored or scandalized by the roots such texts send down into the contingent circumstances of their own historical time, this is surely testimony as to his resistance to his own political unconscious and to his denial (in the United States, the denial of a whole generation) of the reading and the writing of the text of history within himself. An exhibit like Balzac's *Vieille Fille* then implies a significant mutation in such political allegory in the literature of the capitalist period, and show the virtual assimilation of the footnote-subtext of an older web of political allusion into the mechanism of narrative, where the meditation on social classes and political regimes becomes the very *pensée sauvage* of a whole narrative production (see below, Chapter 3). But if this is where the study of "expressive causality" leads, then to switch it off at the source entails the virtual repression of the text of history and the political unconscious in our own cultural and practical experience, just at the moment when increasing privatization has made that dimension so faint as to be virtually inaudible.

This analysis of the function of expressive causality suggests a provisional qualification of Althusser's antiteleological formula for history (neither a subject nor a telos), based as it is on Lacan's notion of the Real as that which "resists symbolization absolutely"[18] and on Spinoza's idea of the "absent cause." The sweeping negativity of the Althusserian formula is misleading insofar as it can readily be assimilated to the polemic themes of a host of contemporary post-structuralisms and post-Marxisms, for which History, in the bad sense—the reference to a "context" or a "ground," an external real world of some kind, the reference, in other words, to the much maligned "referent" itself—is simply one more text among others, something found in history manuals and that chronological presentation of historical sequences so often called "linear history." What Althusser's own insistence on history as an absent cause makes clear, but what is missing from the formula as it is canonically worded, is that he does not at all draw the fashionable conclusion that because history is a text, the "referent" does not exist. We would therefore propose the following revised formulation: that history is *not* a text, not a narrative, master or otherwise, but that, as an absent cause, it is inaccessible to us except in textual form, and that our approach to it and to the Real itself necessarily passes through its prior textualization, its narrativization in the political unconscious.

Such a reformulation acknowledges the powerful Althusserian objections to expressive causality and to interpretation generally, while making a local place for such operations. What we have not yet considered is whether Althusser's position is anything more than a negative and second-degree critical one, a kind of correction of the ever-possible illusions of the Hegelian code, or whether his concept of a properly "structural causality" has content in its own right and implies specific interpretive possibilities distinct from those already outlined. We may perhaps best convey the originality of his model by restructuring the traditional Marxist conception of levels (represented above) in a different way (see following page). This diagram will have served its purpose if it immediately brings out one striking and fundamental difference between Althusser's conception of "levels" and that of traditional Marxism: where the

18. Jacques Lacan, *Le Séminaire, Livre I: Les Ecrits techniques de Freud* (Paris: Seuil, 1975), p. 80; and compare this other remark, on Newton's laws: "Il y a des formules qu'on n'imagine pas; au moins pour un temps, elles font assemblée avec le réel" ("Radiophonie," *Scilicet*, No. 2–3 [1970], p. 75).

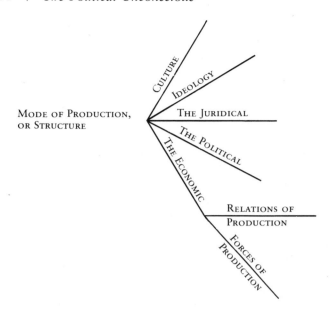

MODE OF PRODUCTION, OR STRUCTURE

CULTURE

IDEOLOGY

THE JURIDICAL

THE POLITICAL

THE ECONOMIC

RELATIONS OF PRODUCTION

FORCES OF PRODUCTION

latter either conceived, or in the absence of rigorous conceptualization perpetuated the impression, of the "ultimately determining instance" or mode of production as the narrowly economic—that is, as one level within the social system which, however, "determines" the others—the Althusserian conception of mode of production identifies this concept with the structure as a whole. For Althusser, then, the more narrowly economic—the forces of production, the labor process, technical development, or relations of production, such as the functional interrelation of social classes—is, however privileged, not identical with the mode of production as a whole, which assigns this narrowly "economic" level its particular function and efficiency as it does all the others. If therefore one wishes to characterize Althusser's Marxism as a structuralism, one must complete the characterization with the essential proviso that it is a structuralism for which only *one* structure exists: namely the mode of production itself, or the synchronic system of social relations as a whole. This is the sense in which this "structure" is an absent cause, since it is nowhere empirically present as an element, it is not a part of the whole or one of the levels, but rather the entire system of *relationships* among those levels.

This conception of structure should make it possible to understand the otherwise incomprehensible prestige and influence of the Althusserian revolution—which has produced powerful and challenging oppositional currents in a host of disciplines, from philosophy proper to political science, anthropology, legal studies, economics, and cultural studies—as well as to restore its political content, easily lost in translation and disguised by the coded fashion in which its battles have been fought. The insistence on the "semiautonomy" of these various levels—which can so easily strike the unwary as a scholastic quibble, but which we have now been able to grasp as the correlative of the attack on Hegelian expressive causality in which all those levels are somehow "the same" and so many expressions and modulations of one another—may now be understood as a coded battle waged within the framework of the French Communist Party against Stalinism. As paradoxical as it may seem, therefore, "Hegel" here is a secret code word for Stalin (just as in Lukács' work, "naturalism" is a code word for "socialist realism"); Stalin's "expressive causality" can be detected, to take one example, in the productionist ideology of Soviet Marxism, as an insistence on the primacy of the forces of production. In other words, if all the levels are "expressively" the same, then the infrastructural change in forces of production—nationalization and the elimination of private property relations, as well as industrialization and modernization—will be enough "more or less rapidly to transform the whole superstructure," and cultural revolution is unnecessary, as is the collective attempt to invent new forms of the labor process.[19] Another crucial example can be found in the theory of the state: if the state is a mere epiphenomenon of the economy, then the repressive apparatus of certain socialist revolutions needs no par-

19. See, for a discussion of the ideological consequences of "expressive causality" in the Stalin period, Charles Bettelheim, *Class Struggles in the USSR*, Vol. II, trans. Brian Pearce (New York: Monthly Review, 1978), esp. pp. 500–566. Commenting on "the affirmation made in [Stalin's] *Dialectical and Historical Materialism* that changes in production '*always* begin with changes and developments in the productive forces, and in the first place, with changes and development of the *instruments of production*,'" Bettelheim observes that such formulations "make the totality of social relations and practices the 'expression' of the 'productive forces.' 'Society' is here presented as an 'expressive totality,' which is not contradictory, and the changes in which seem to depend upon 'development in production.' The central role played by the revolutionary struggle of the masses in the process of social change does not appear here" (Bettelheim, pp. 516, 514).

ticular attention and can be expected to begin to "wither" when the appropriate stage of productivity is reached. The current Marxist emphasis on the "semi-autonomy" of the state and its apparatuses, which we owe to the Althusserians, is intended to cast the gravest doubts on these interpretations of the "text" of the state (seen as simply replicating other levels), and to encourage attention both to the semi-autonomous dynamics of bureaucracy and the state apparatus in the Soviet system, and to the new and enlarged apparatus of the state under capitalism as a locus for class struggle and political action, rather than a mere obstacle which one "smashes."[20] These illustrations should make clear that, in all the disciplinary fields enumerated above, a dilemma emerges analogous to that of cultural studies proper: is the text a free-floating object in its own right, or does it "reflect" some context or ground, and in that case does it simply replicate the latter ideologically, or does it possess some autonomous force in which it could also be seen as negating that context? It is only because we are all so irredeemably locked in our disciplinary specializations that we fail to see the similarity of these issues; and the obvious place for Marxism to reassert its claim to being an interdisciplinary and a universal science lies within this particular problematic. Indeed, the privileged status of cultural studies might be conveyed by the way in which such textual and interpretive problems are in them more immediately visible and available for study and reflection than in more apparently empirical sciences.

On the other hand, the issue of the academic disciplines serves to dramatize the ambiguity of the Althusserian position. For in its insistence on the semi-autonomy of the levels or instances—and in particular in its notorious and self-serving attempt to reinvent a privileged place for philosophy proper, in a tradition in which the latter was supposed to have been overcome and subsumed by the "unity of theory and practice"—the Althusserian conception of structure has often seemed to its adversaries to constitute a renewed defense of the reified specialization of the bourgeois academic dis-

---

20. Here, the form taken by "expressive causality" is "the conception of the state as agent of the monopolies in state monopoly capitalism"; see in particular Nicos Poulantzas, *Political Power and Social Classes,* trans. Timothy O'Hagan (London: New Left Books, 1973), esp. pp. 273–274.

ciplines, and thereby an essentially antipolitical alibi.[21] It is true that a somewhat different Althusser has himself (in the seminal essay "Ideological State Apparatuses") taught us that in this society what look like ideas require vigilant demystification as the messages of so many institutional or bureaucratic infrastructures (for example, the University). But his critics turn this view against him by reading his own system of semi-autonomous levels as a legitimation of the French Communist Party, henceforth one more inert institution among others within the bourgeois state. It would be frivolous to try to choose between these antithetical evaluations of the Althusserian operation (anti-Stalinist or Stalinist); rather, they mark out a space in which that operation is objectively and functionally ambiguous.

We can, however, locate the source of this ambiguity. It is to be found in an area strategic for any literary or cultural analysis, namely in the concept of *mediation:* that is, the relationship between the levels or instances, and the possibility of adapting analyses and findings from one level to another. Mediation is the classical dialectical term for the establishment of relationships between, say, the formal analysis of a work of art and its social ground, or between the internal dynamics of the political state and its economic base. It should be understood from the outset that Althusser himself assimilates the concept of "mediation" to expressive causality in the Hegelian sense; that is, he grasps the process of mediation exclusively as the establishment of symbolic *identities* between the various levels, as a process whereby each level is folded into the next, thereby losing its constitutive autonomy and functioning as an expression of its homologues. Thus, state power is seen as the mere expression of the economic system that underlies it, as is the juridical apparatus in a somewhat different way; culture is seen as the expression of the underlying political, juridical and economic instances, and so forth. Starting from this point, the analysis of mediations aims to demonstrate what is not evident in the appearance of things, but rather in their underlying reality, namely that *the same* essence is at work in the specific languages of

---

21. Jacques Rancière, *La Leçon d'Althusser* (Paris: Gallimard, 1974), chap. 2; and E. P. Thompson, *The Poverty of Theory* (London: Merlin, 1978), pp. 374–379.

culture as in the organization of the relations of production. This Althusserian attack on mediation is central, insofar as its targets are no longer limited to Hegel and the Lukácsean tradition, but also include thinkers such as Sartre and (more guardedly) Gramsci.

But the concept of mediation has traditionally been the way in which dialectical philosophy and Marxism itself have formulated their vocation to break out of the specialized compartments of the (bourgeois) disciplines and to make connections among the seemingly disparate phenomena of social life generally. If a more modern characterization of mediation is wanted, we will say that this operation is understood as a process of *transcoding:* as the invention of a set of terms, the strategic choice of a particular code or language, such that the same terminology can be used to analyze and articulate two quite distinct types of objects or "texts," or two very different structural levels of reality. Mediations are thus a device of the analyst, whereby the fragmentation and autonomization, the compartmentalization and specialization of the various regions of social life (the separation, in other words, of the ideological from the political, the religious from the economic, the gap between daily life and the practice of the academic disciplines) is at least locally overcome, on the occasion of a particular analysis. Such momentary reunification would remain purely symbolic, a mere methodological fiction, were it not understood that social life is in its fundamental reality one and indivisible, a seamless web, a single inconceivable and transindividual process, in which there is no need to invent ways of linking language events and social upheavals or economic contradictions because on that level they were never separate from one another. The realm of separation, of fragmentation, of the explosion of codes and the multiplicity of disciplines is merely the reality of the appearance: it exists, as Hegel would put it, not so much *in itself* as rather *for us,* as the basic logic and fundamental law of our daily life and existential experience in late capitalism. The appeal to some ultimate underlying unity of the various "levels" is therefore a merely formal and empty one, except insofar as it supplies the rationale and the philosophical justification for that more concrete and local practice of mediations with which we are here concerned.

Now what must be said about the Althusserian conception of

structure in this respect is that the notion of "semi-autonomy" necessarily has to *relate* as much as it *separates*. Otherwise the levels will simply become autonomous *tout court*, and break into the reified space of the bourgeois disciplines; and we have seen that for some readers this last is precisely the thrust of Althusserianism. But in that case it is hard to see why Althusser would insist on a determination by the structural totality: it is clear that he means to underscore some ultimate structural interdependency of the levels, but that he grasps this interdependency in terms of a mediation that passes through the structure, rather than a more *immediate* mediation in which one level folds into another directly. This suggests that the philosophical thrust of the Althusserian notion of structural causality strikes less at the concept of mediation as such, than at what the dialectical tradition would call unreflected immediacy: and in that case, Althusser's real polemic target is at one with that of Hegel, whose whole work is one long critique of premature immediacy and the establishment of unreflected unities. This can perhaps be said in a less technical way by observing that Althusserian structure, like all Marxisms, necessarily insists on the interrelatedness of all elements in a social formation; only it relates them by way of their structural *difference* and distance from one another, rather than by their ultimate identity, as he understands expressive causality to do. Difference is then here understood as a relational concept, rather than as the mere inert inventory of unrelated diversity.

The practice of expressive causality, in which similar processes are observed in two distinct regions of social life, is one of the forms mediation can take, but it is surely not the only one. The point that must be made against Althusser's own formulation of the problem is that the distinguishing of two phenomena from each other, their structural separation, the affirmation that they are not the same, and that in quite specific and determinate ways, is *also* a form of mediation. Althusserian structural causality is therefore just as fundamentally a practice of mediation as is the "expressive causality" to which it is opposed. To describe mediation as the strategic and local invention of a code which can be used about two distinct phenomena does not imply any obligation for the same message to be transmitted in the two cases; to put it another way, one cannot enumerate the differences between things except against the background of some more general identity. Mediation undertakes to establish this initial identity, against which then—but only then—local identification or differentiation can be registered.

These interpretive possibilities explain why the practice of mediation is particularly crucial for any literary or cultural criticism which seeks to avoid imprisonment in the windless closure of the formalisms, which aims at inventing ways of opening the text onto its *hors-texte* or extratextual relationships in less brutal and purely contingent fashion than was the case with the mechanical causality touched on above. To invent (as we will frequently do in these pages) a terminology of reification, of fragmentation and monadization, which can be used alternately to characterize social relations in late capitalism and formal relations and verbal structures within the latter's cultural and literary products, is not necessarily to affirm the identity of both these things (expressive causality) and thereby to conclude that the latter, the superstructural phenomena, are mere reflexes, epiphenomenal projections of infrastructural realities. At some level this is certainly true, and modernism and reification are parts of the same immense process which expresses the contradictory inner logic and dynamics of late capitalism. Yet even if our aim, as literary analysts, is rather to demonstrate the ways in which modernism—far from being a mere reflection of the reification of late nineteenth-century social life—is also a revolt against that reification and a symbolic act which involves a whole Utopian compensation for increasing dehumanization on the level of daily life, we are first obliged to establish a continuity between these two regional zones or sectors—the practice of language in the literary work, and the experience of *anomie,* standardization, rationalizing desacralization in the *Umwelt* or world of daily life—such that the latter can be grasped as that determinate situation, dilemma, contradiction, or subtext, to which the former comes as a symbolic resolution or solution.

We must therefore repudiate a conception of the process of mediation which fails to register its capacity for differentiation and for revealing structural oppositions and contradictions through some overemphasis on its related vocation to establish identities. Even in the practice of Sartre, whom Althusser denounces, along with Gramsci, as the very "prototype of the philosopher of mediations," the characteristic account[22] of the institution of the family as the basic mediation between the experience of the child (object of psychoanalysis) and the class structure of the society at large (object of a Marxist analysis) by no means has the result of reducing these three distinct realities to a common denominator or assimilating them in such a way as to lose the quite different specificities of the destiny of the individual subject, the history of the bourgeois cellular family, and the "conjuncture" of class relations obtaining at that particular moment in the development of the national capitalism in question. On the contrary, the very force of this mediation presupposes your sense of the relative autonomy of each of the sectors or regions in question: it is an identificatory transcoding which requires you at one and the same time to maintain these three "levels" at some absolute structural distance from one another.

This lengthy discussion of mediation should not be taken to mean that Althusser's critique of expressive causality is wholly unjustified; rather, it has been displaced, and its genuine power can be recovered only when its appropriate object is determined. The true target of the Althusserian critique would seem to me not the practice of mediation, but something else, which presents superficial similarities to it but is in reality a very different kind of concept, namely the structural notion of *homology* (or isomorphism, or structural parallelism)—a term currently in wide use in a variety of literary and cultural analyses. Here the Althusserian strictures provide the occasion for a reevaluation of this particular interpretive mechanism, introduced to the critical public by Lucien Goldmann, whose *Hidden God* posited homologies between class situations, world views, and artistic forms (the object of study was Jansenism, with its social origins in the *noblesse de robe,* and its cultural emanation in the new ideology of the *Augustinus,* as well as in the *Pensées* of Pascal and the tragedies of Racine). What is unsatisfactory about this work of Goldmann's is not the establishment of a historical relationship among these three zones or sectors, but rather the simplistic and mechanical model which is constructed in order to articulate that relationship, and in which it is affirmed that

22. Jean-Paul Sartre, *Search for a Method,* trans. Hazel Barnes (New York: Vintage, 1968), p. 38: "It is, then, inside the particularity of a history, through the peculiar contradictions of *this* family, that Gustave Flaubert unwittingly served his class apprenticeship."

at some level of abstraction the "structure" of the three quite different realities of social situation, philosophical or ideological position, and verbal and theatrical practice are "the same." Even more glaring, in this respect, is Goldmann's suggestion, in his later *Sociology of the Novel*, of a "rigorous homology" between the novel as a form and the "daily life of an individualistic society born of market production."[23] Here, if anywhere, the Althusserian reminder of the need to respect the relative autonomy of the various structural levels is timely; and it would seem to me that the related injunction to build a hierarchical model in which the various levels stand in determinate relations of domination or subordination to one another can best be fulfilled, in the area of literary and cultural analysis, by a kind of fiction of the process whereby they are generated. So the Russian Formalists showed us how to construct a picture of the emergence of a given complex form in which a certain feature is seen as being generated in order to compensate for and rectify a structural lack at some lower or earlier level of production. To anticipate the example of Conrad developed in Chapter 5, it would certainly be possible to posit some static homology or parallelism between the three levels of social reification, stylistic invention, and narrative or diegetic categories; but it seems more interesting to grasp the mutual relationships between these three dimensions of the text and its social subtext in the more active terms of production, projection, compensation, repression, displacement, and the like. In the case of Conrad, for instance, we will suggest that the stylistic mannerisms have the function of symbolically resolving the contradiction in the subtext, while at the same time actively generating or projecting their narrative pretext (the Formalists called this the "motivation of the device") in the form of a specific category of event to be narrated.

The practice of homologies may, however, be observed in far more sophisticated contexts than that of Goldmann's work: for instance, in current ideologies of production whose interpretive practice it is useful to distinguish from the model of formal genera-

---

23. Lucien Goldmann, "Sociology of the Novel," *Telos*, No. 18 (Winter, 1973–74), p. 127. These critical observations should be accompanied by a reminder of the historic and indeed incomparable role played by Lucien Goldmann in the reawakening of Marxist theory in contemporary France, and of Marxist cultural theory generally.

tion or projective construction outlined above. Whatever the value of current efforts to fashion a "materialist theory of language,"[24] it is clear that most such efforts are based on a tacit homology between the "production" of language in writing and speech, and economic production (sometimes a secondary homology is also asserted, between the "economic" topology in Freud and "economics" itself). These assertions strike me as misguided in two different ways. Certainly, insofar as the idea of textual production helps us break the reifying habit of thinking of a given narrative as an object, or as a unified whole, or as a static structure, its effect has been positive; but the active center of this idea is in reality a conception of the text as *process,* and the notion of productivity is a metaphorical overlay which adds little enough to the methodological suggestivity of the idea of process, but a great deal to its potential for use or misappropriation by a new ideology. One cannot without intellectual dishonesty assimilate the "production" of texts (or in Althusser's version of this homology, the "production" of new and more scientific concepts) to the production of goods by factory workers: writing and thinking are not alienated labor in that sense, and it is surely fatuous for intellectuals to seek to glamorize their tasks—which can for the most part be subsumed under the rubric of the elaboration, reproduction, or critique of ideology—by assimilating them to real work on the assembly line and to the experience of the resistance of matter in genuine manual labor.

The term *matter* suggests a second misconception at work in such theories, in which the Lacanian notion of a "material signifier" (in Lacan the phallus) and a few feeble allusions to the sonorous vibration of language in air and space are appealed to as a grounding for some genuinely materialistic view. Marxism is, however, not a mechanical but a historical materialism: it does not assert the primacy of matter so much as it insists on an ultimate determination by the mode of production. Indeed, if one likes to brandish epithets, it must be remarked that the grounding of materialism in one or another conception of matter is rather the hallmark of bourgeois ideology from the eighteenth-century mate-

24. Most notably in Rosalind Coward and John Ellis, *Language and Materialism* (London: Routledge & Kegan Paul, 1977). A similar homology ultimately limits the rich and suggestive work of Ferruccio Rossi-Landi, which turns explicitly on the exploration of language production.

rialisms all the way to nineteenth-century positivism and determinism (itself a bourgeois rather than a Marxian term and concept). The assertion of homologies is at fault here at least in so far as
it encourages the most comfortable solutions (the production of
language is "the same" as the production of goods), and forestalls
the laborious—but surely alone productive—detour of a theory of
language through the mode of production as a whole, or, in Althusser's language, through structure, as an ultimate cause only
visible in its effects or structural elements, of which linguistic practice is one.

Given its methodological importance in the present volume, I
must make a preliminary observation here on the semiotics of A. J.
Greimas, in which homology plays an important part, and which
will surely appear to some readers as being far more static and
ahistorical than the analyses of Goldmann criticized above. I would
not disagree with this view, provided it is understood that in
Greimas, the conception of levels and their homology is posited as a
methodological starting point, as a set of categories to be explored,
rather than as a forecast of the shape of the results of analysis.
Thus, to take the terms of his fundamental essay "The Interaction
of Semiotic Constraints."[25] the various superposed and homologous quadrants—e.g., for sexual relations, the four logical possibilities of marital relations, normal relations, abnormal relations
and extramarital relations; for rule systems, those of prescriptions,
taboos, nonprescriptions, nontaboos—far from designating the
concrete kinship or legal systems of any specific and historical
human community, on the contrary constitute the empty slots and
logical possibilities necessarily obtaining in all of them, against
which the content of a given social text is to be measured and sorted
out. In this sense, the semantic or semiotic structures articulated in
Greimas' scheme seem to map out what he takes to be the logical
structure of reality itself, and stand as the fundamental categories of
that reality, whatever its particular historical form; if this is the
case, then his would be what Umberto Eco has termed an "ontological structuralism," one for which structure is transhistorical and
endowed with at least the being and the permanence of the
categories of logic or mathematical thought. The "levels" are then

25. *Yale French Studies*, No. 41 (1968); or in *Du Sens*, pp. 135–155.

in Greimas homologous because they are all crisscrossed and organized by the same fundamental conceptual or semiotic categories, those of his "elementary structure of signification" or semiotic rectangle (or hexagon).

One of the essential themes of this book will be the contention that Marxism subsumes other interpretive modes or systems; or, to put it in methodological terms, that the limits of the latter can always be overcome, and their more positive findings retained, by a radical historicizing of their mental operations, such that not only the content of the analysis, but the very method itself, along with the analyst, then comes to be reckoned into the "text" or phenomenon to be explained. In the case of Greimas, we will show[26] how this apparently static analytical scheme, organized around binary oppositions rather than dialectical ones, and continuing to posit the relationship between levels in terms of homology, can be reappropriated for a historicizing and dialectical criticism by designating it as the very locus and model of ideological closure. Seen in this way, the semiotic rectangle becomes a vital instrument for exploring the semantic and ideological intricacies of the text—not so much because, as in Greimas' own work, it yields the objective possibilities according to which landscape and the physical elements, say, must necessarily be perceived, as rather because it maps the limits of a specific ideological consciousness and marks the conceptual points beyond which that consciousness cannot go, and between which it is condemned to oscillate. This is the perspective in which, in Chapter 3, we will examine the vision of history which

26. See below pp. 82–83, and also pp. 165–169, and 253–257. The position argued here—on the distinction as well as the possible coordination between a static or semiotic method and a dialectical one—is consistent with Sartre's interesting critique of structuralism generally: "Althusser, like Foucault, limits himself to the analysis of structure. From the epistemological point of view, that amounts to privileging the *concept* over against the *notion*. [Sartre is here alluding to the variously translated Hegelian opposition of *Begriff* and *Idee*, respectively.] The concept is atemporal. One can study how concepts are engendered one after the other within determined categories. But neither time itself nor, consequently, history, can be made the object of a concept. There is a contradiction in terms. When you introduce temporality, you come to see that within a temporal development the concept modifies itself. *Notion*, on the contrary, can be defined as the synthetic effort to produce an idea which develops itself by contradiction and its successive overcoming, and therefore is homogeneous to the development of things" ("Replies to Structuralism," trans. R. D'Amico, *Telos*, No. 9 [Fall, 1971], p. 114, or *L'Arc*, No. 30 [1966], p. 94).

informs *La Vieille Fille*—a binary opposition between aristocratic elegance and Napoleonic energy, which the political imagination seeks desperately to transcend, generating the contradictories of each of these terms, mechanically generating all the syntheses logically available to it, while remaining locked into the terms of the original double bind. Such a vision is not to be taken as the logical articulation of all the political positions or ideological possibilities objectively present in the situation of the Restoration, but rather as the structure of a particular political fantasy, as the mapping of that particular "libidinal apparatus" in which Balzac's political thinking becomes invested—it being understood that we are not here distinguishing between fantasy and some objective reality onto which it would be "projected," but rather, with Deleuze or with J.-F. Lyotard, asserting such fantasy or protonarrative structure as the vehicle for our experience of the real.[27] When Greimas' system is used in this fashion, its closure ceases to pose the problems traditionally raised for a more dialectical position by static and analytic thought; on the contrary, it furnishes the graphic embodiment of ideological closure as such, and allows us to map out the inner limits of a given ideological formation and to construct the basic terms of this particular libidinal apparatus or "desiring machine" which is Balzac's commitment to history. More than this, the very closure of the "semiotic rectangle" now affords a way into the text, not by positing mere logical possibilities and permutations, but rather through its diagnostic revelation of terms or nodal points implicit in the ideological system which have, however, remained unrealized in the surface of the text, which have failed to become manifest in the logic of the narrative, and which we can therefore read as what the text represses. Thus appropriated, or perhaps indeed misappropriated, by a dialectical criticism, Greimas' scheme, constructed by means of purely logical or analytical negations, by its very exhaustiveness opens a place for the practice of a more genuinely dialectical negation in the tension between the realized and the unrealized terms; what for Greimas is to be formulated as a structural homology between the various levels on which the semiotic rectangle reproduces itself, for us on the contrary be-

27. A fuller demonstration of the critical uses of the concept of a "libidinal apparatus" may be found in my *Fables of Aggression: Wyndham Lewis, The Modernist as Fascist* (Berkeley: University of California Press, 1979).

comes powerfully restructured into a relationship of tension between presence and absence, a relationship that can be mapped according to the various dynamic possibilities (generation, projection, compensation, repression, displacement) indicated above. So the literary structure, far from being completely realized on any one of its levels tilts powerfully into the underside or *impensé* or *non-dit*, in short, into the very political unconscious, of the text, such that the latter's dispersed semes—when reconstructed according to this model of ideological closure—themselves then insistently direct us to the informing power of forces or contradictions which the text seeks in vain wholly to control or master (or *manage*, to use Norman Holland's suggestive term). Thus, by means of a radically historicizing reappropriation, the ideal of logical closure which initially seemed imcompatible with dialectical thinking, now proves to be an indispensable instrument for revealing those logical and ideological centers a particular historical text fails to realize, or on the contrary seeks desperately to repress.

These qualifications tend to suggest that Althusser's program for a structural Marxism must be understood as a modification within the dialectical tradition, rather than a complete break with it, a kind of genetic mutation in which some wholly new Marxism emerges that has no relationship at all to the classical categories in which dialectical philosophy has been couched. But they by no means exhaust the issues and problems of what may be called the Althusser-Lukács debate; nor can we fully do so here. At best, a checklist of those issues can be suggested, in order to prevent the impression that some easy synthesis is readily available. Six major themes come to mind, some of which have already been touched on: (1) the problem of representation, and most particularly of the representation of History: as has already been suggested, this is essentially a narrative problem, a question of the adequacy of any storytelling framework in which History might be represented; (2) the related problem of the "characters" of historical narrative, or more precisely, that of the status of the concept of social class, and its availability as a "subject of history" or prime actor in such a collective historical narrative; (3) the relationship of praxis to structure, and the possible contamination of the first of these concepts by categories of purely individual action, as opposed to the possible imprisonment of the second of these concepts in an ultimately static and reified vision of some "total system"; (4) the more general problem, issuing from this last one, of the status of the synchronic, and its adequacy as a framework for analysis; or, correlatively, of the adequacy of the older dialectical vision of diachronic transformation and periodization, most notably in the account to be given of *transition* from one mode of production to another; (5) the related issue of the status of a category no less central to the classical dialectic than mediation, namely that of *contradiction,* and its formulation within the new structural or synchronic framework (a category about which we must insist that it be radically distinguished from the semiotic categories of opposition, antinomy, or aporia); (6) and finally the notion of a totality, a term which Althusser continues to use, all the while seeking radically to differentiate his concept of a properly structural totality from the older expressive totality alleged to be the organizing category of Hegelian idealism and Hegelian Marxism (Lukács, Sartre) alike. As this term is the most dramatic battleground of the confrontation between Hegelian and structural Marxisms, we must conclude this section with a few brief remarks about the issues it raises.

Lukács' notion of totality (outlined in *History and Class Consciousness*) and Sartre's methodological ideal of totalization (described in the *Critique of Dialectical Reason*) have generally been condemned by association with Hegel's Absolute Spirit, a space in which all contradictions are presumably annulled, the gap between subject and object abolished, and some ultimate and manifestly idealistic form of Identity is established. The attack on so-called identity theory, then—a theory attributed to Lukács, Sartre, and other so-called Hegelian Marxists—takes its inspiration from Marx's critique of Hegel in the *Economic and Philosophical Manuscripts of 1844.* Marx there argued that Hegel mistakenly assimilated objectification, a universal human process, with its unique historical form under capitalism, which is rather to be designated as alienation: given this assimilation, the Hegelian ideal of Absolute Spirit then seeks to overcome alienation by projecting a clearly idealistic vision of the end of objectification as such, the return of all externalizing relations back into the indistinction of Spirit. In its contemporary form, the critique of such identity theory argues not merely that the concept of "totality" is here a code word for Absolute Spirit, but that a whole vision of history is herein perpetuated, in which Utopia (read: communism) is understood as achieving its ultimate identity by the obliteration of difference through sheer force; or, in the memorable words of the *nouveaux philosophes,* in which a direct line runs from Hegel's Absolute Spirit to Stalin's Gulag. This fashionable polemic stereotype has, of course, no historical or textual justification whatsoever. The two major Marxian studies of Hegel have for one thing argued convincingly that Hegel's "conception" of Absolute Spirit is little more than a symptom of a historical situation in which his thinking could go no further[28]: less an idea in its own right than an attempt to resolve an impossible historical contradiction, and to project some impossible third term beyond the alternatives of romantic reaction and bourgeois utilitarianism. Rather than diagnosing some irremediable vice of "idealism" in Hegel's thought, we must more modestly accuse him of not having been able, in his historical moment, to become Marx. The content of Absolute Spirit may better be understood in the for us far more local context of a projection of the mind of the historian and his relationship to the past; yet even this retroactive account of the dialectical vision as the "Sunday of life" and as the Rememoration (*Er-innerung*) of a history already terminated (the owl of Minerva taking her flight at dusk) must be grasped in the historical context of the failure of the Napoleonic revolution, and of Hegel's discouragement at what was to him in a very real way the end of the history on which he placed his own political and visionary hopes.

The philosophical evolution of Hegel himself makes it clear that the Hegelian dialectic emerges precisely from his own assault on "identity theory," in the form of Schelling's system, which he stigmatized in the famous remark about "the night in which all cows are gray": a "reconciliation" of subject with object in which both are obliterated, and ultimately a philosophical orientation that ends in a mystical vision of Identity. From this very polemic emerges the central mechanism of the dialectic, the notion of objectification, without which neither the historical content of Hegel's own work nor the Marxian dialectic is conceivable. It is thus inaccurate or

28. See Georg Lukács, *The Young Hegel*, trans. Rodney Livingstone (Cambridge: MIT Press, 1976); and Herbert Marcuse, *Reason and Revolution* (Boston: Beacon, 1960).

dishonest to associate Hegel himself with what is attacked under the term "identity theory."[29]

As far as Lukács is concerned, the conception of totality outlined in *History and Class Consciousness* must be read, not as some positive vision of the end of history in the sense of Schelling's Absolute, but as something quite different, namely a methodological standard. It has not been sufficiently grasped, indeed, that Lukács' method of ideological critique—like the Hegelian dialectic itself and its Sartrean variant, in the methodological imperative of totalization proposed in the *Critique*—is an essentially critical and negative, demystifying operation. Lukács' central analysis of the ideological character of classical German philosophy may from this perspective be seen as a creative and original variant on Marx's theory of ideology, which is not, as is widely thought, one of false consciousness, but rather one of structural limitation and ideological closure. Nor is Marx's seminal analysis of petty-bourgeois ideology in *The Eighteenth Brumaire* predicated on class affiliation or origins: "What makes [petty-bourgeois intellectuals] the representatives of the petty bourgeoisie is the fact that in their minds they do not get beyond the limits which the latter do not get beyond in life, that they are consequently driven, theoretically, to the same problems and solutions to which material interest and social position drive the latter politically. This is, in general, the relationship between the political and literary representatives of a class and the class they represent."[30]

We will suggest that such an approach posits ideology in terms of

---

29. Thus, I must feel that Martin Jay's valuable history of the Frankfurt School to 1950, *The Dialectical Imagination* (Boston: Little, Brown, 1973), by overstressing the leitmotif of non-identity theory, ends up conveying the misleading impression that the fundamental target of "critical theory" was Marxism rather than capitalism. The non-identity between subject and object often means little more than a materialist and "decentering" approach to knowledge. Meanwhile, unless one grasps "negative dialectics" as an essentially aesthetic ideal, as I do, it would be best to seek Adorno's most authentic practice of the dialectic in *Philosophy of Modern Music* (trans. A. G. Mitchell and W. V. Blomster [New York: Seabury, 1973]), rather than in the philosophical works (see, on the tension between the musical and the philosophical analyses, Susan Buck-Morss, *The Origin of Negative Dialectics* [New York: Free Press, 1977], pp. 33–49). But compare Martin Jay, "The Concept of Totality," in *Telos* No. 32 (Summer, 1977).

30. Karl Marx, *The Eighteenth Brumaire of Louis Bonaparte* (New York: International, 1963), pp. 50–51.

strategies of containment, whether intellectual or (in the case of narratives) formal. Lukács' achievement was to have understood that such strategies of containment—which Marx himself described principally in his critiques of classical political economy and the ingenious frames the latter constructed in order to avoid the ultimate consequences of such insights as the relationship between labor and value—can be unmasked only by confrontation with the ideal of totality which they at once imply and repress. From this perspective, Hegel's notion of Absolute Spirit is seen as just such a strategy of containment, which allows what can be thought to seem internally coherent in its own terms, while repressing the unthinkable (in this case, the very possibility of collective praxis) which lies beyond its boundaries. Here Marxism is no doubt implied as that thinking which knows no boundaries of this kind, and which is infinitely totalizable, but the ideological critique does not depend on some dogmatic or "positive" conception of Marxism as a system. Rather, it is simply the place of an imperative to totalize, and the various historical forms of Marxism can themselves equally effectively be submitted to just such a critique of their own local ideological limits or strategies of containment. In this sense, Hegel's great dictum, "the true is the whole," is less an affirmation of some place of truth which Hegel himself (or others) might occupy, than it is a perspective and a method whereby the "false" and the ideological can be unmasked and made visible.

This negative and methodological status of the concept of "totality" may also be shown at work in those very post-structural philosophies which explicitly repudiate such "totalizations" in the name of difference, flux, dissemination, and heterogeneity; Deleuze's conception of the schizophrenic text and Derridean deconstruction come to mind. If such perceptions are to be celebrated in their intensity, they must be accompanied by some initial appearance of continuity, some ideology of unification already in place, which it is their mission to rebuke and to shatter. The value of the molecular in Deleuze, for instance, depends structurally on the preexisting molar or unifying impulse against which its truth is read. We will therefore suggest that these are second-degree or critical philosophies, which reconfirm the status of the concept of totality by their very reaction against it; such a movement is worked out even more explicitly in Adorno's "negative dialectic," with its counteraffirmation—"the whole is the untrue"—in which the classical dialectic seeks, by biting its own tail, to deconstruct itself.

Thus understood, Lukács' critical conception of the "totality" may immediately be transformed into an instrument of narrative analysis, by way of attention to those narrative frames or containment strategies which seek to endow their objects of representation with formal unity. Indeed, the overfamiliar essays on realism of Lukács' middle period—often simply read as exercises in "reflection theory"—recover their interest if they are rewritten in this way, as studies of those privileged narrative instances (the so-called "great realists") in which the elaborate frames and strategies of containment of a later modernism did for whatever reason not yet seem necessary.[31]

Indeed, in some paradoxical or dialectical fashion, Lukács' con-

---

31. We must add a final comment about the coded political resonance of this debate, which the critics of "totalization" have so often construed as an attack on a monolithic or totalitarian ideology. Such instant "ideological analysis" may profitably be juxtaposed with a social reading of the debate, as a symbolic index of the distinct situations faced by the Left in the structurally different national contexts of France and the United States. The critique of totalization in France goes hand in hand with a call for a "molecular" or local, nonglobal, nonparty politics: and this repudiation of the traditional forms of class and party action evidently reflects the historic weight of French centralization (at work both in the institutions and in the forces that oppose them), as well as the belated emergence of what can very loosely be called a "countercultural" movement, with the breakup of the old cellular family apparatus and a proliferation of subgroups and alternate "life-styles." In the United States, on the other hand, it is precisely the intensity of social fragmentation of this latter kind that has made it historically difficult to unify Left or "antisystemic" forces in any durable and effective organizational way. Ethnic groups, neighborhood movements, feminism, various "countercultural" or alternative life-style groups, rank-and-file labor dissidence, student movements, single-issue movements—all have in the United States seemed to project demands and strategies which were theoretically incompatible with each other and impossible to coordinate on any practical political basis. The privileged form in which the American Left can develop today must therefore necessarily be that of an *alliance politics;* and such a politics is the strict practical equivalent of the concept of totalization on the theoretical level. In practice, then, the attack on the concept of "totality" in the American framework means the undermining and the repudiation of the only realistic perspective in which a genuine Left could come into being in this country. There is therefore a real problem about the importation and translation of theoretical polemics which have a quite different semantic content in the national situation in which they originate, as in that of France, where the various nascent movements for regional autonomy, women's liberation and neighborhood organization are perceived as being repressed, or at least hampered in their development, by the global or "molar" perspectives of the traditional Left mass parties.

ception of totality may here be said to rejoin the Althusserian notion of History or the Real as an "absent cause." Totality is not available for representation, any more than it is accessible in the form of some ultimate truth (or moment of Absolute Spirit). And since Sartre has figured in this discussion, we can do no better to illustrate the complex process whereby the "whole" is kept faith with and "represented" in its very absence, than to quote an agonized and self-canceling passage from *Les Chemins de la liberté*, in which totality is affirmed in the very movement whereby it is denied, and represented in the same language that denies it all possible representation:

> A vast entity, a planet, in a space of a hundred million dimensions; three-dimensional beings could not so much as imagine it. And yet each dimension was an autonomous consciousness. Try to look directly at that planet, it would disintegrate into tiny fragments, and nothing but consciousnesses would be left. A hundred million free consciousnesses, each aware of walls, the glowing stump of a cigar, familiar faces, and each constructing its destiny on its own responsibility. And yet each of those consciousnesses, by imperceptible contacts and insensible changes, realizes its existence as a cell in a gigantic and invisible coral. War: everyone is free, and yet the die is cast. It is there, it is everywhere, it is the totality of all my thoughts, of all Hitler's words, of all Gomez's acts; but no one is there to add it up. It exists solely for God. But God does not exist. And yet the war exists.[32]

If it is overhasty to characterize the traditional concept of a totality as organic, and even less adequate to characterize its opposite number, the concept of structure, as mechanical, what can at least be stressed is the significance of the areas of aesthetics and linguistics in which these concepts were initially adapted[33] and prepared for their later, more immediately figural uses in fields such as social theory. It would therefore seem legitimate to conclude this provisional juxtaposition of the two in terms of the *aesthetic* that each projects. We are now, in the midst of a post-structuralist culture, in a better

32. Jean-Paul Sartre, *The Reprieve,* trans. Eric Sutton (New York: Vintage, 1973), p. 326.

33. See, for a discussion of the aesthetic origins of the dialectic, Georg Lukács, *Beiträge zur Geschichte der Aesthetik,* and in particular the essay on Schiller's aesthetics, in *Probleme der Aesthetik* (Neuwied: Luchterhand, 1969).

position to see that the expressive totality associated here with
Hegel and Lukács implies the value of what is sometimes called
organic form, and projects the notion of a work of art as an ordered
whole: the critic's business—the task of interpretation viewed from
the standpoint of expressive causality—is accordingly to seek a
unified meaning to which the various levels and components of the
work contribute in a hierarchical way.

It follows, then, that the interpretive mission of a properly structural causality will on the contrary find its privileged content in rifts
and discontinuities within the work, and ultimately in a conception
of the former "work of art" as a heterogeneous and (to use the most
dramatic recent slogan) a schizophrenic text. In the case of Althusserian literary criticism proper, then, the appropriate object of
study emerges only when the appearance of formal unification is
unmasked as a failure or an ideological mirage. The authentic function of the cultural text is then staged rather as an *interference*
between levels, as a subversion of one level by another; and for
Althusser and Pierre Macherey the privileged form of this disunity
or dissonance is the objectification of the ideological by the work of
aesthetic production.[34] The aim of a properly structural interpretation or exegesis thus becomes the explosion of the seemingly unified
text into a host of clashing and contradictory elements. Unlike
canonical post-structuralism, however, whose emblematic gesture
is that by which Barthes, in *S/Z*, shatters a Balzac novella into a
random operation of multiple codes, the Althusserian/Marxist conception of culture requires this multiplicity to be reunified, if not at
the level of the work itself, then at the level of its process of production, which is not random but can be described as a coherent
functional operation in its own right. The current post-structural
celebration of discontinuity and heterogeneity is therefore only an
initial moment in Althusserian exegesis, which then requires the
fragments, the incommensurable levels, the heterogeneous impulses, of the text to be once again related, but in the mode of
structural difference and determinate contradiction. In the interpretive chapters of the following work, I have found it possible without

34. These positions are enunciated in Althusser's "Letter on Art," in *Lenin and
Philosophy*, trans. Ben Brewster (New York: Monthly Review, 1971), pp. 221–227;
and in Pierre Macherey, *Pour une théorie de la production litteraire* (Paris: Maspéro,
1970), most notably in the chapter on Jules Verne.

any great inconsistency to respect both the methodological imperative implicit in the concept of totality or totalization, and the quite
different attention of a "symptomal" analysis to discontinuities,
rifts, actions at distance, within a merely apparently unified cultural
text.

But these distinct aesthetics—which we have just characterized in
terms of continuity and discontinuity, homogeneity and
heterogeneity, unification and dispersal—can also be grasped and
differentiated according to the immanent or transcendent nature of
the interpretations they propose. Rightly or wrongly, a totalizing
criticism has been felt to be transcendent in the bad sense, or in
other words to make appeal, for its interpretive content, to spheres
and levels outside the text proper. We have seen that such apparently extrinsic operations are then drawn back into the dialectical
framework as the latter expands and is systematically totalized.
Thus, it can be argued that this type of interpretation, while con-
taining a transcendent moment, foresees that moment as merely
provisionally extrinsic, and requires for its completion a movement
to the point at which that apparently external content (political
attitudes, ideological materials, juridical categories, the raw materials of history, the economic processes) is then at length drawn
back within the process of reading.

The ideal of a purely immanent criticism is clearly not unique to
post-structuralism but dominates a host of critical methods from
the older New Criticism on. We will argue in subsequent sections
that an immanent criticism in this sense is a mirage. But the originality of Althusserian interpretation, particularly as it is developed
in Macherey's work, may be formulated in a quite different way,
and may be understood as a deductive operation. From this point of
view, the work or the text is not inserted into a genetic process in
which it is understood as emerging from this or that prior moment
of form or style; nor is it "extrinsically" related to some ground or
context which is at least initially given as something lying beyond it.
Rather, the data of the work are interrogated in terms of their
formal and logical and, most particularly, their *semantic* conditions
of possibility. Such analysis thus involves the hypothetical *reconstruction* of the materials—content, narrative paradigms, stylistic
and linguistic practices—which had to have been given in advance
in order for that particular text to be produced in its unique histori-

cal specificity. We will demonstrate what is at stake in such an operation in subsequent chapters; what we have been concerned to argue here is that this is also, but in some new and unexpected sense, an interpretive or hermeneutic act: and with this assertion—that a mode of interpretation exists which is specific to Althusser's third or structural form of causality—this lengthy digression is complete.

II

Nonetheless, the distinction argued by Deleuze and Guattari, between "old-fashioned" interpretation and contemporary "deconstruction," suggests a useful means for sorting out the various critical or interpretive methods with which we must now come to terms. Leaving aside for the moment the possibility of any genuinely immanent criticism, we will assume that a criticism which asks the question "What does it mean?" constitutes something like an allegorical operation in which a text is systematically *rewritten* in terms of some fundamental master code or "ultimately determining instance." On this view, then, all "interpretation" in the narrower sense demands the forcible or imperceptible transformation of a given text into an allegory of its particular master code or "transcendental signified": the discredit into which interpretation has fallen is thus at one with the disrepute visited on allegory itself.

Yet to see interpretation this way is to acquire the instruments by which we can force a given interpretive practice to stand and yield up its name, to blurt out its master code and thereby reveal its metaphysical and ideological underpinnings. It should not, in the present intellectual atmosphere, be necessary laboriously to argue the position that every form of practice, including the literary-critical kind, implies and presupposes a form of theory; that empiricism, the mirage of an utterly nontheoretical practice, is a contradiction in terms; that even the most formalizing kinds of literary or textual analysis carry a theoretical charge whose denial unmasks it as ideological. Unfortunately, such a position, which we will take for granted in what follows, must always be reargued and refought. We will now, however, move on to the even more outrageous assertion that the working theoretical framework or presuppositions of a given method are in general the ideology which that method seeks to perpetuate. Thus, in another place, I have suggested that even so apparently ahistorical a "method" as the older New Criticism pre-supposes a specific "vision" or "theory" of history.[35] I will here go much further than this, and argue that even the most innocently formalizing readings of the New Criticism have as their essential and ultimate function the propagation of this particular view of what history is. Indeed, no working model of the functioning of language, the nature of communication or of the speech act, and the dynamics of formal and stylistic change is conceivable which does not imply a whole philosophy of history.

In the present work, we will be less concerned with those modes of formal or stylistic, purely textual, analysis which are generally strategically limited to lyric poetry than with the various types of "strong" rewritings implied by interpretations that identify them-selves as such and wear a particular label. Yet we must make some initial place for what is still the predominant form of literary and cultural criticism today, in spite of its repudiation by every succes-sive generation of literary theorists (each for a different reason). This is what we will call *ethical* criticism, and it constitutes the predominant code in terms of which the question "What does it mean?" tends to be answered. Ethical analysis is a vaster category than two other currently stigmatized types of thinking that it in-cludes and subsumes: metaphysical thought, which presupposes the possibility of questions about the "meaning" of life (even where these questions are answered in the negative, by the various existen-tialisms), and so-called humanism, which is always grounded on a certain conception of "human nature."[36] In its narrowest sense, ethical thought projects as permanent features of human "experi-ence," and thus as a kind of "wisdom" about personal life and interpersonal relations, what are in reality the historical and institu-tional specifics of a determinate type of group solidarity or class cohesion. We will return at some length, in the next chapter, to the

35. See *Marxism and Form* (Princeton: Princeton University Press, 1971), pp. 323, 331–333.
36. "Metaphysics" and "humanism" are the negative critical categories of the Derridean and Althusserian groups respectively, explicitly ranged by each under the more global materialist category of "idealism." To my mind, such philosophical categories are useful when they are taken to refer, as literally as possible, to the most banal everyday attitudes and presuppositions: it would seem "idealistic" to ab-solutize any historical category of idealism and to thematize any form of error or false consciousness as a transhistorical category.

way in which all ethics lives by exclusion and predicates certain types of Otherness or evil; that these must ultimately have political consequences is obvious, and one of the subthemes of the present work will indeed be the temptation of ethics to recontain itself by assigning hostile and more properly political impulses to the ultimate negative category of *ressentiment*.

Still, it may strike the reader as paradoxical or even perverse to characterize the bulk of garden-variety literary criticism today as "ethical," by which we normally understand a moralizing, or moralistic, didactic gesture of the type presumably extinct with the *Scrutiny* group if not with the Victorian age. This is to misrecognize the dominant form taken by ethics in our own situation, which is essentially psychological and psychologizing, even where it appeals for its authority to this or that version of psychoanalysis. Here notions of personal identity, myths of the reunification of the psyche, and the mirage of some Jungian "self" or "ego" stand in for the older themes of moral sensibility and ethical awareness and reconfirm the aptness of that other contemporary continental theme which, as we shall see further in the Chapter 3, turns upon the critique of the "center" and the "centered" self. Still, these various post-structural motifs should not be understood as a wholesale endorsement of post-structuralism, the anti-Marxist character of which is increasingly evident in France today. On the contrary, I will argue that only the dialectic provides a way for "decentering" the subject concretely, and for transcending the "ethical" in the direction of the political and the collective.

Interpretation proper—what we have called "strong" rewriting, in distinction from the weak rewriting of ethical codes, which all in one way or another project various notions of the unity and the coherence of consciousness—always presupposes, if not a conception of the unconscious itself, then at least some mechanism of mystification or repression in terms of which it would make sense to seek a latent meaning behind a manifest one, or to rewrite the surface categories of a text in the stronger language of a more fundamental interpretive code. This is perhaps the place to answer the objection of the ordinary reader, when confronted with elaborate and ingenious interpretations, that the text means just what it says. Unfortunately, no society has ever been quite so mystified in quite so many ways as our own, saturated as it is with messages and information, the very vehicles of mystification (language, as Talleyrand put it, having been given us in order to conceal our thoughts). If everything were transparent, then no ideology would be possible, and no domination either: evidently that is not our case. But above and beyond the sheer fact of mystification, we must point to the supplementary problem involved in the study of cultural or literary texts, or in other words, essentially, of narratives: for even if discursive language were to be taken literally, there is always, and constitutively, a problem about the "meaning" of narrative as such; and the problem about the assessment and subsequent formulation of the "meaning" of this or that narrative is the hermeneutic question, which leaves us as deeply involved in our present inquiry as we were when the objection was raised.

It can be argued that all of the original philosophical systems or positions in recent times have in one way or another projected a hermeneutic which is specific to them. Thus, I have argued in another place that most classical structuralisms practice a hermeneutic whose master code or interpretive key is simply Language itself.[37] Similarly, one could point to other local attempts to construct a universal hermeneutic, as in the short-lived interpretive system of the classical period of Sartrean existentialism, according to which it was possible to read literary styles, the structure of imagery, characterological traits, and ideological values in terms of anxiety and the fear of freedom.[38] Meanwhile, a phenomenological criticism not unrelated to the various existentialisms found a master code in the experience and thematics of temporality: a thematics which seems oddly dated, an experience which no longer seems particularly obsessive, in the post-modernist world of today.

But it is clear that the most influential and elaborate interpretive system of recent times is that of psychoanalysis, which may indeed lay claim to the distinction of being the only really new and original hermeneutic developed since the great patristic and medieval system of the four senses of scripture. So great has been the suggestiveness

37. See *The Prison-House of Language* (Princeton: Princeton University Press, 1972), pp. 195–205.
38. See my "Three Methods in Jean-Paul Sartre's Literary Criticism," in John K. Simon, ed., *Modern French Criticism* (Chicago: University of Chicago, Press, 1972), pp. 9–27. We will return to the ideological functions of existentialism, as well as to the possibility of a sociological analysis of this philosophy, in Chapter 5.

of the Freudian model that terms and secondary mechanisms drawn from it are to be found strewn at great distance from their original source, pressed into the service of quite unrelated systems, and not least in the following pages.

To come to some ultimate reckoning with psychoanalysis would require us radically to historicize Freudianism itself, and to reach a reflexive vantage point from which the historical and social conditions of possibility both of Freudian method and of its objects of study came into view. This is not achieved simply by resituating Freud in the Vienna and the Central Europe of his period, although such material is clearly of the greatest interest.[39] Nor is it even achieved when we stress the dependency of the psychoanalytic master code but also of its raw materials—childhood traumas, primal scene fantasies, Oedipal conflicts, "period" illnesses such as hysteria—on the historical institution of the nuclear family.[40] The conditions of possibility of psychoanalysis become visible, one would imagine, only when you begin to appreciate the extent of psychic fragmentation since the beginnings of capitalism, with its systematic quantification and rationalization of experience, its instrumental reorganization of the subject just as much as of the outside world. That the structure of the psyche is historical, and has a history, is, however, as difficult for us to grasp as that the senses are not themselves natural organs but rather the results of a long process of differentiation even within human history.[41] For the dynamic of *rationalization*—Weber's term, which Lukács will

39. See, for example, Juliet Mitchell, *Psychoanalysis and Feminism* (London: Allen Lane, 1974), pp. 419–435; and Stephen Toulmin and A. Janik, *Wittgenstein's Vienna* (New York: Simon & Schuster, 1973).

40. Jacques Lacan has suggestively underscored the relationship between emergent psychoanalysis and its historical raw material: hysteria as the "desire to desire." (See Lacan, *Le Séminaire, Livre XI: Les quatre concepts fondamentaux de la psychanalyse* [Paris: Seuil, 1973], p. 16: "hysteria puts us, so to speak, on the track of a certain original sin of psychoanalysis," by which he evidently means the relationship of this "science" to its historical situation and conditions of possibility. Hysteria in this sense may be understood as a historically new feature of the more general phenomenon of reification discussed in Chapter 5.)

41. "The *senses* have therefore become *theoreticians* in their immediate praxis. They relate to the *thing* for its own sake, but the thing itself is an *objective human* relation to itself and to man, and vice-versa" (Karl Marx, *Economic and Philosophical Manuscripts*, Second Manuscript, "Private Property and Communism," section 4, in *Early Writings*, trans. Rodney Livingstone and Gregor Benton [London: Penguin/NLB, 1975], p. 352. The whole section is of the greatest interest).

strategically retranslate as *reification* in *History and Class Consciousness*—is a complex one in which the traditional or "natural" [*naturwüchsige*] unities, social forms, human relations, cultural events, even religious systems, are systematically broken up in order to be reconstructed more efficiently, in the form of new post-natural processes or mechanisms; but in which, at the same time, these now isolated broken bits and pieces of the older unities acquire a certain autonomy of their own, a semi-autonomous coherence which, not merely a reflex of capitalist reification and rationalization, also in some measure serves to compensate for the dehumanization of experience reification brings with it, and to rectify the otherwise intolerable effects of the new process. So, to take an obvious example, as sight becomes a separate activity in its own right, it acquires new objects that are themselves the products of a process of abstraction and rationalization which strips the experience of the concrete of such attributes as color, spatial depth, texture, and the like, which in their turn undergo reification. The history of forms evidently reflects this process, by which the visual features of ritual, or those practices of imagery still functional in religious ceremonies, are secularized and reorganized into ends in themselves, in easel painting and new genres like landscape, then more openly in the perceptual revolution of the impressionists, with the autonomy of the visual finally triumphantly proclaimed in abstract expressionism. So Lukács is not wrong to associate the emergence of this modernism with the reification which is its precondition; but he oversimplifies and deproblematizes a complicated and interesting situation by ignoring the Utopian vocation of the newly reified sense, the mission of this heightened and autonomous language of color to restore at least a symbolic experience of libidinal gratification to a world drained of it, a world of extension, gray and merely quantifiable. Much the same might be said of the heightened experience of language in the modern world; and it would be desirable for those who celebrate the discovery of the Symbolic to reflect on the historical conditions of possibility of this new and specifically modern sense of the linguistic, semiotic, textual construction of reality. The "discovery" of Language is at one with its structural abstraction from concrete experience, with its hypostasis as an autonomous object, power, or activity (the work of the later Wittgenstein, who is so often numbered among the ideologues of the Symbolic, may also be read in the very different sense of a critique of just this conceptualization of language as a thing in itself).[42]

To return to that new event which was the emergence of psychoanalysis, it should be clear that the autonomization of the family as a private space within the nascent public sphere of bourgeois society, and as the "specialization" by which childhood and the family situation are qualitatively differentiated from other biographical experiences, are only features of a far more general process of social development, which also includes the autonomization of sexuality. Freud's object of study is, to be sure, less sexuality as such than desire and its dynamics as a whole; but once again, the precondition for the articulation and analysis of the mechanisms of desire according to such key themes or signifiers as the phallus, castration, the primal scene, the psychosexual stages, narcissism, repression, Eros vs. Thanatos, and the like—which can be taken as the thematics of the Freudian hermeneutic—lies in the preliminary isolation of sexual experience, which enables its constitutive features to carry a wider symbolic meaning. The psychoanalytic demonstration of the sexual dimensions of overtly nonsexual conscious experience and behavior is possible only when the sexual "dispositif" or apparatus has by a process of isolation, autonomization, specialization, developed into an independent sign system or symbolic dimension in its own right; as long as sexuality remains as integrated into social life in general as, say, eating, its possibilities of symbolic extension are to that degree limited, and the sexual retains its status as a banal inner-worldly event and bodily function. Its symbolic possibilities are dependent on its preliminary exclusion from the social field. As for primitive sexuality, if we were able imaginatively to grasp the symbolic trajectory that leads from tattoos and ritual mutilation to the constitution of erogenous zones in modern men and women,[43] we would have gone a long way toward sensing the historicity of the sexual phenomenon.

42. E.g.: "The paradox disappears only if we make a radical break with the idea that language always functions in one way, always serves the same purpose: to convey thoughts—which may be about houses, pains, good and evil, or anything else you please" (Ludwig Wittgenstein, *Philosophical Investigations* [Oxford: Blackwell, 1958], para. 304, p. 102). And see also Ferruccio Rossi-Landi, "Per un uso marxiano di Wittgenstein," in *Linguaggio come lavoro e come mercato* (Milan: Bompiani, 1968), pp. 11–60.

43. See Serge Leclerc, "La Mi-prise de la lettre," in *Démasquer le réel* (Paris: Seuil, 1971), pp. 63–69.

As I have suggested above, however, the sexual and its thematics are to be considered as the occasion for the Freudian hermeneutic, and as the source of its particular semiotic or symbolic system, rather than its fundamental mechanism. Indeed, this structural rift in the psychoanalytic hermeneutic between its interpretive code and its basic functioning model (or models, for Freud proposed a whole series of them throughout his career[44]) may explain the paradoxical situation of Freudian criticism today, about which we may affirm that the only people still seriously interested in it are the Freudians themselves, at the same time that the prestige and influence of the Freudian oeuvre and of psychoanalysis as a method and a model has never been so immense at any moment of its history. Having learned the Freudian lesson about sexual symbolism, in other words, our interest has been satisfied in this specialized area and can be displaced onto the more general but also more burning question of interpretation itself, and the contribution that such fundamental hermeneutic manuals as *The Interpretation of Dreams* and *Jokes and the Unconscious* have made to it.

The center around which the Freudian interpretive system turns is not sexual experience but rather wish-fulfillment, or its more metaphysical variant, "desire," posited as the very dynamic of our being as individual subjects. Is it necessary to stress the dependence of this "discovery" on the increasing abstraction of experience in modern society? Yet the same might be said of other interpretive themes developed during this period, and in particular the meditation, from Nietzsche to Weber, on the nature of value as such. The Nietzschean "transvaluation of all values" and also Weber's own notion of "value-free science" (commonly misconstrued as neutral scientific "objectivity"[45]) constitute so many attempts to project some Archimedean standpoint outside of social life, from which the inner-worldly values of the latter might be abstracted and studied in a kind of experimental or laboratory isolation. Like the rather different Freudian abstractions, then, such conceptions of value are subjectively possible only on the basis of some preliminary objective dissociation within action or behavior itself; and in a later chapter

44. Paul Ricoeur, *Freud and Philosophy* (New Haven: Yale University Press, 1970), pp. 65–157.

45. See Eugène Fleischmann, "De Nietzsche à Weber," *Archives européennes de sociologie*, 5 (1964), 190–238; and also my "Vanishing Mediator: Narrative Structure in Max Weber," *New German Critique*, No. 1 (Winter, 1973), 52–89.

we will see how strongly Joseph Conrad's work is marked by the dialectic of value, which unexpectedly reveals him to be the contemporary of both Nietzsche and Weber.

For with the coming of secular society and the desacralization of life paths and of the various rituals of traditional activity, with the new mobility of the market and the freedom of hesitation before a whole range of professions as well as the even more fundamental and increasingly universal commodification of labor power (on which the central discovery of the labor theory of value was itself dependent), it became possible for the first time to separate the unique quality and concrete content of a particular activity from its abstract organization or end, and to study the latter in isolation. To claim that Freud's conception of wish-fulfillment is a late stage in this process of abstraction (and that it has as epistemological predecessors the Marxian theory of labor power, and the subsequent Nietzschean and Weberian conceptions of value) is simply to observe that you cannot talk about wish-fulfillment or desire except by way of a powerful abstraction performed on a host of concrete and irreducible wishes or desires; and the possibility of performing such a conceptual abstraction subjectively is dependent on the preliminary objective realization of such a process within the raw materials or objects of study. We can think abstractly about the world only to the degree to which the world itself has already become abstract.

From the point of view of a political hermeneutic, measured against the requirements of a "political unconscious," we must conclude that the conception of wish-fulfillment remains locked in a problematic of the individual subject and the individual psychobiography which is only indirectly useful to us. The Lacanian rewriting of Freud should not be read as a mere variant on that Freudian hermeneutic, but rather a substantial and reflexive shift from the Freudian proposition about the nature of the dynamics of the subject (wish-fulfillment) to the interrogation of that problematic itself, foregrounding the category of the subject and studying the process whereby this psychic reality (consciousness)—as well as its buttressing ideologies and illusions (the feeling of personal identity, the myth of the ego or the self, and so forth)—become rigorous and self-imposed limitations on Freud's notion of individual wish-fulfillment. But the ideology of desire in its most fully realized forms is less an interpretive mode than a whole world-view, a genuine metaphysic, at its most resonant and attractive in its most extreme and grandiose versions, such as that, rich with death and the archaic, of Freud's own late metapsychology, with its vision of the immortal struggle between Eros and Thanatos. Such "theories" certainly rewrite the work; in the various ideologies of desire that have been proposed from Georges Bataille to Deleuze, and passing through such American variants as Norman O. Brown, the object of commentary is effectively transformed into an allegory whose master narrative is the story of desire itself, as it struggles against a repressive reality, convulsively breaking through the grids that were designed to hold it in place or, on the contrary, succumbing to repression and leaving the dreary wasteland of *aphanasis* behind it. At this level, it is to be wondered whether we have to do with a mere interpretation any longer, whether it is not a question here of the production of a whole new aesthetic object, a whole new mythic narrative. It is clear at least that such allegories of desire (generally the products of the Freudian Left) have a great deal more in common with Jungianism and myth criticism proper than they do with the older orthodox Freudian analyses. To such allegories of desire, indeed, may be applied Norman Holland's powerful critique of myth criticism as a whole, about which he observes that it works only if we have been told the work is mythic ahead of time, the unquestionable "resonance" of the mythic rewriting presupposing not the operation of some mythic unconscious but rather our own preliminary conscious "set" toward the reading in question.[46]

Yet, it will be observed, even if the theory of desire is a metaphysic and a myth, it is one whose great narrative events—repression and revolt—ought to be congenial to a Marxist perspective, one whose ultimate Utopian vision of the liberation of desire and of libidinal transfiguration was an essential feature of the great mass revolts of the 1960s in Eastern and Western Europe as well as in China and the United States. But precisely because of this, and more particularly on account of the theoretical as well as political difficulties encountered by the sequels to these movements as they tried to adapt to the very different circumstances of the present

46. Norman Holland, *The Dynamics of Literary Response* (New York: Oxford, 1968), pp. 243–261, 331–332.

period, such myths must be carefully reexamined. If they have affinities with Marxism, they have even greater ones with anarchism, with whose vital renewal today a contemporary Marxism must also come to terms.

The theoretical objection to the theory of desire has for the most part taken the form of a critique of the notion of transgression on which such theories are inevitably based. It is as though "genuine" desire needed repression in order for us to come to consciousness of it as such: but then in that case desire must always be transgressive, must always have a repressive norm or law through which to burst and against which to define itself. Yet it is a commonplace that transgressions, presupposing the laws or norms or taboos against which they function, thereby end up precisely reconfirming such laws. (For example, blasphemy not only requires you to have a strong sense of the sacred quality of the divine name, but may even be seen as a kind of ritual by which that strength is reawakened and revitalized.) From the point of view of interpretation, what this means is that desire is always outside of time, outside of narrative: it has no content, it is always the same in its cyclical moments of emergence, and the event in question takes on historicity only to the degree that the context of the explosion, the nature of that particular and historical repressive apparatus, knows specification.

What is more damaging, from the present perspective, is that desire, like its paler and more well behaved predecessor, wish-fulfillment, remains locked into the category of the individual subject, even if the form taken by the individual in it is no longer the ego or self, but rather the individual body. We must now argue this objective more consequently, since the need to transcend individualistic categories and modes of interpretation is in many ways the fundamental issue for any doctrine of the political unconscious, of interpretation in terms of the collective or associative. We will do so, however, by shifting from the Freudian hermeneutic to a quite different interpretive system, comparable only to the psychoanalytic one in the persistence of just such a valorization of desire. This is the archetypal system of Northrop Frye, which has the additional interest for us of conceiving of the function of culture explicitly in social terms.

I have suggested elsewhere that ideology leaves its mark on myth criticism insofar as the latter proposes an unbroken continuity between the social relations and narrative forms of primitive society and the cultural objects of our own.[47] For Marxism, on the contrary, it is the radical break between the two social formations which must be stressed, if we are to begin to grasp the degree to which capitalism has effectively dissolved all the older forms of collective relations, leaving their cultural expressions and their myths as incomprehensible to us as so many dead languages or undecipherable codices. In the present context, however, Frye's work comes before us as a virtual contemporary reinvention of the four-fold hermeneutic associated with the theological tradition.

Indeed, in this sense the trajectory of our discussion, from Freud to Northrop Frye, is an emblematic one: for any contemporary reevaluation of the problem of interpretation, the most vital exchange of energies inevitably takes place between the two poles of the psychoanalytic and the theological, between the rich and concrete practice of interpretation contained in the Freudian texts and dramatized in the diagnostic genius of Freud himself, and the millenary theoretical reflection on the problems and dynamics of interpretation, commentary, allegory, and multiple meanings, which, primarily organized around the central text of the Bible, is preserved in the religious tradition.[48]

The greatness of Frye, and the radical difference between his work and that of the great bulk of garden-variety myth criticism, lies in his willingness to raise the issue of community and to draw basic, essentially social, interpretive consequences from the nature of religion as collective representation. In so doing, Frye rejoins, although he would probably not enjoy the association, that more positive approach to religious symbolism which in the nineteenth century succeeded the essentially negative and destructive stance

---

47. "Criticism in History," in Norman Rudich, ed., *The Weapons of Criticism* (Palo Alto: Ramparts, 1976), pp. 38–40.

48. This, rather than any lingering or residual "religious" content, explains the strategic function of theological language in Walter Benjamin: to suggest that the "automaton" called "historical materialism" needs to harbor the "wizened dwarf" called theology within it in order to win every chess game it plays ("Theses on the Philosophy of History," in *Illuminations*, trans. H. Zohn, [New York: Schocken, 1969], p. 253) is to note, in coded language, the unnatural divorce between Stalinism and the tradition of a more properly hermeneutic Marxism, driven underground in the 1920s and 1930s. See below, Conclusion.

toward it of the Enlightenment, whose sapping of the ideological foundations of the *ancien régime* involved a systematic demystification and debunking of religious phenomena and a clear perception of the legitimizing relationship between what the philosophes conceived as "error" and "superstition" and the arbitrary power of hierarchical political institutions. But for thinkers as diverse as Feuerbach and Durkheim—the one emerging from the radicalism of pre-1848 Germany, the other within a still unstable Third Republic anxiously and in a conservative spirit meditating on the sources of social stability in general—the "illusions" of religion were to be read as the complement of a positive social functionality, and decoded as the figure and the projection of an essentially human energy—whether the latter is grasped as that full and nonalienated development of the human personality and of human potentialities which was the supreme value of German idealism, or, in the case of Durkheim, as a symbol for and confirmation of the organic human community. To be sure, any doctrine of figurality must necessarily be ambiguous: a symbolic expression of a truth is also, at the same time, a distorted and disguised expression, and a theory of figural expression is also a theory of mystification or false consciousness. Religion is thus here the distorted or symbolic coming to consciousness of itself, of the human community, and the critic's distance from religious figures will vary depending on whether, as is the case with Feuerbach (and with Hegel), stress is laid on its symbolic and alienating function, or whether, as in Durkheim's far more retrospective and anthropological account, its vocation as the locus of group identity is foregrounded.[49] The religious figures then become the symbolic space in which the collectivity thinks itself and celebrates its own unity; so that it does not seem a very difficult next step, if, with Frye, we see literature as a weaker form of myth or a later stage of ritual, to conclude that in that sense all literature, no matter how weakly, must be informed by what we have called a political unconscious, that all literature must be read as a symbolic meditation on the destiny of community.

Yet it is precisely this second step which Frye, on the one hand

49. See the sections on religion in Hegel's *Phenomenology of Spirit*, as well as Feuerbach's *Kleine Schriften* (translated as *The Fiery Brook: Selected Writings of Ludwig Feuerbach* by Zawar Hanfi [New York: Anchor, 1972]), and the "Conclusion" to Durkheim's *Elementary Forms of Religious Life*.

powerfully arguing it, then in a curious afterthought seems once more to withdraw; and this movement of recontainment, this impulse to stem the possibilities of collective and social interpretation which his hermeneutic had seemed to open, will serve us as a strategic occasion on which to interrogate religious hermeneutics in general. In this respect, Frye's restructuring of the traditional medieval four levels of meaning is instructive and symptomatic: it will be recalled that his "Theory of Symbols" rewrites the older fourfold scheme as four "phases": the Literal and Descriptive; the Formal; the Mythical or Archetypal; and the Anagogic. By phase, Frye means to designate not so much an interpretive code of a distinct type, as a certain type of attention—what we will shortly term the "horizon" or the "set" of the reading mind toward one particular order of textual phenomena, "a sequence of contexts or relationships in which the whole work of literary art can be placed"[50] such that this particular context determines a particular type of interpretation. His first two phases, the Literal and the Formal, remain essentially particular modalities of the attention of the reading mind, the first an attention to verbal organization and to the order of language, the second marking the shift to something like a phenomenological awareness of content as image, of the work's vocation to convey a symbolic structure or symbolic world by way of the first-level verbal constructions.

It is only at the third level, the Mythical or Archetypal, on which the concepts of both desire and society make their appearance that we reach interpretation proper. As in the medieval system, however, these have been somehow liberated or generated by the first two levels (which are for Frye the enabling institution of literature):

> The archetypal critic studies the poem as part of poetry, and poetry as part of the total human imitation of nature that we call civilization. Civilization is not merely an imitation of nature, and it is impelled by the force that we have just called desire. . . . [Desire] is neither limited to nor satisfied by objects, but is the energy that leads human society to develop its own form. Desire in this sense is the social aspect of what we met on the literal level as emotion, an impulse towards expression which would have remained amorphous if the poem had

50. Northrop Frye, *The Anatomy of Criticism* (Princeton: Princeton University Press, 1957), p. 73.

not liberated it by providing the form of its expression [or in other words, the Second or Formal Phase]. The form of desire, similarly, is liberated and made apparent by civilization. The efficient cause of civilization is work, and poetry in its social aspect has the function of expressing, as a verbal hypothesis, a vision of the goal of work and the forms of desire.[51]

And Frye goes on to enumerate some of the privileged archetypes, "the city, the garden, the farm, the sheep-fold, and the like, as well as human society itself,"[52] through which a symbolic or a heightened consciousness of the collective expresses itself.

Yet paradoxically this level—which the medieval theorists called the anagogic level, and in which the ultimate allegorical coding in terms of the destiny of the human race was achieved—is not yet for Frye the outer limit of what the literary text can do, not yet the final form of "what once, what each time, was *said*, when meaning appeared new, when meaning was at its fullest."[53] For Frye, this final level of meaning begins to emerge only when beyond the natural or inner-wordly archetypes of community we glimpse the human body itself, when in Joycean fashion the landscape slowly turns into a sleeping giant and with allegorical literality the various "members" of society knit themselves together into a genuine organism:

When we pass into anagogy, nature becomes, not the container, but the thing contained, and the archetypal universal symbols, the city, the garden, the quest, the marriage, are no longer the desirable forms that man constructs inside nature, but are themselves the forms of nature. Nature is now inside the mind of an infinite man who builds his cities out of the Milky Way. This is not reality, but it is the imaginative limit of desire, which is infinite, eternal, and hence apocalyptic. By an apocalypse I mean primarily the imaginative conception of the whole of nature as the content of an infinite and eternal living body which, if not human, is closer to being human than to being inanimate. "The desire of man being infinite," said Blake, "the possession is infinite and himself infinite."[54]

51. Ibid., pp. 105–106.
52. Ibid., p. 113.
53. Ricoeur, *Freud and Philosophy*, p. 27.
54. Frye, *Anatomy*, p. 119. The fundamental work on the body as a symbol of the organic community is Mary Douglas, *Natural Symbols* (New York: Pantheon, 1970).

Thus, not only does Frye's Blakean anagogy rejoin by a paradoxical movement that whole metaphysic of desire of which we spoke
above; the very concept of apocalypse as the end of history and the
culminating struggle of the collectivity is here curiously redirected,
rechanneled and indeed recontained, by the image of Blakean absolute "man" and transfigured body projected out upon the universe.
Yet equally paradoxically, the association lends Frye's metaphysic
of desire a kind of collective and Utopian resonance which the more
purely Freudian versions of the metaphysic lacked: when we come
to it from the more purely anarchistic and individualizing limits of
the left Freudians, this transfigured libidinal body glows and expands with all the political energies of a Blake engraving, and
makes it clear that the program of libidinal revolution is political
only to the degree that it is itself the figure for social revolution. Yet
this movement of figurality is precisely what from the other point of
view the arrangement of Frye's allegorical levels recontains: for,
being the final "phase" of the allegory, the image of the cosmic
body cannot stand for anything further, for anything other than
itself. Its figural and political momentum is broken, and the collective content of the image has been reprivatized in the henceforth
purely individual terms of the isolated body and the merely personal ecstasy.

This is not to suggest that a Marxian hermeneutic can do without
the symbolism and the impulse of libidinal transfiguration. Indeed,
radical politics has traditionally alternated between these two classical options or "levels," between the image of the triumph of the
collectivity and that of the liberation of the "soul" or "spiritual
body"; between a Saint-Simonian vision of social and collective
engineering and a Fourieresque Utopia of libidinal gratification;
between a 1920s Leninist formulation of communism as "the
soviets plus electrification" and some more properly Marcusean
1960s celebration of an instinctual "body politic." The problem is
not merely that of the respective priorities of these two "levels," not
merely interpretive and hermeneutic, but also practical and political, as the fate of the countercultural movement of the 1960s
demonstrates.

As far as Frye's own allegorical method is concerned, its terminological uncertainties may stand as something like an implicit
self-critique. We have seen above that in the system of the medieval

four levels of scripture, the third, that of the individual soul is designated as the *moral* level, while it is the fourth or last level—which embraces the whole history of the human race and the last judgment—that is termed the *anagogical* one. In Frye's appropriation of this system, the terms have been reversed: what Frye calls the Mythical or Archetypal level is that of the community—what the medieval exegetes called the *anagogical*—and is now positioned as a third level or phase subsumed under the final one, that of the libidinal body (which Frye, however, designates as the *Anagogical* level[55]). This terminological shift is thus a significant strategic and ideological move, in which political and collective imagery is transformed into a mere relay in some ultimately privatizing celebration of the category of individual experience. The essentially historical interpretive system of the church fathers has here been recontained, and its political elements turned back into the merest figures for the Utopian realities of the individual subject.

A social hermeneutic will, on the contrary, wish to keep faith with its medieval precursor in just this respect, and must necessarily restore a perspective in which the imagery of libidinal revolution and of bodily transfiguration once again becomes a figure for the perfected community. The unity of the body must once again prefigure the renewed organic identity of associative or collective life, rather than, as for Frye, the reverse. Only the community, indeed, can dramatize that self-sufficient intelligible unity (or "structure") of which the individual body, like the individual "subject," is a decentered "effect," and to which the individual organism, caught in the ceaseless chain of the generations and the species, cannot, even in the most desperate Renaissance or Neoplatonic visions of hermaphroditism (or in their contemporary counterpart, the Deleuze-Guattari "bachelor machine"), lay claim.

III

At this point it might seem appropriate to juxtapose a Marxist method of literary and cultural interpretation with those just outlined, and to document its claims to greater adequacy and validity. For better or for worse, however, as I warned in the Preface, this

55. "Our fourth level, the study of myths, and of poetry as a technique of social communication, is the third medieval level of moral and tropological meaning" (*Anatomy*, p. 116).

obvious next step is not the strategy projected by the present book, which rather seeks to argue the perspectives of Marxism as necessary preconditions for adequate literary comprehension. Marxist critical insights will therefore here be defended as something like an ultimate *semantic* precondition for the intelligibility of literary and cultural texts. Even this argument, however, needs a certain specification: in particular we will suggest that such semantic enrichment and enlargement of the inert givens and materials of a particular text must take place within three concentric frameworks, which mark a widening out of the sense of the social ground of a text through the notions, first, of political history, in the narrow sense of punctual event and a chroniclelike sequence of happenings in time; then of society, in the now already less diachronic and time-bound sense of a constitutive tension and struggle between social classes; and, ultimately, of history now conceived in its vastest sense of the sequence of modes of production and the succession and destiny of the various human social formations, from prehistoric life to whatever far future history has in store for us.[56]

These distinct semantic horizons are, to be sure, also distinct moments of the process of interpretation, and may in that sense be understood as dialectical equivalents of what Frye has called the successive "phases" in our reinterpretation—our rereading and rewriting—of the literary text. What we must also note, however, is that each phase or horizon governs a distinct reconstruction of its

---

56. A useful discussion of the phenomenological concept of "horizon" may be found in Hans-Georg Gadamer, *Truth and Method,* trans. G. Barden and J. Cumming (New York: Seabury, 1975), pp. 216–220, 267–274. It will become clear in the course of my subsequent discussion that a Marxian conception of our relationship to the past requires a sense of our radical difference from earlier cultures which is not adequately allowed for in Gadamer's influential notion of *Horizontverschmelzung* (fusion of horizons). This is perhaps also the moment to add that from the perspective of Marxism as an "absolute historicism," the stark antithesis proposed by E. D. Hirsch, Jr., between Gadamer's historicist "relativism" and Hirsch's own conception of a more absolute interpretive validity, will no longer seem particularly irreconcilable. Hirsch's distinction between *Sinn* and *Bedeutung,* between the scientific analysis of a text's intrinsic "meaning" and what he is pleased to call our "ethical" evaluation of its "significance" for us (see, for example, *The Aims of Interpretation* [Chicago: University of Chicago Press, 1976]), corresponds to the traditional Marxist distinction between science and ideology, particularly as it has been retheorized by the Althusserians. It is surely a useful working distinction, although in the light of current revisions of the idea of science one should probably make no larger theoretical claims for it than this operative one.

object, and construes the very structure of what can now only in a general sense be called "the text" in a different way.

Thus, within the narrower limits of our first, narrowly political or historical, horizon, the "text," the object of study, is still more or less construed as coinciding with the individual literary work or utterance. The difference between the perspective enforced and enabled by this horizon, however, and that of ordinary *explication de texte,* or individual exegesis, is that here the individual work is grasped essentially as a *symbolic act.*

When we pass into the second phase, and find that the semantic horizon within which we grasp a cultural object has widened to include the social order, we will find that the very object of our analysis has itself been thereby dialectically transformed, and that it is no longer construed as an individual "text" or work in the narrow sense, but has been reconstituted in the form of the great collective and class discourses of which a text is little more than an individual *parole* or utterance. Within this new horizon, then, our object of study will prove to be the *ideologeme,* that is, the smallest intelligible unit of the essentially antagonistic collective discourses of social classes.

When finally, even the passions and values of a particular social formation find themselves placed in a new and seemingly relativized perspective by the ultimate horizon of human history as a whole, and by their respective positions in the whole complex sequence of the modes of production, both the individual text and its ideologemes know a final transformation, and must be read in terms of what I will call the *ideology of form,* that is, the symbolic messages transmitted to us by the coexistence of various sign systems which are themselves traces or anticipations of modes of production.

The general movement through these three progressively wider horizons will largely coincide with the shifts in focus of the final chapters in this book, and will be felt, although not narrowly and programmatically underscored, in the methodological transformations determined by the historical transformations of their textual objects, from Balzac to Gissing to Conrad.

We must now briefly characterize each of these semantic or interpretive horizons. We have suggested that it is only in the first narrowly political horizon—in which history is reduced to a series of punctual events and crises in time, to the diachronic agitation of the year-to-year, the chroniclelike annals of the rise and fall of political regimes and social fashions, and the passionate immediacy of struggles between historical individuals—that the "text" or object of study will tend to coincide with the individual literary work or cultural artifact. Yet to specify this individual text as a symbolic act is already fundamentally to transform the categories with which traditional *explication de texte* (whether narrative or poetic) operated and largely still operates.

The model for such an interpretive operation remains the readings of myth and aesthetic structure of Claude Lévi-Strauss as they are codified in his fundamental essay "The Structural Study of Myth."[57] These suggestive, often sheerly occasional, readings and speculative glosses immediately impose a basic analytical or interpretive principle: the individual narrative, or the individual formal structure, is to be grasped as the imaginary resolution of a real contradiction. Thus, to take only the most dramatic of Lévi-Strauss's analyses—the "interpretation" of the unique facial decorations of the Caduveo Indians—the starting point will be an immanent description of the formal and structural peculiarities of this body art; yet it must be a description already pre-prepared and oriented toward transcending the purely formalistic, a movement which is achieved not by abandoning the formal level for something extrinsic to it— such as some inertly social "content"—but rather immanently, by construing purely formal patterns as a symbolic enactment of the social within the formal and the aesthetic. Such symbolic functions are, however, rarely found by an aimless enumeration of random formal and stylistic features; our discovery of a text's symbolic efficacity must be oriented by a formal description which seeks to grasp it as a determinate structure of still properly formal *contradictions*. Thus, Lévi-Strauss orients his still purely visual analysis

---

57. Claude Lévi-Strauss, *Structural Anthropology,* trans. C. Jacobson and B. G. Schoepf (New York: Basic, 1963), pp. 206–231. The later four-volume *Mythologiques* reverse the perspective of this analysis: where the earlier essay focused on the individual mythic *parole* or utterance, the later series models the entire system or *langue* in terms of which the various individual myths are related to each other. *Mythologiques* should therefore rather be used as suggestive material on the historical difference between the narrative mode of production of primitive societies and that of our own: in this sense, the later work would find its place in the third and final horizon of interpretation.

of Caduveo facial decorations toward this climactic account of their contradictory dynamic: "the use of a design which is symmetrical but yet lies across an oblique axis . . . a complicated situation based upon two contradictory forms of duality, and resulting in a compromise brought about by a secondary opposition between the ideal axis of the object itself [the human face] and the ideal axis of the figure which it represents."[58] Already on the purely formal level, then, this visual text has been grasped as a contradiction by way of the curiously provisional and asymmetrical resolution it proposes for that contradiction.

Lévi-Strauss's "interpretation" of this formal phenomenon may now, perhaps overhastily, be specified. Caduveo are a hierarchical society, organized in three endogamous groups or castes. In their social development, as in that of their neighbors, this nascent hierarchy is already the place of the emergence, if not of political power in the strict sense, then at least of relations of domination: the inferior status of women, the subordination of youth to elders, and the development of a hereditary aristocracy. Yet whereas this latent power structure is, among the neighboring Guana and Bororo, masked by a division into moieties which cuts across the three castes, and whose exogamous exchange appears to function in a nonhierarchical, essentially egalitarian way, it is openly present in Caduveo life, as surface inequality and conflict. The social institutions of the Guana and Bororo, on the other hand, provide a realm of appearance, in which real hierarchy and inequality are dissimulated by the reciprocity of the moieties, and in which, therefore, "asymmetry of class is balanced . . . by symmetry of 'moieties.'"

As for the Caduveo,

> they were never lucky enough to resolve their contradictions, or to disguise them with the help of institutions artfully devised for that purpose. On the social level, the remedy was lacking . . . but it was never completely out of their grasp. It was within them, never objectively formulated, but present as a source of confusion and disquiet. Yet since they were unable to conceptualize or to live this solution directly, they began to dream it, to project it into the imaginary. . . . We must therefore interpret the graphic art of Caduveo

58. Claude Lévi-Strauss, *Tristes tropiques,* trans. John Russell (New York: Atheneum, 1971), p. 176.

women, and explain its mysterious charm as well as its apparently gratuitous complication, as the fantasy production of a society seeking passionately to give symbolic expression to the institutions it might have had in reality, had not interest and superstition stood in the way.[59]

In this fashion, then, the visual text of Caduveo facial art constitutes a symbolic act, whereby real social contradictions, insurmountable in their own terms, find a purely formal resolution in the aesthetic realm.

This interpretive model thus allows us a first specification of the relationship between ideology and cultural texts or artifacts: a specification still conditioned by the limits of the first, narrowly historical or political horizon in which it is made. We may suggest that from this perspective, ideology is not something which informs or invests symbolic production; rather the aesthetic act is itself ideological, and the production of aesthetic or narrative form is to be seen as an ideological act in its own right, with the function of inventing imaginary or formal "solutions" to unresolvable social contradictions.

Lévi-Strauss's work also suggests a more general defense of the proposition of a political unconscious than we have hitherto been able to present, insofar as it offers the spectacle of so-called primitive peoples perplexed enough by the dynamics and contradictions of their still relatively simple forms of tribal organization to project decorative or mythic resolutions of issues that they are unable to articulate conceptually. But if this is the case for pre-capitalist and even pre-political societies, then how much more must it be true for the citizen of the modern *Gesellschaft,* faced with the great constitutional options of the revolutionary period, and with the corrosive and tradition-annihilating effects of the spread of a money and market economy, with the changing cast of collective characters which oppose the bourgeoisie, now to an embattled aristocracy, now to an urban proletariat, with the great fantasms of the various nationalisms, now themselves virtual "subjects of history" of a rather different kind, with the social homogenization and psychic constriction of the rise of the industrial city and its "masses," the sudden appearance of the great

59. Ibid., pp. 179–180.

transnational forces of communism and fascism, followed by the advent of the superstates and the onset of that great ideological rivalry between capitalism and communism, which, no less passionate and obsessive than that which, at the dawn of modern times, seethed through the wars of religion, marks the final tension of our now global village? It does not, indeed, seem particularly farfetched to suggest that these texts of history, with their fantasmatic collective "actants," their narrative organization, and their immense charge of anxiety and libidinal investment, are lived by the contemporary subject as a genuine politico-historical *pensée sauvage* which necessarily informs all of our cultural artifacts, from the literary institutions of high modernism all the way to the products of mass culture. Under these circumstances, Lévi-Strauss's work suggests that the proposition whereby all cultural artifacts are to be read as symbolic resolutions of real political and social contradictions deserves serious exploration and systematic experimental verification. It will become clear in later chapters of this book that the most readily accessible formal articulation of the operations of a political *pensée sauvage* of this kind will be found in what we will call the structure of a properly political *allegory,* as it develops from networks of topical allusion in Spenser or Milton or Swift to the symbolic narratives of class representatives or "types" in novels like those of Balzac. With political allegory, then, a sometimes repressed ur-narrative or master fantasy about the interaction of collective subjects, we have moved to the very borders of our second horizon, in which what we formerly regarded as individual texts are grasped as "utterances" in an essentially collective or class discourse.

We cannot cross those borders, however, without some final account of the critical operations involved in our first interpretive phase. We have implied that in order to be consequent, the will to read literary or cultural texts as symbolic acts must necessarily grasp them as resolutions of determinate contradictions; and it is clear that the notion of contradiction is central to any Marxist cultural analysis, just as it will remain central in our two subsequent horizons, although it will there take rather different forms. The methodological requirement to articulate a text's fundamental contradiction may then be seen as a test of the completeness of the analysis: this is why, for example, the conventional sociology of literature or culture, which modestly limits itself to the identification of class motifs or values in a given text, and feels that its work is done when it shows how a given artifact "reflects" its social background, is utterly unacceptable. Meanwhile, Kenneth Burke's play of emphases, in which a symbolic act is on the one hand affirmed as a genuine *act*, albeit on the symbolic level, while on the other it is registered as an act which is "merely" symbolic, its resolutions imaginary ones that leave the real untouched, suitably dramatizes the ambiguous status of art and culture.

Still, we need to say a little more about the status of this external reality, of which it will otherwise be thought that it is little more than the traditional notion of "context" familiar in older social or historical criticism. The type of interpretation here proposed is more satisfactorily grasped as the rewriting of the literary text in such a way that the latter may itself be seen as the rewriting or restructuration of a prior historical or ideological *subtext*, it being always understood that that "subtext" is not immediately present as such, not some common-sense external reality, nor even the conventional narratives of history manuals, but rather must itself always be (re)constructed after the fact. The literary or aesthetic act therefore always entertains some active relationship with the Real; yet in order to do so, it cannot simply allow "reality" to persevere inertly in its own being, outside the text and at distance. It must rather draw the Real into its own texture, and the ultimate paradoxes and false problems of linguistics, and most notably of semantics, are to be traced back to this process, whereby language manages to carry the Real within itself as its own intrinsic or immanent subtext. Insofar, in other words, as symbolic action—what Burke will map as "dream," "prayer," or "chart"[60]—is a way of doing something to the world, to that degree what we are calling "world" must inhere within it, as the content it has to take up into itself in order to submit it to the transformations of form. The symbolic act therefore begins by generating and producing its own context in the same moment of emergence in which it steps back from it, taking its measure with a view toward its own projects of transformation. The whole paradox of what we have here called the

---

60. Kenneth Burke, *The Philosophy of Literary Form* (Berkeley: University of California Press, 1973), pp. 5–6; and see also my "Symbolic Inference; or, Kenneth Burke and Ideological Analysis," *Critical Inquiry,* 4 (Spring, 1978), 507–523.

subtext may be summed up in this, that the literary work or cultural object, as though for the first time, brings into being that very situation to which it is also, at one and the same time, a reaction. It articulates its own situation and textualizes it, thereby encouraging and perpetuating the illusion that the situation itself did not exist before it, that there is nothing but a text, that there never was any extra- or con-textual reality before the text itself generated it in the form of a mirage. One does not have to argue the reality of history: necessity, like Dr. Johnson's stone, does that for us. That history—Althusser's "absent cause," Lacan's "Real"—is *not* a text, for it is fundamentally non-narrative and nonrepresentational; what can be added, however, is the proviso that history is inaccessible to us except in textual form, or in other words, that it can be approached only by way of prior (re)textualization. Thus, to insist on either of the two inseparable yet incommensurable dimensions of the symbolic act without the other: to overemphasize the active way in which the text reorganizes its subtext (in order, presumably, to reach the triumphant conclusion that the "referent" does not exist); or on the other hand to stress the imaginary status of the symbolic act so completely as to reify its social ground, now no longer understood as a subtext but merely as some inert given that the text passively or fantasmatically "reflects"—to overstress either of these functions of the symbolic act at the expense of the other is surely to produce sheer ideology, whether it be, as in the first alternative, the ideology of structuralism, or, in the second, that of vulgar materialism.

Still, this view of the place of the "referent" will be neither complete nor methodologically usable unless we specify a supplementary distinction between several types of subtext to be (re)constructed. We have implied, indeed, that the social contradiction addressed and "resolved" by the formal prestidigitation of narrative must, however reconstructed, remain an absent cause, which cannot be directly or immediately conceptualized by the text. It seems useful, therefore, to distinguish, from this ultimate subtext which is the place of social *contradiction,* a secondary one, which is more properly the place of ideology, and which takes the form of the *aporia* or the *antinomy:* what can in the former be resolved only through the intervention of praxis here comes before the purely contemplative mind as logical scandal or double bind, the unthinkable and the conceptually paradoxical, that which cannot be unknotted by the operation of pure thought, and which must therefore generate a whole more properly narrative apparatus—the text itself—to square its circles and to dispel, through narrative movement, its intolerable closure. Such a distinction, positing a system of antinomies as the symptomatic expression and conceptual reflex of something quite different, namely a social contradiction, will now allow us to reformulate that coordination between a semiotic and a dialectical method, which was evoked in the preceding section. The operational validity of semiotic analysis, and in particular of the Greimassian semiotic rectangle,[61] derives, as was suggested there, not from its adequacy to nature or being, nor even from its capacity to map all forms of thinking or language, but rather from its vocation specifically to model ideological closure and to articulate the workings of binary oppositions, here the privileged form of what we have called the antinomy. A dialectical reevaluation of the findings of semiotics intervenes, however, at the moment in which this entire system of ideological closure is taken as the symptomatic projection of something quite different, namely of social contradiction.

We may now leave this first textual or interpretive model behind, and pass over into the second horizon, that of the social. The latter becomes visible, and individual phenomena are revealed as social facts and institutions, only at the moment in which the organizing categories of analysis become those of social class. I have in another place described the dynamics of ideology in its constituted form as a function of social class:[62] suffice it only to recall here that for Marxism classes must always be apprehended relationally, and that the ultimate (or ideal) form of class relationship and class struggle is always dichotomous. The constitutive form of class relationships is always that between a dominant and a laboring class: and it is only in terms of this axis that class fractions (for example, the petty

---

61. See Chapter 3, note 13, and above, pp. 46–49.

62. *Marxism and Form*, pp. 376–382; and see below, pp. 288–291. The most authoritative contemporary Marxist statement of this view of social class is to be found in E. P. Thompson, *The Making of the English Working Classes* (New York: Vintage, 1966), pp. 9–11; in *The Poverty of Theory*, Thompson has argued that his view of classes is incompatible with "structural" Marxism, for which classes are not "subjects" but rather "positions" within the social totality (see, for the Althusserian position, Nicos Poulantzas, *Political Power and Social Classes*).

bourgeoisie) or ec-centric or dependent classes (such as the peasantry) are positioned. To define class in this way is sharply to differentiate the Marxian model of classes from the conventional sociological analysis of society into strata, subgroups, professional elites and the like, each of which can presumably be studied in isolation from one another in such a way that the analysis of their "values" or their "cultural space" folds back into separate and independent *Weltanschauungen,* each of which inertly reflects its particular "stratum." For Marxism, however, the very content of a class ideology is relational, in the sense that its "values" are always actively in situation with respect to the opposing class, and defined against the latter: normally, a ruling class ideology will explore various strategies of the *legitimation* of its own power position, while an oppositional culture or ideology will, often in covert and disguised strategies, seek to contest and to undermine the dominant "value system."

This is the sense in which we will say, following Mikhail Bakhtin, that within this horizon class discourse—the categories in terms of which individual texts and cultural phenomena are now rewritten—is essentially *dialogical* in its structure.[63] As Bakhtin's (and Voloshinov's) own work in this field is relatively specialized, focusing primarily on the heterogeneous and explosive pluralism of moments of carnival or festival (moments, for example, such as the immense resurfacing of the whole spectrum of the religious or political sects in the English 1640s or the Soviet 1920s) it will be necessary to add the qualification that the normal form of the dialogical is essentially an *antagonistic* one, and that the dialogue of class struggle is one in which two opposing discourses fight it out within the general unity of a shared code. Thus, for instance, the shared master code of religion becomes in the 1640s in England the place in which the dominant formulations of a hegemonic theology are reappropriated and polemically modified.[64]

---

63. Mikhail Bakhtin, *Problems of Dostoyevsky's Poetics,* trans. R. W. Rotsel (Ann Arbor: Ardis, 1973), pp. 153–169. See also Bakhtin's important book on linguistics, written under the name of V. N. Voloshinov, *Marxism and the Philosophy of Language,* trans. L. Matejka and I. R. Titunik (New York: Seminar Press, 1973), pp. 83–98; and Bakhtin's posthumous collection, *Esthétique et théorie du roman,* trans. Daria Olivier (Paris: Gallimard, 1978), esp. pp. 152–182.

64. See Christopher Hill, *The World Turned Upside Down* (London: Temple Smith, 1972).

Within this new horizon, then, the basic formal requirement of dialectical analysis is maintained, and its elements are still restructured in terms of *contradiction* (this is essentially, as we have said, what distinguishes the relationality of a Marxist class analysis from static analysis of the sociological type). Where the contradiction of the earlier horizon was univocal, however, and limited to the situation of the individual text, to the place of a purely individual symbolic resolution, contradiction here appears in the form of the dialogical as the irreconcilable demands and positions of antagonistic classes. Here again, then, the requirement to prolong interpretation to the point at which this ultimate contradiction begins to appear offers a criterion for the completeness or insufficiency of the analysis.

Yet to rewrite the individual text, the individual cultural artifact, in terms of the antagonistic dialogue of class voices is to perform a rather different operation from the one we have ascribed to our first horizon. Now the individual text will be refocused as a *parole,* or individual utterance, of that vaster system, or *langue,* of class discourse. The individual text retains its formal structure as a symbolic act: yet the value and character of such symbolic action are now significantly modified and enlarged. On this rewriting, the individual utterance or text is grasped as a symbolic move in an essentially polemic and strategic ideological confrontation between the classes, and to describe it in these terms (or to reveal it in this form) demands a whole set of different instruments.

For one thing, the illusion or appearance of isolation or autonomy which a printed text projects must now be systematically undermined. Indeed, since by definition the cultural monuments and masterworks that have survived tend necessarily to perpetuate only a single voice in this class dialogue, the voice of a hegemonic class, they cannot be properly assigned their relational place in a dialogical system without the restoration or artificial reconstruction of the voice to which they were initially opposed, a voice for the most part stifled and reduced to silence, marginalized, its own utterances scattered to the winds, or reappropriated in their turn by the hegemonic culture.

This is the framework in which the reconstruction of so-called popular cultures must properly take place—most notably, from the fragments of essentially peasant cultures: folk songs, fairy tales, popular festivals, occult or oppositional systems of belief such as magic and witchcraft. Such reconstruction is of a piece with the reaffirmation of the existence of marginalized or oppositional cultures in our own time, and the reaudition of the oppositional voices of black or ethnic cultures, women's and gay literature, "naive" or marginalized folk art, and the like. But once again, the affirmation of such nonhegemonic cultural voices remains ineffective if it is limited to the merely "sociological" perspective of the pluralistic rediscovery of other isolated social groups: only an ultimate rewriting of these utterances in terms of their essentially polemic and subversive strategies restores them to their proper place in the dialogical system of the social classes. Thus, for instance, Bloch's reading of the fairy tale, with its magical wish-fulfillments and its Utopian fantasies of plenty and the *pays de Cocagne*,[65] restores the dialogical and antagonistic content of this "form" by exhibiting it as a systematic deconstruction and undermining of the hegemonic aristocratic form of the epic, with its somber ideology of heroism and baleful destiny; thus also the work of Eugene Genovese on black religion restores the vitality of these utterances by reading them, not as the replication of imposed beliefs, but rather as a process whereby the hegemonic Christianity of the slave-owners is appropriated, secretly emptied of its content and subverted to the transmission of quite different oppositional and coded messages.[66]

Moreover, the stress on the dialogical then allows us to reread or rewrite the hegemonic forms themselves; they also can be grasped as a process of the reappropriation and neutralization, the cooptation and class transformation, the cultural universalization, of forms which originally expressed the situation of "popular," subordinate, or dominated groups. So the slave religion of Christianity is transformed into the hegemonic ideological apparatus of the medieval system; while folk music and peasant dance find themselves transmuted into the forms of aristocratic or court festivity and into the cultural visions of the pastoral; and popular narrative from time immemorial—romance, adventure story, melodrama, and the like—is ceaselessly drawn on to restore vitality to an enfeebled and

---

65. Ernst Bloch, "Zerstörung, Rettung des Mythos durch Licht," in *Verfremdungen* I (Frankfurt: Suhrkamp, 1963), pp. 152–162.
66. Eugene Genovese, *Roll Jordan Roll* (New York: Vintage, 1976), pp. 161–284.

asphyxiating "high culture." Just so, in our own time, the vernacular and its still vital sources of production (as in black language) are reappropriated by the exhausted and media-standardized speech of a hegemonic middle class. In the aesthetic realm, indeed, the process of cultural "universalization" (which implies the repression of the oppositional voice, and the illusion that there is only one genuine "culture") is the specific form taken by what can be called the process of legitimation in the realm of ideology and conceptual systems.

Still, this operation of rewriting and of the restoration of an essentially dialogical or class horizon will not be complete until we specify the "units" of this larger system. The linguistic metaphor (rewriting texts in terms of the opposition of a *parole* to a *langue*) cannot, in other words, be particularly fruitful until we are able to convey something of the dynamics proper to a class *langue* itself, which is evidently, in Saussure's sense, something like an ideal construct that is never wholly visible and never fully present in any one of its individual utterances. This larger class discourse can be said to be organized around minimal "units" which we will call *ideologemes*. The advantage of this formulation lies in its capacity to mediate between conceptions of ideology as abstract opinion, class value, and the like, and the narrative materials with which we will be working here. The ideologeme is an amphibious formation, whose essential structural characteristic may be described as its possibility to manifest itself either as a pseudoidea—a conceptual or belief system, an abstract value, an opinion or prejudice—or as a protonarrative, a kind of ultimate class fantasy about the "collective characters" which are the classes in opposition. This duality means that the basic requirement for the full description of the ideologeme is already given in advance: as a construct it must be susceptible to both a conceptual description and a narrative manifestation all at once. The ideologeme can of course be elaborated in either of these directions, taking on the finished appearance of a philosophical system on the one hand, or that of a cultural text on the other; but the ideological analysis of these finished cultural products requires us to demonstrate each one as a complex work of transformation on that ultimate raw material which is the ideologeme in question. The analyst's work is thus first that of the identification of the ideologeme, and, in many cases, of its initial naming in instances where for whatever reason it had not yet been registered as such. The immense preparatory task of identifying and inventorying such ideologemes has scarcely even begun, and to it the present book will make but the most modest contribution: most notably in its isolation of that fundamental nineteenth-century ideologeme which is the "theory" of *ressentiment,* and in its "unmasking" of ethics and the ethical binary opposition of good and evil as one of the fundamental forms of ideological thought in Western culture. However, our stress here and throughout on the fundamentally narrative character of such ideologemes (even where they seem to be articulated only as abstract conceptual beliefs or values) will offer the advantage of restoring the complexity of the transactions between opinion and protonarrative or libidinal fantasy. Thus we will observe, in the case of Balzac, the generation of an overt and constituted ideological and political "value system" out of the operation of an essentially narrative and fantasy dynamic; the chapter on Gissing, on the other hand, will show how an already constituted "narrative paradigm" emits an ideological message in its own right without the mediation of authorial intervention.

This focus or horizon, that of class struggle and its antagonistic discourses, is, as we have already suggested, not the ultimate form a Marxist analysis of culture can take. The example just alluded to— that of the seventeenth-century English revolution, in which the various classes and class fractions found themselves obliged to articulate their ideological struggles through the shared medium of a religious master code—can serve to dramatize the shift whereby these objects of study are reconstituted into a structurally distinct "text" specific to this final enlargement of the analytical frame. For the possibility of a displacement in emphasis is already given in this example: we have suggested that within the apparent unity of the theological code, the fundamental difference of antagonistic class positions can be made to emerge. In that case, the inverse move is also possible, and such concrete semantic differences can on the contrary be focused in such a way that what emerges is rather the all-embracing unity of a single code which they must share and which thus characterizes the larger unity of the social system. This new object—code, sign system, or system of the production of signs and codes—thus becomes an index of an entity of study which greatly transcends those earlier ones of the narrowly political (the symbolic act), and the social (class discourse and the ideologeme), and which we have proposed to term the historical in the larger sense of this word. Here the organizing unity will be what the Marxian tradition designates as a *mode of production*.

I have already observed that the "problematic" of modes of production is the most vital new area of Marxist theory in all the disciplines today; not paradoxically, it is also one of the most traditional, and we must therefore, in a brief preliminary way, sketch in the "sequence" of modes of production as classical Marxism, from Marx and Engels to Stalin, tended to enumerate them.[67] These modes, or "stages" of human society, have traditionally included the following: primitive communism or tribal society (the horde), the *gens* or hierarchical kinship societies (neolithic society), the Asiatic mode of production (so-called Oriental despotism), the *polis* or an oligarchical slaveholding society (the ancient mode of production), feudalism, capitalism, and communism (with a good deal of debate as to whether the "transitional" stage between these last—sometimes called "socialism"—is a genuine mode of production in its own right or not). What is more significant in the present context is that even this schematic or mechanical conception of historical "stages" (what the Althusserians have systematically criticized under the term "historicism") includes the notion of a cultural dominant or form of ideological coding specific to each mode of production. Following the same order these have generally been conceived as magic and mythic narrative, kinship, religion or the sacred, "politics" according to the narrower category of citi-

---

67. The "classical" texts on modes of production, besides Lewis Henry Morgan's *Ancient Society* (1877), are Karl Marx, *Pre-Capitalist Economic Formations,* a section of the *Grundrisse* (1857–58) published separately by Eric Hobsbawm (New York: International, 1965), and Friedrich Engels, *The Family, Private Property, and the State* (1884). Important recent contributions to the mode of production "debate" include Etienne Balibar's contribution to Althusser's collective volume, *Reading Capital;* Emmanuel Terray, *Marxism and "Primitive" Societies,* trans. M. Klopper (New York: Monthly Review, 1972); Maurice Godelier, *Horizon: trajets marxistes en anthropologie* (Paris: Maspéro, 1973); J. Chesneaux, ed., *Sur le "mode de production asiatique"* (Paris: Editions Sociales, 1969); and Barry Hindess and Paul Hirst, *Pre-Capitalist Modes of Production* (London: Routledge & Kegan Paul, 1975).

zenship in the ancient city state, relations of personal domination, commodity reification, and (presumably) original and as yet nowhere fully developed forms of collective or communal association.

Before we can determine the cultural "text" or object of study specific to the horizon of modes of production, however, we must make two preliminary remarks about the methodological problems it raises. The first will bear on whether the concept of "mode of production" is a synchronic one, while the second will address the temptation to use the various modes of production for a classifying or typologizing operation, in which cultural texts are simply dropped into so many separate compartments.

Indeed, a number of theorists have been disturbed by the apparent convergence between the properly Marxian notion of an all-embracing and all-structuring mode of production (which assigns everything within itself—culture, ideological production, class articulation, technology—a specific and unique place), and non-Marxist visions of a "total system" in which the various elements or levels of social life are programmed in some increasingly constricting way. Weber's dramatic notion of the "iron cage" of an increasingly bureaucratic society,[68] Foucault's image of the gridwork of an ever more pervasive "political technology of the body,"[69] but also more traditional "synchronic" accounts of the cultural programming of a given historical "moment," such as those that have variously been proposed from Vico and Hegel to Spengler and Deleuze—all such monolithic models of the cultural unity of a given historical period have tended to confirm the suspicions of a dialecti-

68. "The Puritan wanted to work in a calling; we are forced to do so. For when asceticism was carried out of monastic cells into everyday life, and began to dominate worldly morality, it did its part in building the tremendous cosmos of the modern economic order. This order is now bound to the technical and economic conditions of machine production which today determine the lives of all the individuals who are born into this mechanism, not only those directly concerned with economic acquisition, with irresistible force. Perhaps it will so determine them until the last ton of fossilized coal is burnt. In Baxter's view the care for external goods should only lie on the shoulders of the saint 'like a light cloak, which can be thrown aside at any moment.' But fate decreed that the cloak should become an iron cage." *The Protestant Ethic and the Spirit of Capitalism*, trans. T. Parsons (New York: Scribners, 1958), p. 181.

69. Michel Foucault, *Surveiller et punir* (Paris: Gallimard, 1975), pp. 27–28 and passim.

cal tradition about the dangers of an emergent "synchronic" thought, in which change and development are relegated to the marginalized category of the merely "diachronic," the contingent or the rigorously nonmeaningful (and this, even where, as with Althusser, such models of cultural unity are attacked as forms of a more properly Hegelian and idealistic "expressive causality"). This theoretical foreboding about the limits of synchronic thought can perhaps be most immediately grasped in the political area, where the model of the "total system" would seem slowly and inexorably to eliminate any possibility of the *negative* as such, and to reintegrate the place of an oppositional or even merely "critical" practice and resistance back into the system as the latter's mere inversion. In particular, everything about class struggle that was anticipatory in the older dialectical framework, and seen as an emergent space for radically new social relations, would seem, in the synchronic model, to reduce itself to practices that in fact tend to reinforce the very system that foresaw and dictated their specific limits. This is the sense in which Jean Baudrillard has suggested that the "total-system" view of contemporary society reduces the options of resistance to anarchist gestures, to the sole remaining ultimate protests of the wildcat strike, terrorism, and death. Meanwhile, in the framework of the analysis of culture also, the latter's integration into a synchronic model would seem to empty cultural production of all its antisystemic capacities, and to "unmask" even the works of an overtly oppositional or political stance as instruments ultimately programmed by the system itself.

It is, however, precisely the notion of a series of enlarging theoretical horizons proposed here that can assign these disturbing synchronic frameworks their appropriate analytical places and dictate their proper use. This notion projects a long view of history which is inconsistent with concrete political action and class struggle only if the specificity of the horizons is not respected; thus, even if the concept of a mode of production is to be considered a synchronic one (and we will see in a moment that things are somewhat more complicated than this), at the level of historical abstraction at which such a concept is properly to be used, the lesson of the "vision" of a total system is for the short run one of the structural limits imposed on praxis rather than the latter's impossibility.

The theoretical problem with the synchronic systems enumerated above lies elsewhere, and less in their analytical framework than in what in a Marxist perspective might be called their infrastructural regrounding. Historically, such systems have tended to fall into two general groups, which one might term respectively the hard and soft visions of the total system. The first group projects a fantasy future of a "totalitarian" type in which the mechanisms of domination—whether these are understood as part of the more general process of bureaucratization, or on the other hand derive more immediately from the deployment of physical and ideological force—are grasped as irrevocable and increasingly pervasive tendencies whose mission is to colonize the last remnants and survivals of human freedom—to occupy and organize, in other words, what still persists of Nature objectively and subjectively (very schematically, the Third World and the Unconscious).

This group of theories can perhaps hastily be associated with the central names of Weber and Foucault; the second group may then be associated with names such as those of Jean Baudrillard and the American theorists of a "post-industrial society."[70] For this second group, the characteristics of the total system of contemporary world society are less those of political domination than those of cultural programming and penetration: not the iron cage, but rather the *société de consommation* with its consumption of images and simulacra, its free-floating signifiers and its effacement of the older structures of social class and traditional ideological hegemony. For both groups, world capitalism is in evolution toward a system which is not socialist in any classical sense, on the one hand the nightmare of total control and on the other the polymorphous or schizophrenic intensities of some ultimate counterculture (which may be no less disturbing for some than the overtly threatening characteristics of the first vision). What one must add is that neither kind of analysis respects the Marxian injunction of the "ultimately determining instance" of economic organization and tendencies: for both, indeed, economics (or political economy) of that type is in the new total system of the contemporary world at an end, and the economic finds itself in

---

70. Jean Baudrillard, *Le Système des objets* (Paris: Gallimard, 1968); *La Société de consommation* (Paris: Denöel, 1970); *Pour une économie politique du signe* (Paris: Gallimard, 1972). The most influential statement of the American version of this "end of ideology"/consumer society position is, of course, that of Daniel Bell: see his *Coming of Post-Industrial Society* (New York: Basic, 1973) and *The Cultural Contradictions of Capitalism* (New York: Basic, 1976).

both reassigned to a secondary and nondeterminant position beneath the new dominant of political power or of cultural production respectively.

There exist, however, within Marxism itself precise equivalents to these two non-Marxian visions of the contemporary total system: rewritings, if one likes, of both in specifically Marxian and "economic" terms. These are the analyses of late capitalism in terms of *capitalogic*[71] and of *disaccumulation*,[72] respectively; and while this book is clearly not the place to discuss such theories at any length, it must be observed here that both, seeing the originality of the contemporary situation in terms of systemic tendencies *within* capitalism, reassert the theoretical priority of the organizing concept of the mode of production which we have been concerned to argue.

We must therefore now turn to the second related problem about this third and ultimate horizon, and deal briefly with the objection that cultural analysis pursued within it will tend toward a purely typological or classificatory operation, in which we are called upon to "decide" such issues as whether Milton is to be read within a "precapitalist" or a nascent capitalist context, and so forth. I have insisted elsewhere on the sterility of such classificatory procedures, which may always, it seems to me, be taken as symptoms and indices of the repression of a more genuinely dialectical or historical practice

71. See, for a review and critique of the basic literature, Stanley Aronowitz, "Marx, Braverman, and the Logic of Capital," *Insurgent Sociologist,* viii, No. 2/3 (Fall, 1978), pp. 126–146; and see also Hans-Georg Backhaus, "Zur Dialektik der Wertform," in A. Schmidt, ed., *Beiträge zur marxistischen Erkenntnistheorie* (Frankfurt: Suhrkamp, 1969), pp. 128–152; and Helmut Reichelt, *Zur logischen Struktur des Kapitalbegriffs bei Karl Marx* (Frankfurt: Europäische Verlagsanstalt, 1970). For the Capitalogicians, the "materialist kernel" of Hegel is revealed by grasping the concrete or objective reality of Absolute Spirit (the Notion in-and-for-itself) as none other than capital (Reichelt, pp. 77–78). This tends, however, to force them into the post-Marxist position for which the dialectic is seen as the thought-mode proper only to capitalism (Backhaus, pp. 140–141): in that case, of course, the dialectic would become unnecessary and anachronistic in a society that had abolished the commodity form.

72. The basic texts on "disaccumulation theory" are Martin J. Sklar, "On the Proletarian Revolution and the End of Political-Economic Society," *Radical America,* iii, No. 3 (May-June, 1969), pp. 1–41; Jim O'Connor, "Productive and Unproductive Labor," *Politics and Society,* 5 (1975), pp. 297–336; Fred Block and Larry Hirschhorn, "New Productive Forces and the Contradictions of Contemporary Capitalism," *Theory and Society,* 7 (1979), 363–395; and Stanley Aronowitz, "The End of Political Economy," *Social Text,* No. 2 (1980), pp. 3–52.

of cultural analysis. This diagnosis may now be expanded to cover all three horizons at issue here, where the practice of homology, that of a merely "sociological" search for some social or class equivalent, and that, finally, of the use of some typology of social and cultural systems, respectively, may stand as examples of the misuse of these three frameworks. Furthermore, just as in our discussion of the first two we have stressed the centrality of the category of contradiction for any Marxist analysis (seen, within the first horizon, as that which the cultural and ideological artifact tries to "resolve," and in the second as the nature of the social and class conflict within which a given work is one act or gesture), so too here we can effectively validate the horizon of the mode of production by showing the form contradiction takes on this level, and the relationship of the cultural object to it.

Before we do so, we must take note of more recent objections to the very concept of the mode of production. The traditional schema of the various modes of production as so many historical "stages" has generally been felt to be unsatisfactory, not least because it encourages the kind of typologizing criticized above, in political quite as much as in cultural analysis. (The form taken in political analysis is evidently the procedure which consists in "deciding" whether a given conjuncture is to be assigned to a moment within feudalism—the result being a demand for bourgeois and parliamentary rights—or within capitalism—with the accompanying "reformist" strategy—or, on the contrary, a genuine "revolutionary" moment—in which case the appropriate revolutionary strategy is then deduced.)

On the other hand, it has become increasingly clear to a number of contemporary theorists that such classification of "empirical" materials within this or that abstract category is impermissible in large part because of the level of abstraction of the concept of a mode of production: no historical society has ever "embodied" a mode of production in any pure state (nor is *Capital* the description of a historical society, but rather the construction of the abstract concept of capitalism). This has led certain contemporary theorists, most notably Nicos Poulantzas,[73] to insist on the distinction between a "mode of production" as a purely theoretical construction

73. Poulantzas, *Political Power and Social Classes*, pp. 13–16.

and a "social formation" that would involve the description of some historical society at a certain moment of its development. This distinction seems inadequate and even misleading, to the degree that it encourages the very empirical thinking which it was concerned to denounce, in other words, subsuming a particular or an empirical "fact" under this or that corresponding "abstraction." Yet one feature of Poulantzas' discussion of the "social formation" may be retained: his suggestion that every social formation or historically existing society has in fact consisted in the overlay and structural coexistence of *several* modes of production all at once, including vestiges and survivals of older modes of production, now relegated to structurally dependent positions within the new, as well as anticipatory tendencies which are potentially inconsistent with the existing system but have not yet generated an autonomous space of their own.

But if this suggestion is valid, then the problems of the "synchronic" system and of the typological temptation are both solved at one stroke. What is synchronic is the "concept" of the mode of production; the moment of the historical coexistence of several modes of production is not synchronic in this sense, but open to history in a dialectical way. The temptation to classify texts according to the appropriate mode of production is thereby removed, since the texts emerge in a space in which we may expect them to be crisscrossed and intersected by a variety of impulses from contradictory modes of cultural production all at once.

Yet we have still not characterized the specific object of study which is constructed by this new and final horizon. It cannot, as we have shown, consist in the concept of an individual mode of production (any more than, in our second horizon, the specific object of study could consist in a particular social class in isolation from the others). We will therefore suggest that this new and ultimate object may be designated, drawing on recent historical experience, as *cultural revolution*, that moment in which the coexistence of various modes of production becomes visibly antagonistic, their contradictions moving to the very center of political, social, and historical life. The incomplete Chinese experiment with a "proletarian" cultural revolution may be invoked in support of the proposition that previous history has known a whole range of equivalents for similar processes to which the term may legitimately be extended. So the

Western Enlightenment may be grasped as part of a properly bourgeois cultural revolution, in which the values and the discourses, the habits and the daily space, of the *ancien régime* were systematically dismantled so that in their place could be set the new conceptualities, habits and life forms, and value systems of a capitalist market society. This process clearly involved a vaster historical rhythm than such punctual historical events as the French Revolution or the Industrial Revolution, and includes in its *longue durée* such phenomena as those described by Weber in *The Protestant Ethic and the Spirit of Capitalism*—a work that can now in its turn be read as a contribution to the study of the bourgeois cultural revolution, just as the corpus of work on romanticism is now repositioned as the study of a significant and ambiguous moment in the resistance to this particular "great transformation," alongside the more specifically "popular" (precapitalist as well as working-class) forms of cultural resistance.

But if this is the case, then we must go further and suggest that all previous modes of production have been accompanied by cultural revolutions specific to them of which the neolithic "cultural revolution," say, the triumph of patriarchy over the older matriarchal or tribal forms, or the victory of Hellenic "justice" and the new legality of the *polis* over the vendetta system are only the most dramatic manifestations. The concept of cultural revolution, then—or more precisely, the reconstruction of the materials of cultural and literary history in the form of this new "text" or object of study which is cultural revolution—may be expected to project a whole new framework for the humanities, in which the study of culture in the widest sense could be placed on a materialist basis.

This description is, however, misleading to the degree to which it suggests that "cultural revolution" is a phenomenon limited to so-called "transitional" periods, during which social formations dominated by one mode of production undergo a radical restructuration in the course of which a different "dominant" emerges. The problem of such "transitions" is a traditional crux of the Marxian problematic of modes of production, nor can it be said that any of the solutions proposed, from Marx's own fragmentary discussions to the recent model of Etienne Balibar, are altogether satisfactory, since in all of them the inconsistency between a "synchronic" description of a given system and a "diachronic" account of the passage from one system to another seems to return with undiminished intensity. But our own discussion began with the idea that a given social formation consisted in the coexistence of various synchronic systems or modes of production, each with its own dynamic or time scheme—a kind of metasynchronicity, if one likes—while we have now shifted to a description of cultural revolution which has been couched in the more diachronic language of systemic transformation. I will therefore suggest that these two apparently inconsistent accounts are simply the twin perspectives which our thinking (and our presentation or *Darstellung* of that thinking) can take on this same vast historical object. Just as overt revolution is no punctual event either, but brings to the surface the innumerable daily struggles and forms of class polarization which are at work in the whole course of social life that precedes it, and which are therefore latent and implicit in "prerevolutionary" social experience, made visible as the latter's deep structure only in such "moments of truth"—so also the overtly "transitional" moments of cultural revolution are themselves but the passage to the surface of a permanent process in human societies, of a permanent struggle between the various coexisting modes of production. The triumphant moment in which a new systemic dominant gains ascendency is therefore only the diachronic manifestation of a constant struggle for the perpetuation and reproduction of its dominance, a struggle which must continue throughout its life course, accompanied at all moments by the systemic or structural antagonism of those older and newer modes of production that resist assimilation or seek deliverance from it. The task of cultural and social analysis thus construed within this final horizon will then clearly be the rewriting of its materials in such a way that this perpetual cultural revolution can be apprehended and read as the deeper and more permanent constitutive structure in which the empirical textual objects know intelligibility.

Cultural revolution thus conceived may be said to be beyond the opposition between synchrony and diachrony, and to correspond roughly to what Ernst Bloch has called the *Ungleichzeitigkeit* (or "nonsynchronous development") of cultural and social life.[74] Such

---

74. Ernst Bloch, "Nonsynchronism and Dialectics," *New German Critique*, No. 11 (Spring, 1977), pp. 22–38; or *Erbschaft dieser Zeit* (Frankfurt: Suhrkamp, 1973). The "nonsynchronous" use of the concept of mode of production outlined above is in my opinion the only way to fulfill Marx's well-known program for

a view imposes a new use of concepts of periodization, and in particular of that older schema of the "linear" stages which is here preserved and canceled all at once. We will deal more fully with the specific problems of periodization in the next chapter: suffice it to say at this point that such categories are produced within an initial diachronic or narrative framework, but become usable only when that initial framework has been annulled, allowing us now to coordinate or articulate categories of diachronic origin (the various distinct modes of production) in what is now a synchronic or meta-synchronic way.

We have, however, not yet specified the nature of the textual object which is constructed by this third horizon of cultural revolution, and which would be the equivalent within this dialectically new framework of the objects of our first two horizons—the symbolic act, and the ideologeme or dialogical organization of class discourse. I will suggest that within this final horizon the individual text or cultural artifact (with its appearance of autonomy which was dissolved in specific and original ways within the first two horizons as well) is here restructured as a field of force in which the dynamics of sign systems of several distinct modes of production can be registered and apprehended. These dynamics—the newly constituted "text" of our third horizon—make up what can be termed *the ideology of form,* that is, the determinate contradiction of the specific messages emitted by the varied sign systems which

---

dialectical knowledge "of rising from the abstract to the concrete" (1857 Introduction, *Grundrisse,* p. 101). Marx there distinguished three stages of knowledge: (1) the notation of the particular (this would correspond to something like empirical history, the collection of data and descriptive materials on the variety of human societies); (2) the conquest of abstraction, the coming into being of a properly "bourgeois" science or of what Hegel called the categories of the Understanding (this moment, that of the construction of a static and purely classificatory concept of "modes of production," is what Hindess and Hirst quite properly criticize in *Precapitalist Modes of Production*); (3) the transcendence of abstraction by the dialectic, the "rise to the concrete," the setting in motion of hitherto static and typologizing categories by their reinsertion in a concrete historical situation (in the present context, this is achieved by moving from a classificatory use of the categories of modes of production to a perception of their dynamic and contradictory coexistence in a given cultural moment). Althusser's own epistemology, incidentally—Generalities I, II, and III (*Pour Marx* [Paris: Maspéro, 1965], pp. 187–190)—is a gloss on this same fundamental passage of the 1857 Introduction, but one which succeeds only too well in eliminating its dialectical spirit.

coexist in a given artistic process as well as in its general social formation.

What must now be stressed is that at this level "form" is apprehended as content. The study of the ideology of form is no doubt grounded on a technical and formalistic analysis in the narrower sense, even though, unlike much traditional formal analysis, it seeks to reveal the active presence within the text of a number of discontinuous and heterogeneous formal processes. But at the level of analysis in question here, a dialectical reversal has taken place in which it has become possible to grasp such formal processes as sedimented content in their own right, as carrying ideological messages of their own, distinct from the ostensible or manifest content of the works; it has become possible, in other words, to display such formal operations from the standpoint of what Louis Hjelmslev will call the "content of form" rather than the latter's "expression," which is generally the object of the various more narrowly formalizing approaches. The simplest and most accessible demonstration of this reversal may be found in the area of literary genre. Our next chapter, indeed, will model the process whereby generic specification and description can, in a given historical text, be transformed into the detection of a host of distinct generic messages—some of them objectified survivals from older modes of cultural production, some anticipatory, but all together projecting a formal conjuncture through which the "conjuncture" of coexisting modes of production at a given historical moment can be detected and allegorically articulated.

Meanwhile, that what we have called the ideology of form is something other than a retreat from social and historical questions into the more narrowly formal may be suggested by the relevance of this final perspective to more overtly political and theoretical concerns; we may take the much debated relation of Marxism to feminism as a particularly revealing illustration. The notion of overlapping modes of production outlined above has indeed the advantage of allowing us to short-circuit the false problem of the priority of the economic over the sexual, or of sexual oppression over that of social class. In our present perspective, it becomes clear that sexism and the patriarchal are to be grasped as the sedimentation and the virulent survival of forms of alienation specific to the oldest mode of production of human history, with its division of labor between men and women, and its division of power between youth and elder. The analysis of the ideology of form, properly completed, should reveal the formal persistence of such archaic structures of alienation—and the sign systems specific to them—beneath the overlay of all the more recent and historically original types of alienation—such as political domination and commodity reification—which have become the dominants of that most complex of all cultural revolutions, late capitalism, in which all the earlier modes of production in one way or another structurally coexist. The affirmation of radical feminism, therefore, that to annul the patriarchal is the most *radical* political act—insofar as it includes and subsumes more partial demands, such as the liberation from the commodity form—is thus perfectly consistent with an expanded Marxian framework, for which the transformation of our own dominant mode of production must be accompanied and completed by an equally radical restructuration of all the more archaic modes of production with which it structurally coexists.

With this final horizon, then, we emerge into a space in which History itself becomes the ultimate ground as well as the untranscendable limit of our understanding in general and our textual interpretations in particular. This is, of course, also the moment in which the whole problem of interpretive priorities returns with a vengeance, and in which the practitioners of alternate or rival interpretive codes—far from having been persuaded that History is an interpretive code that includes and transcends all the others—will again assert "History" as simply one more code among others, with no particularly privileged status. This is most succinctly achieved when the critics of Marxist interpretation, borrowing its own traditional terminology, suggest that the Marxian interpretive operation involves a thematization and a reification of "History" which is not markedly different from the process whereby the other interpretive codes produce their own forms of thematic closure and offer themselves as absolute methods.

It should by now be clear that nothing is to be gained by opposing one reified theme—History—by another—Language—in a polemic debate as to ultimate priority of one over the other. The influential forms this debate has taken in recent years—as in Jürgen Habermas' attempt to subsume the "Marxist" model of production beneath a more all-embracing model of "communication" or inter-subjectivity,[75] or in Umberto Eco's assertion of the priority of the Symbolic in general over the technological and productive systems which it must organize as *signs* before they can be used as *tools*[76]—are based on the misconception that the Marxian category of a "mode of production" is a form of technological or "pro-ductionist" determinism.

It would seem therefore more useful to ask ourselves, in conclu-sion, how History as a ground and as an absent cause can be conceived in such a way as to resist such thematization or reifica-tion, such transformation back into one optional code among oth-ers. We may suggest such a possibility obliquely by attention to what the Aristotelians would call the generic satisfaction specific to the form of the great monuments of historiography, or what the semioticians might call the "history-effect" of such narrative texts. Whatever the raw material on which historiographic form works (and we will here only touch on that most widespread type of material which is the sheer chronology of fact as it is produced by the rote-drill of the history manual), the "emotion" of great his-toriographic form can then always be seen as the radical restructur-ation of that inert material, in this instance the powerful reorgani-zation of otherwise inert chronological and "linear" data in the form of Necessity: why what happened (at first received as "empiri-cal" fact) had to happen the way it did. From this perspective, then, causality is only one of the possible tropes by which this formal restructuration can be achieved, although it has obviously been a privileged and historically significant one. Meanwhile, should it be objected that Marxism is rather a "comic" or "romance" paradigm, one which sees history in the salvational perspective of some ultimate liberation, we must observe that the most powerful realizations of a Marxist historiography—from Marx's own narra-tives of the 1848 revolution through the rich and varied canonical studies of the dynamics of the Revolution of 1789 all the way to Charles Bettelheim's study of the Soviet revolutionary experience—remain visions of historical Necessity in the sense

75. See Jürgen Habermas, *Knowledge and Human Interests*, trans. J. Shapiro (Boston: Beacon, 1971), esp. Part I.

76. Umberto Eco, *A Theory of Semiotics* (Bloomington: Indiana University Press, 1976), pp. 21–26.

evoked above. But Necessity is here represented in the form of the inexorable logic involved in the determinate failure of all the revolutions that have taken place in human history: the ultimate Marxian presupposition—that socialist revolution can only be a total and worldwide process (and that this in turn presupposes the completion of the capitalist "revolution" and of the process of commodification on a global scale)—is the perspective in which the failure or the blockage, the contradictory reversal or functional inversion, of this or that local revolutionary process is grasped as "inevitable," and as the operation of objective limits.

History is therefore the experience of Necessity, and it is this alone which can forestall its thematization or reification as a mere object of representation or as one master code among many others. Necessity is not in that sense a type of content, but rather the inexorable *form* of events; it is therefore a narrative category in the enlarged sense of some properly narrative political unconscious which has been argued here, a retextualization of History which does not propose the latter as some new representation or "vision," some new content, but as the formal effects of what Althusser, following Spinoza, calls an "absent cause." Conceived in this sense, History is what hurts, it is what refuses desire and sets inexorable limits to individual as well as collective praxis, which its "ruses" turn into grisly and ironic reversals of their overt intention. But this History can be apprehended only through its effects, and never directly as some reified force. This is indeed the ultimate sense in which History as ground and untranscendable horizon needs no particular theoretical justification: we may be sure that its alienating necessities will not forget us, however much we might prefer to ignore them.

2

MAGICAL NARRATIVES:
On the Dialectical Use of Genre Criticism

O, she's warm!
If this be magic, let it be an art
Lawful as eating.

—*The Winter's Tale*

The Marxian vision of history outlined in the previous chapter has sometimes, as we have observed, been described as a "comic" archetype or a "romance" paradigm.[1] What is meant thereby is the salvational or redemptive perspective of some secure future, from which, with William Morris' Time Traveller, we can have our "fill of the pleasure of the eyes without any of that sense of incongruity, that dread of approaching ruin, which had always beset me hitherto when I had been among the beautiful works of art of the past."[2] In such a future, indeed, or from its perspective, our own cultural

---

1. Hayden White, *Metahistory* (Baltimore: Johns Hopkins University Press, 1973); pp. 281–282: "Hegel's Comic conception of history was based ultimately on his belief in the right of life over death; 'life' guaranteed to Hegel the possibility of an ever more adequate form of social life throughout the historical future. Marx carried this Comic conception even further; he envisioned nothing less than the dissolution of that 'society' in which the contradiction between consciousness and being had to be entertained as a fatality for all men in all times. It would not, then, be unjust to characterize the final vision of history which inspired Marx in his historical and social theorizing as a Romantic one. But his conception did not envisage humanity's redemption as a deliverance from time itself. Rather, his redemption took the form of a reconciliation of man with a nature denuded of its fantastic and terrifying powers, submitted to the rule of technics, and turned to the creation of a genuine community."

2. William Morris, *News from Nowhere,* chap. xx (London: Longmans, Green, 1903), p. 188.

tradition—the monuments of power societies (for Goethe, the *Iliad* was a glimpse into hell) as well as the stories of fierce market competition and the expressions of commodity lust and of the triumph of the commodity form—will be read as children's books, recapitulating the barely comprehensible memory of ancient dangers.

Even from the standpoint of an ideal of realism (traditionally in one form or another the central model of Marxist aesthetics as a narrative discourse which unites the experience of daily life with a properly cognitive, mapping, or well-nigh "scientific" perspective[3]) this apparently contradictory valorization of romance has much to be said for it. Let Scott, Balzac, and Dreiser serve as the non-chronological markers of the emergence of realism in its modern form; these first great realisms are characterized by a fundamental and exhilarating heterogeneity in their raw materials and by a corresponding versatility in their narrative apparatus. In such moments, a generic confinement to the existent has a paradoxically liberating effect on the registers of the text, and releases a set of heterogeneous historical perspectives—the past for Scott, the future for Balzac, the process of commodification for Dreiser—normally felt to be inconsistent with a focus on the historical present. Indeed, this multiple temporality tends to be sealed off and recontained again in "high" realism and naturalism, where a perfected narrative apparatus (in particular the threefold imperatives of authorial depersonalization, unity of point of view, and restriction to scenic representation) begins to confer on the "realistic" option the appearance of an asphyxiating, self-imposed penance. It is in the context of the gradual reification of realism in late capitalism that romance once again comes to be felt as the place of narrative heterogeneity and of freedom from that reality principle to which a now oppressive realistic representation is the hostage. Romance now again seems to offer the possibility of sensing other historical rhythms, and of demonic or Utopian transformations of a real now unshakably set in place; and Frye is surely not wrong to assimilate

---

3. The canonical statements are those of Georg Lukács; see in particular, *Studies in European Realism,* (New York: Grosset & Dunlap, 1964), and *Realism in Our Time,* trans. J. and N. Mander (New York: Harper, 1964). See also my "Reflections in Conclusion" to the collection of materials on the so-called Brecht-Lukács debate, *Aesthetics and Politics* (London: New Left Books, 1977), pp. 196–213.

the salvational perspective of romance to a reexpression of Utopian longings, a renewed meditation on the Utopian community, a reconquest (but at what price?) of some feeling for a salvational future.

The association of Marxism and romance therefore does not discredit the former so much as it explains the persistence and vitality of the latter, which Frye takes to be the ultimate source and paradigm of all storytelling.[4] On this view, the oral tales of tribal society, the fairy tales that are the irrepressible voice and expression of the underclasses of the great systems of domination, adventure stories and melodrama, and the popular or mass culture of our own time are all syllables and broken fragments of some single immense story.

Yet Frye's identification of narrative in general with the particular narrative genre of romance raises the apparently unrelated issue of genre criticism, which, though thoroughly discredited by modern literary theory and practice, has in fact always entertained a privileged relationship with historical materialism. The first extended exercise in Marxist literary criticism—the letters of Marx and Engels to Lassalle about the latter's verse tragedy, *Franz von Sickingen*[5]—was indeed essentially generic; while the most developed corpus of Marxist literary analysis in our own time, the work of Georg Lukács, spanning some sixty years, is dominated by concepts of genre from beginning to end. I take it, indeed, as one of the moments of "high seriousness" in the history of recent Marxist thought that when the aging Lukács felt the urgency of supporting Solzhenitsyn's denunciation of Stalinism but also of responding to the religious and antisocialist propaganda to which the latter lent his talent and the authority of his personal suffering, he did so by sitting down at his desk and producing a piece of genre criticism. The strategic value of generic concepts for Marxism clearly lies in the mediatory function of the notion of a genre, which allows the coordination of immanent formal analysis of the individual text with the twin diachronic perspective of the history of forms and the evolution of social life.

4. Northrop Frye, *The Secular Scripture* (Cambridge: Harvard University Press, 1976), pp. 28–31.

5. Karl Marx and Friedrich Engels, *Über Kunst und Literatur* (Berlin: Henschelverlag, 1953), pp. 129–167.

Meanwhile, in the other traditions of contemporary literary criticism, generic perspectives live something like a "return of the repressed." Frye's own work, so resolutely organized around narrative, owed its widespread influence to the New Critical context in which it first appeared, and in which the fundamental object of literary study had been only too narrowly construed as the lyric, or poetic language. Contemporary structural and semiotic methods also, with their rigorous self-imposed restriction to discrete individual texts, have known the reemergence of a meditation on hitherto marginalized types of discourse: legal language, the fragment, the anecdote, autobiography, Utopian discourse, the fantastic, novelistic description (or *ekphrasis*), the preface, the scientific treatise, which are increasingly conceived as so many distinct generic modes.

What literary criticism seems unable to do without completely, however, literary production has in modern times ceaselessly and systematically undermined. The emancipation of the "realistic novel" from its generic restrictions (in the tale, the letter, the framed *récit*), the emergence, first of modernism, with its Joycean or Mallarmean ideal of a single Book of the world, then of the postmodernist aesthetic of the text or of *écriture,* of "textual productivity" or schizophrenic writing—all seem rigorously to exclude traditional notions of the literary kinds, or of systems of the fine arts, as much by their practice as by their theory.

Nor is it difficult to see why this has been so. Genres are essentially literary *institutions,* or social contracts between a writer and a specific public, whose function is to specify the proper use of a particular cultural artifact. The speech acts of daily life are themselves marked with indications and signals (intonation, gesturality, contextual deictics and pragmatics) which ensure their appropriate reception. In the mediated situations of a more complicated social life—and the emergence of writing has often been taken as paradigmatic of such situations—perceptual signals must be replaced by conventions if the text in question is not to be abandoned to a drifting multiplicity of uses (as *meanings* must, according to Wittgenstein, be described). Still, as texts free themselves more and more from an immediate performance situation, it becomes ever more difficult to enforce a given generic rule on their readers. No small part of the art of writing, indeed, is absorbed by this (impossible) attempt to devise a foolproof mechanism for the automatic exclusion of undesirable responses to a given literary utterance.

It is not merely the performance situation, but the generic contract and institution itself, which, along with so many other institutions and traditional practices, falls casualty to the gradual penetration of a market system and a money economy. With the elimination of an institutionalized social status for the cultural producer and the opening of the work of art itself to commodification, the older generic specifications are transformed into a brand-name system against which any authentic artistic expression must necessarily struggle. The older generic categories do not, for all that, die out, but persist in the half-life of the subliterary genres of mass culture, transformed into the drugstore and airport paperback lines of gothics, mysteries, romances, bestsellers, and popular biographies, where they await the resurrection of their immemorial, archetypal resonance at the hands of a Frye or a Bloch. Meanwhile, it would seem necessary to invent a new, historically reflexive, way of using categories, such as those of genre, which are so clearly implicated in the literary history and the formal production they were traditionally supposed to classify and neutrally to describe.

I

When we look at the practice of contemporary genre criticism, we find two seemingly incompatible tendencies at work, which we will term the *semantic* and the *syntactic* or structural, respectively, and which can conveniently be illustrated by traditional theories of comedy. For a first group, the object of study is less the individual comic text than some ultimate comic vision of which the texts of Molière, Aristophanes, Joyce, and Rabelais offer so many embodiments. Accounts of such a vision, to be sure, seem to oscillate between the repressive and the liberatory; thus for Bergson comedy has the function of preserving social norms by castigating deviancy with ridicule, while for Emil Staiger the comic serves to make the fundamental absurdity of human existence tolerable. Such approaches, whatever their content, aim to describe the essence or meaning of a given genre by way of the reconstruction of an imaginary entity—the "spirit" of comedy or tragedy, the melodramatic or epic "world view," the pastoral "sensibility" or the satiric "vision"—which is something like the generalized existential experience behind the individual texts. In what follows we will take Frye's work as the richest idiosyncratic elaboration of such an approach, for which genre is essentially apprehended as a *mode*.

The second, syntactic approach to genre, which condemns the semantic option as intuitive and impressionistic, proposes rather to analyze the mechanisms and structure of a genre such as comedy, and to determine its laws and its limits. Analyses of this kind, which range from the lost chapters of Aristotle's *Poetics* to Freud's joke book, aim less at discovering the meaning of the generic mechanism or process than at constructing its model. The two approaches are thus no mere inversions of each other, but are fundamentally incommensurable, as may be judged from the fact that each projects a quite distinct dialectical opposite or negation. For the semantic or phenomenological approach, the contrary in terms of which comedy will be defined always proves to be another mode: tragedy, say, or irony. For structural analyses, the "opposite" of comedy will simply be the noncomic or the unfunny, the joke that falls flat or the farce that remains a dead letter. Our basic text for this second approach to the generic problem will be Vladimir Propp's *Morphology of the Folk Tale,* where genre is apprehended in terms of a series of determinate functions, or what we will call a structure or a *fixed form*.

It will have become evident that these two approaches correspond to what, in our first chapter, has been described as the rivalry between old-fashioned "interpretation," which still asks the text what it *means,* and the newer kinds of analysis which, according to Deleuze, ask how it *works.* Yet similar methodological hesitations and alternations in stylistics and in the history of linguistics suggest that we can now locate the source of such antinomies in the very nature of language, which, uniquely ambiguous, both subject and object all at once, or in Humboldt's terms, both *energeia* and *ergon,* intentional meaning and articulated system, necessarily projects two distinct and discontinuous dimensions (or "objects of study") which can never be conceptually unified.[6] We assume that the objective source of these twin projections, language, is somehow a

6. These two dimensions, and the methodological alternatives that accompany them, essentially correspond to what Voloshinov-Bakhtin calls the two tendencies or "two trends of thought in the philosophy of language": see *Marxism and the Philosophy of Language,* pp. 45–63.

unified phenomenon. Unfortunately, as the burden of Wittgenstein's later work teaches, any attempt prematurely to think it as such—in the form of Language—always reifies it. Thus, our meditation on language must henceforth take the mediatory path of the separate specialized disciplines which each of these perspectives on language has generated: logic and linguistics, semantics and grammar, phenomenology and semiotics.

This situation apparently condemns genre theory to a methodological double standard, an unavoidable shifting of gears between two irreconcilable options. At best, it would seem, we can make a virtue of necessity, and turn the problem into a relatively sterile hypothesis about the dual nature of genre; the latter would then be defined as that literary discourse which may be examined either in terms of a fixed form or in terms of a mode, but which *must* be susceptible of study from both these perspectives optionally.

In reality, however, this disappointing hypothesis marks a first step forward on the project of this chapter, which is, by rethinking both these interpretive methods dialectically, to historicize their findings, so as, thereby, not merely to gain some sense of the ideological significance and historical destiny of romance as a genre, but, beyond that, to get some feeling for the dialectical use of generic literary history as such.

Dialectical thinking can be characterized as historical reflexivity, that is, as the study of an object (here the romance texts) which also involves the study of the concepts and categories (themselves historical) that we necessarily bring to the object. In the present case these categories have already been described as the semantic and structural approaches. But how do you go about "historicizing" such mental categories or conceptual operations? A first step in this direction has been taken when you come to understand that they are not the result of purely philosophic choices or options in the void, but are objectively determined: and this is what has happened when we come to understand that the apparently philosophical alternative between the two "methods" was in reality the projection of objective antinomies in language.

Now we need to make a further step, which we can call the de-positivizing of these two positions. Every universalizing approach, whether the phenomenological or the semiotic, will from the dialectical point of view be found to conceal its own contradictions and repress its own historicity by strategically framing its perspective so as to omit the negative, absence, contradiction, repression, the *non-dit,* or the *impensé.* To restore the latter requires that abrupt and paradoxical dialectical restructuration of the basic problematic which has often seemed to be the most characteristic gesture and style of dialectical method in general, keeping the terms but standing the problem on its head. So we will show in what follows that Frye's entire discussion of romance turns on a presupposition—the ethical axis of good and evil—which needs to be historically problematized in its turn, and which will prove to be an ideologeme that articulates a social and historical contradiction. An interrogation of Propp's method will, meanwhile, disclose that it is contradictory in its own terms, and fails to come to grips with the basic underlying problem of the *subject,* which it assumes as nonproblematical and as a given from the outset. The dialectical critique of these methods is, however, not a merely negative and destructive one; it leads, as we shall see, to their fulfillment and completion, albeit in a very different spirit from the one they initially propose.

II

Frye's theory of romance, as has been suggested, is the fullest account of this genre as a mode. Romance is for Frye a wish-fulfillment or Utopian fantasy which aims at the transfiguration of the world of everyday life in such a way as to restore the conditions of some lost Eden, or to anticipate a future realm from which the old mortality and imperfections will have been effaced. Romance, therefore, does not involve the substitution of some more ideal realm for ordinary reality (as in mystical experience, or as might be suggested by the partial segments of the romance paradigm to be found in the idyll or the pastoral), but rather a process of *transforming* ordinary reality: "the quest-romance is the search of the libido or desiring self for a fulfillment that will deliver it from the anxieties of reality *but will still contain that reality.*"[7]

Frye's initial emphasis on the transformation of ordinary reality already implies a corollary: if it is possible for the lineaments of the earthly paradise to emerge from ordinary life, then the latter must

---

7. Frye, *Anatomy of Criticism,* p. 193, italics mine.

already have been conceived, not as some humdrum place of secular contingency and "normal" existence, but rather as the end product of curse and enchantment, black magic, baleful spells, and ritual desolation. Romance is thus at once staged as the struggle between higher and lower realms, between heaven and hell, or the angelic and the demonic or diabolic:

> The hero of romance is analogous to the mythical Messiah or deliverer who comes from an upper world, and his enemy is analogous to the demonic powers of a lower world. The conflict however takes place in, or at any rate primarily concerns, *our* world, which is in the middle, and which is characterized by the cyclical movements of nature. Hence the opposite poles of the cycles of nature are assimilated to the opposition of the hero and his enemy. The enemy is associated with winter, darkness, confusion, sterility, moribund life, and old age, and the hero with spring, dawn, order, fertility, vigor, and youth.[8]

This description rewrites the form in terms of three distinct operative elements: its "world," its twin protagonists (hero and villain), and its semic organization (high and low, angelic and demonic, white and black magic, winter and spring), each of which demands comment.

Frye's assimilation of the "world" of romance to nature in its traditional acceptation conceals an interesting problem, which phenomenological accounts of this concept may help to dramatize. For phenomenology, the technical term *world* designates the ultimate frame or *Gestalt,* the overall organizational category or ultimate perceptual horizon, within which empirical, inner-worldly objects and phenomena are perceived and inner-worldly experience takes place; but in that case, "world," in its phenomenological sense, cannot normally be an object of perception in its own right.[9] This view is indeed confirmed by conventional narrative realism, where events take place within the infinite space of sheer Cartesian extension, of the quantification of the market system: a space which like that of film extends indefinitely beyond any particular momentary "still" or setting or larger vista or panorama, and is incapable of symbolic unification.

---

8. Ibid., pp. 187–188.
9. Martin Heidegger, *Sein und Zeit* (Tübingen: Niemeyer, 1957), pp. 131–140.

A first specification of romance would then be achieved if we could account for the way in which, in contrast to realism, its inner-worldly objects such as landscape or village, forest or mansion—mere temporary stopping places on the lumbering coach or express-train itinerary of realistic representation—are somehow transformed into folds in space, into discontinuous pockets of homogeneous time and of heightened symbolic closure, such that they become tangible analoga or perceptual vehicles for *world* in its larger phenomenological sense. Heidegger's account goes on to supply the key to this enigma, and we may borrow his cumbersome formula to suggest that romance is precisely that form in which the *worldness* of *world* reveals or manifests itself, in which, in other words, *world* in the technical sense of the transcendental horizon of our experience becomes visible in an inner-worldly sense. Frye is therefore not wrong to evoke the intimate connection between romance as a mode and the "natural" imagery of the earthly paradise or the waste land, of the bower of bliss or the enchanted wood. What is misleading is the implication that this "nature" is in any sense itself a "natural" rather than a very peculiar and specialized social and historical phenomenon.

The centrality of *worldness* in romance will now lead us to question the primacy Frye attributes to traditional categories of character—in particular, the role of the hero and the villain—in romance. We suggest, on the contrary, that the strangely active and pulsating vitality of the "world" of romance, much like Stanislaw Lem's sentient ocean in *Solaris,* tends to absorb many of the act- and event-producing functions normally reserved for narrative "characters"; to use Kenneth Burke's dramatistic terminology, we might say that in romance the category of Scene tends to capture and to appropriate the attributes of Agency and Act, making the "hero" over into something like a registering apparatus for transformed states of being, sudden alterations of temperature, mysterious heightenings, local intensities, sudden drops in quality, and alarming effluvia, in short, the whole semic range of transformation scenes whereby, in romance, higher and lower worlds struggle to overcome each other.

It will be objected that Frye's description is predicated on his notion of the displacement of romance from some primary register in religious myth all the way to its degraded versions in the irony of a fallen world. We will have more to say about this concept of "displacement" later. Even at present, however, we may suggest that Frye has here projected the later categories of religion—the ideology of centralized and hieratic power societies—back onto myth, which is rather the discourse of decentered, magic-oriented, tribal social formations. Any "first-hand" contact with the original mythic narratives themselves (and for many readers, Lévi-Strauss's four-volume *Mythologiques* will have served as a vast introductory manual of these unfamiliar and unsettling strings of episodes, so utterly unlike what our childhood versions of Greek myth led us to expect) suggests that later notions of "character" are quite inappropriate to the actants of these decentered and preindividual narratives.

Even the traditional heroes of Western art-romance, from Yvain and Parzival to Fabrice del Dongo and the Pierrot of Queneau, or the "grand Meaulnes" of Alain-Fournier and the Oedipa Maas of Pynchon's *Crying of Lot 49,* far from striking us as emissaries of some "upper world," show a naivete and bewilderment that marks them rather as mortal spectators surprised by supernatural conflict, into which they are unwittingly drawn, reaping the rewards of cosmic victory without ever having quite been aware of what was at stake in the first place. In a later study, indeed, Frye himself insists on the essential marginality of the most characteristic protagonists of romance, slaves or women, who, by their necessary recourse to fraud and guile rather than to sheer physical power, are more closely related to the Trickster than to the Solar Hero.[10]

If now we ask how such passive-contemplative *actants* can be conceived as functional units of a narrative system, it is clearly the peculiar semic organization of romance which mediates between character-positions and that more fundamental and narratively "meaningful" entity which is worldness itself. Frye's works provide an immense table of the content of the basic semes of romance, of which it is sufficient for our present purposes to observe that they are all arrayed in binary opposition to one another. A dialectical study of this genre (and of Frye's reading of it) ought then logically to impose a historical reexamination of the binary opposition itself, as a form without content which nonetheless ultimately confers

10. Frye, *Secular Scripture,* pp. 68ff.

signification on the various types of content (geographical, sexual, seasonal, social, perceptual, familial, zoological, physiological, and so on) which it organizes. Such reexamination is in fact underway everywhere in post-structuralism today; we will mention only the influential version of Jacques Derrida, whose entire work may be read, from this point of view, as the unmasking and demystification of a host of unconscious or naturalized binary oppositions in contemporary and traditional thought, the best known of which are those which oppose speech and writing, presence and absence, norm and deviation, center and periphery, experience and supplementarity, and male and female. Derrida has shown how all these axes function to ratify the centrality of a dominant term by means of the marginalization of an excluded or inessential one, a process that he characterizes as a persistence of "metaphysical" thinking.[11] On the face of it, however, it seems paradoxical to describe the ideologies of the decentered and serialized society of consumer capitalism as metaphysical survivals, except to underscore the ultimate origin of the binary opposition in the older "centered" master code of theocentric power societies. To move from Derrida to Nietzsche is to glimpse the possibility of a rather different interpretation of the binary opposition, according to which its positive and negative terms are ultimately assimilated by the mind as a distinction between good and evil. Not metaphysics but ethics is the informing ideology of the binary opposition; and we have forgotten the thrust of Nietzsche's thought and lost everything scandalous and virulent about it if we cannot understand how it is ethics itself which is the ideological vehicle and the legitimation of concrete structures of power and domination.

Yet surely, in the shrinking world of the present day, with its gradual leveling of class and national and racial differences, and its imminent abolition of Nature (as some ultimate term of Otherness or difference), it ought to be less difficult to understand to what

---

11. This theme is perhaps most explicitly stated in his attack on the concept of "parasitism" in J. L. Austin and John Searle ("Limited Inc.," Supplement to *Glyph*, 2 [1977]): "You do not have to be a preacher or a pamphleteer calling for the expulsion of wicked parasites (either of language or of political life, effects of the unconscious, scapegoats, migrant workers, militants and spies) for your language to be ethico-political or—and this is really all I wanted to bring out about Austin—for your ostensibly theoretical discourse to reproduce the basic categories that ground all ethico-political statements" (p. 69).

degree the concept of good and evil is a positional one that co-
incides with categories of Otherness. Evil thus, as Nietzsche taught
us, continues to characterize whatever is radically different from
me, whatever by virtue of precisely that difference seems to constitute a real and urgent threat to my own existence. So from the
earliest times, the stranger from another tribe, the "barbarian" who
speaks an incomprehensible language and follows "outlandish"
customs, but also the woman, whose biological difference stimu-
lates fantasies of castration and devoration, or in our own time, the
avenger of accumulated resentments from some oppressed class or
race, or else that alien being, Jew or Communist, behind whose
apparently human features a malignant and preternatural intelligence is thought to lurk: these are some of the archetypal figures of
the Other, about whom the essential point to be made is not so
much that he is feared because he is evil; rather he is evil *because* he
is Other, alien, different, strange, unclean, and unfamiliar.

The question of some immanent, nonconceptual ideological function of romance as a "pure" narrative is thereby again raised with a
vengeance. Meanwhile, our problematization of Frye's use of these
oppositions has allowed us to complete his analysis in an unexpected and instructive way. We will therefore abstract the following
working hypothesis: that the modal approach to genre must be
pursued, until, by means of radical historicization, the "essence,"
"spirit," "world-view," in question is revealed to be an ideologeme,
that is, a historically determinate conceptual or semic complex
which can project itself variously in the form of a "value system" or
"philosophical concept," or in the form of a protonarrative, a private or collective narrative fantasy.

But we cannot leave this particular ideologeme—ethics, or the
binary opposition between good and evil—without a word on the
ringing and programmatic "solution" ("beyond good and evil!") in
which Nietzsche's diagnosis is cast. This goal, utterly to discredit
and to transcend the ethical binary, remains intact even if we find
unsatisfactory the visions through which Nietzsche tried to articulate it: the energy mutation of the *Übermensch* on the one hand, or
the private and intolerable ethos of the eternal return on the other.
In our present context, we may observe that this transcendence of
ethics is in fact realized by other generic modes, which thereby in
their very form rebuke the ideological core of the romance

paradigm. The ethical opposition is, for instance, wholly absent from tragedy, whose fundamental staging of the triumph of an inhuman destiny or fate generates a perspective which radically transcends the purely individual categories of good and evil. This proposition may be demonstrated by our feeling, when, in something that looks like a tragedy, we encounter judgments of a more properly ethical type (reemergence of "heroes" and "villains"), that the text in question is rather to be considered a melodrama, that is, a degraded form of romance. Neither Creon nor Iago can be read as villains without dispersing the tragic force of the plays; yet our irresistible temptation to do so tells us much about the hold of ethical categories on our mental habits. As for comedy, we will see shortly that its categories are also quite distinct from those of romance, and more resolutely social: the classical conflict in comedy is not between good and evil, but between youth and age, its Oedipal resolution aiming not at the restoration of a fallen world, but at the regeneration of the social order.

Tragedy and comedy are thus already in a special sense "beyond good and evil." As for conceptual thought, if we grasp the problem as one of escaping from the purely individualizing categories of ethics, of transcending the categories into which our existence as individual subjects necessarily locks us and opening up the radically distinct transindividual perspectives of collective life or historical process, then the conclusion seems unavoidable that we already have the ideal of a thinking able to go beyond good and evil, namely the dialectic itself. This is not to say that the inventors-discoverers of the dialectic were themselves completely successful in avoiding the entanglement of ethical categories. Hegel's designation of the ultimate horizon of historical and collective understanding as "Absolute Spirit" still fatally projects the afterimage of the individual consciousness of the philosopher-sage; and the classical aporia of the Marxist vision of revolutionary change—objective social law or voluntarist and Leninist praxis—suggests that those locked into it have been unable fully to realize a vision of history in which the voluntarist actions of individuals and individual groups are themselves grasped as objective forces in history. Moreover, Marx and Engels' attempt, in the *Manifesto,* to formulate their vision of "historical inevitability" by way of a mechanical alternation of older ethical categories (the bourgeoisie as both progressive and dehumanizing, both a necessary and a humanly intolerable stage in social development[12]) sufficiently conveys the hold of the older ethical categories and their language. Yet these historical texts are not the last word on the dialectic itself, but merely prodigious anticipations of the thought mode of a social formation of the future, which has not yet come into being.

A final step, however, needs to be taken if our presentation of the ideologeme is to have any completeness. To leave it at this point would, indeed, paradoxically reopen it to all the idealizing habits we wish to avoid, and in particular would suggest a perspective—the "ethical binary" is "wrong," that is to say, evil—in which the ideological closure in question would end up drawing the entire analysis back into itself. This paradox can be avoided only if we can grasp the ideologeme itself as a form of social praxis, that is, as a symbolic resolution to a concrete historical situation. What, on the level of the ideologeme, remains a conceptual *antinomy,* must now be grasped, on the level of the social and historical subtext, as a *contradiction.*

Nietzsche's analysis, which unmasks the concepts of ethics as the sedimented or fossilized trace of the concrete praxis of situations of domination, gives us a significant methodological precedent. He demonstrated, indeed, that what is really meant by "the good" is simply my own position as an unassailable power center, in terms of which the position of the Other, or of the weak, is repudiated and marginalized in practices which are then ultimately themselves formalized in the concept of evil. The Christian reversal of this situation, the revolt of the weak and the slaves against the strong, and the "production" of the secretly castrating ideals of charity, resignation, and abnegation, are, according to the Nietzschean theory of *ressentiment,* no less locked into the initial power relationship than the aristocratic system of which they are the inversion. But Nietzsche's rewriting of ethics in terms of a concrete situation, suggestive as it is for the more fully developed theory of *sedimentation* we will present shortly, is evidently a mythic one, which has the weakness of taking the ethical code as a mere replication of its concrete subtext.

12. Marx and Engels, "Communist Manifesto," Part i (in K. Marx, *On Revolution,* ed. and trans. S. K. Padover [New York: McGraw-Hill, 1971]), esp. pp. 82–85.

It would seem possible to perform this operation in a different way, by grasping the ideologeme, not as a mere reflex or reduplication of its situational context, but as the imaginary resolution of the objective contradictions to which it thus constitutes an active response. It is clear, for instance, that the positional notion of good and evil so central to romance narrative is not unique to this form alone, but also characterizes the *chanson de geste* from which romance emerged, as well as popular forms such as the American Western with which both have so much in common.[13] Such kinships suggest that this positional thinking has an intimate relationship to those historical periods sometimes designated as the "time of troubles," in which central authority disappears and marauding bands of robbers and brigands range geographical immensities with impunity: this is certainly true of the late Carolingian period, when a population terrorized by barbarian incursions increasingly withdrew into the shelter of local fortresses.

When, in the twelfth century, this kind of social and spatial isolation was overcome, and the feudal nobility became conscious of itself as a universal class or "subject of history," newly endowed with a codified ideology,[14] there must arise what can only be called a contradiction between the older positional notion of good and evil, perpetuated by the *chanson de geste,* and this emergent class solidarity. Romance in its original strong form may then be understood as an imaginary "solution" to this real contradiction, a symbolic answer to the perplexing question of how my enemy can be thought of as being *evil* (that is, as other than myself and marked by some absolute difference), when what is responsible for his being so characterized is quite simply the *identity* of his own conduct with mine, the which—points of honor, challenges, tests of strength—he reflects as in a mirror image.

Romance "solves" this conceptual dilemma by producing a new kind of narrative, the "story" of something like a semic evaporation. The hostile knight, in armor, his identity unknown, exudes that insolence which marks a fundamental refusal of recognition

13. And also that curious Brazilian "high literary" variant of the Western which is Guimarães Rosa's *Grande Sertão: Veredas* (translated as *The Devil to Pay in the Backlands* [New York: Knopf, 1963]).

14. Marc Bloch, *Feudal Society,* trans. L. A. Manyon (Chicago: University of Chicago Press, 1961), pp. 320ff.

and stamps him as the bearer of the category of evil, up to the moment when, defeated and unmasked, he asks for mercy by *telling his name:* "Sire, Yidiers, li filz Nut, ai non" (*Erec et Enide,* 1042), at which point, reinserted into the unity of the social class, he becomes one more knight among others and loses all his sinister unfamiliarity. This moment, in which the antagonist ceases to be a villain, distinguishes the romance narrative from those of *chanson de geste* and the Western at the same time that it raises a new and productive dilemma for the future development and adaptation of this form. For now that the "experience" or the seme of evil can no longer be permanently assigned or attached to this or that human agent, it must find itself expelled from the realm of interpersonal or inner-worldly relations in a kind of Lacanian *forclusion* and thereby be projectively reconstituted into a free-floating and disembodied element, a baleful optical illusion, in its own right: that "realm" of sorcery and magical forces which constitutes the semic organization of the "world" of romance and henceforth determines the provisional investment of its anthropomorphic bearers and its landscapes alike. With this development, something like a history of the form may be said already to have begun.

III

It is one matter to historicize Frye's interpretation of romance, and quite another to historicize Propp's "structural" method, to which we now turn. Propp's seminal work, although explicitly limited to the Russian folk tale, has in fact generally been evoked as the paradigm of narrative as such, and of so-called quest-romance in particular, in that it allows us to reformulate or rewrite the episodes of individual romance texts as an invariable sequence of "functions," or in other words, as a fixed form. Propp summarizes his findings as follows:

(1) Functions of characters serve as stable, constant elements in a tale, independent of how and by whom they are fulfilled.
(2) The number of functions known to the fairy tale is limited.
(3) The sequence of functions is always identical.
(4) All fairy tales are of one type in regard to their structure.[15]

15. Vladimir Propp, *Morphology of the Folk Tale,* trans. L. Scott (Austin: University of Texas Press, 1968), pp. 21–23.

This final proposition in particular, suggesting a circular movement whereby the analyst studies his corpus of tales in order to verify their structural homology with one another—that is to say, in order to exclude what does not belong, and thus triumphantly to validate the corpus with which he began!—seems to reduce Propp's method to a classificatory operation, thereby setting a direction for our own discussion as well. We will want to see, in what follows, whether any more productive (let alone historicizing) use can be found for Propp's scheme than the purely typologizing or classificatory.

Lévi-Strauss, in his important review article,[16] has shown that Propp's model suffers from a twofold (and paradoxical) weakness. On the one hand, even on its own terms, it is insufficiently formalized: Propp's "functions," in other words, fail to attain an adequate level of abstraction. Yet what was powerful and attractive about the method from the outset was precisely the possibility it offered of reducing a wealth of empirical or surface narrative events to a much smaller number of abstract or "deep-structural" moments. Such a reduction allows us not only to compare narrative texts which seem very different from one another; it also allows us to simplify a single involved narrative into redundant surface manifestations of a single recurrent function. Thus it is useful to be able to rewrite Fabrice's episodic difficulties, in the early part of *La Chartreuse de Parme*—episodes that we might otherwise be tempted to lay out in the form of a picaresque narrative—as so many versions of one of Propp's basic functions: "the hero is tested, interrogated, attacked, etc., which prepares the way for his receiving either a magical agent or helper (first function of the donor)."[17] Thus, a significant remark by the Duchess, on Fabrice's departure for Napoleon's armies, helps us sort out some of the essential functions of the figures he meets in his adventures: "Speak with more respect of the sex that will make your fortune: for you will always displease men, having too much fire for prosaic souls."[18] The distinction then allows us to extend and to deepen this process of analytic reduction until donor and villain can at last be specified:

16. "La Structure et la forme," in Claude Lévi-Strauss, *Anthropologie structurale*, II (Paris: Plon, 1973), 139–173.

17. Propp, *Morphology:* Function XII (p. 39).

18. Stendhal, *La Chartreuse de Parme*, chap. II (Paris: Cluny, 1940), p. 34.

women will be the donors in this quest-romance and men the villains.

Still, from Lévi-Strauss's point of view, Propp's functions are inadequately "reduced" or formalized because they are still formulated in storytelling categories, no matter how general these may be. When we compare Propp's account of the function that inaugurates the main sequence of the tale ("one member of a family either lacks something or desires to have something [definition: *lack*]")[19] with its equivalents in Lévi-Strauss or Greimas (disequilibrium, contract broken, disjunction), it will be clear, not only that the latter are of a quite different level of abstraction—metalinguistic rather than merely generalizing—but also that a different type of narrative analysis will follow from such a starting point. Propp's follow-up can only be a set of subsequent episodes. That of Greimas or Lévi-Strauss moves at once to the level of semes and semic interactions of a more properly synchronic or systemic type, in which narrative episodes are no longer privileged as such, but play their part along with other kinds of semic transformations, inversions, exchanges and the like. To sum up this aspect of Lévi-Strauss's critique, then, we may say that Propp's series of functions is *still too meaningful,* or, in other words, is still not sufficiently distanced methodologically from the surface logic of the storytelling text.

Paradoxically, however, the other objection to be raised about Propp's method is the opposite one, namely that his analysis is *not yet meaningful enough.* This is Lévi-Strauss's charge of "empiricism," which strikes at the discovery that constitutes the heart of Propp's book, namely the fixed and irreversible sequence of a limited number of functions. From Lévi-Strauss's standpoint, the observation that the sequence in the fairy tale is "thus and not otherwise," even if true, confronts us with something as final and enigmatic, and as ultimately "meaningless," as the constants of modern science, for example, pi or the velocity of light. If we juxtapose Propp's narratological DNA with Lévi-Strauss's own reading of the Oedipus legend[20]—in which functions are reshuffled like a deck of cards and laid out in suits which henceforth entertain

---

19. Propp, *Morphology:* Function viiia (p. 35).
20. Lévi-Strauss, "Structural Analysis of Myth," pp. 213–216.

purely logical or semic relations with one another—it becomes clear that what is ultimately irreducible in Propp's analysis is simply narrative diachrony itself, the movement of storytelling in time. To characterize this movement in terms of "irreversibility" is then to produce not a solution, but rather the problem itself.

From the later, methodologically far more self-conscious points of view of Lévi-Strauss and Greimas, who insist on a radical distinction between the narrative surface (or manifestation) and some underlying deep narrative structure, the irreducible diachrony of Propp's version of the deep structure of the fairy tale is simply the shadow thrown by the surface manifestation upon his narrative model. The two objections are thus essentially the same: both the insufficient formalization of the model (its anthropomorphic traces) and the irreversibility it attributes to its functions are different aspects of the same basic error, namely to have rewritten the primary narratives *in terms of another narrative,* rather than in terms of a synchronic system. Paradoxically, in this Propp rejoins Frye, whose "method" also amounts to the rewriting of a body of varied texts in the form of a single master narrative.

But Propp's model and the developments to which it has led, particularly in Greimassian semiotics, impose rather different questions from those we have raised about Frye. In particular, we will want to ask whether the ideal of formalization, projected by, yet imperfectly realized in, Propp's model, is ultimately realizable. We have already characterized Propp's findings as "anthropomorphic." It now remains to be seen whether a narrative system is conceivable from which the anthropomorphic or the traces of surface representation or narrative "manifestation" have been completely eliminated. Both Propp and Greimas distinguish between narrative "functions" and narrative characters, or between narrative unities and *actants:*[21] but it is clear that the former, as sheer event, present

---

21. Greimas' conception of the *actant* is based on a distinction between narrative syntax (or "deep structure") and that "surface" narrative discourse in which "actors" or recognizable "characters" are the visible unities: *actants,* which correspond to the necessarily far more limited functions of the narrative syntagm, are generally reduced by Greimas to three groups: Sender/Receiver, Subject-Hero/Object-Value, and Auxiliary/Villain. See A. J. Greimas, *Sémantique structurale* (Paris: Larousse, 1966), pp. 172–191; or more recently, "Les Actants, les acteurs, et les figures," in C. Chabrol, ed., *Sémiotique narrative et textuelle* (Paris: Larousse, 1973), pp. 161–176.

no real problems for some ultimate formalization, since events can always in one way or another be rewritten in terms of semic categories. I believe, therefore, that the ultimate blind spot or aporia of such *narrative analysis* is rather to be found in the problem of the character, or in even more basic terms, in its incapacity to make a place for the subject.

Yet this is already a paradoxical reproach: it will be objected that, on the contrary, the aim of the work of Propp and Greimas—and their signal achievement—has been precisely to displace the emphasis that an older, more representational narrative theory put on character. To insist on seeing characters in terms of those more basic unities which are narrative functions, or, in the case of Greimas, to propose the new concept of the *actant* for the structural "operators" of underlying semic transformations, would seem to mark a real advance toward the deanthropomorphization of the study of narrative. Unfortunately, the relationship between function and *actant* necessarily works both ways; and if the latter is thereby displaced and made structurally subordinate to the former, the fact remains that, perhaps even more irrevocably than in less self-conscious interpretations of narrative such as Frye's, the concept of the narrative function is shackled to some ultimately irreducible nucleus of anthropomorphic representation,—call it *actant,* structural role, character-effect, or whatever you like—which then fatally retransforms narrative function into so many acts or deeds of a human figure. The anthropomorphic figure, however, necessarily resists and is irreducible to the formalization which was always the ideal of such analysis.

We need to take seriously the more naive objection to such "scientific" ideals: namely that stories are always about people and that it is perverse, even for purposes of analysis, to seek to eliminate the very anthropomorphism which uniquely characterizes narrative as such. But here the work of Lévi-Strauss has a useful lesson for us; the *Mythologiques* are unique in the way in which they achieve two things apparently incompatible from the point of view of this objection. For at the same time that this corpus of narrative analysis restores to us, as few other works have, an immense body of narratives which enlarge our reading habits and reconfirm the status of storytelling as the supreme function of the human mind, *Mythologiques* also performs the tour de force of eliminating precisely those working concepts of *actant* and of narrative diachrony which we have held to be the strategic weaknesses of Propp's model.

The key to this paradoxical achievement is, I think, to be found in the social origins of the narrative material with which Lévi-Strauss deals. These are evidently preindividualistic narratives; that is, they emerge from a social world in which the psychological subject has not yet been constituted as such, and therefore in which later categories of the subject, such as the "character," are not relevant. Hence the bewildering fluidity of these narrative strings, in which human characters are ceaselessly transformed into animals or objects and back again; in which nothing like narrative "point of view," let alone "identification" or "empathy" with this or that protagonist, emerges; in which not even the position of an individual storyteller or "sender" (*destinataire*) can be conceptualized without contradiction.

But if the emergence of narrative characters requires such social and historical preconditions, then the dilemmas of Propp and Greimas are themselves less methodological than historical ones; they result from projecting later categories of the individual subject back anachronistically onto narrative forms which precede the subject's emergence when they do not unreflexively admit into the logic of their narrative analyses precisely those ideological categories that it was the secret purpose of later texts (for example, nineteenth-century novels) to produce and to project. This is to say that a dialectical critique of the categories of semiotic and narrative method must historicize these categories by relating what are apparently purely methodological issues and dilemmas to the whole current philosophical critique of the subject, as it emerges from Lacan, Freud, and Nietzsche, and is developed in poststructuralism. These philosophical texts, with their attacks on humanism (Althusser), their celebration of the "end of Man" (Foucault), their ideals of *dissémination* or *dérive* (Derrida, Lyotard), their valorization of schizophrenic writing and schizophrenic experience (Deleuze), may in the present context be taken as symptoms of or testimony to a modification of the experience of the subject in consumer or late monopoly capitalism: an experience which is evidently able to accommodate a far greater sense of psychic dispersal, fragmentation, drops in "niveau," fantasy and projective dimensions, hallucinogenic sensations, and temporal discontinuities than the Victorians, say, were willing to acknowledge. From a Marxist point of view, this experience of the decentering of the subject and the theories, essentially psychoanalytic, which have been devised to map it are to be seen as the signs of the dissolution of an essentially bourgeois ideology of the subject and of psychic unity or identity (what used to be called bourgeois "individualism"); but we may admit the descriptive value of the poststructuralist critique of the "subject" without necessarily endorsing the schizophrenic ideal it has tended to project. For Marxism, indeed, only the emergence of a post-individualistic social world, only the reinvention of the collective and the associative, can concretely achieve the "decentering" of the individual subject called for by such diagnoses; only a new and original form of collective social life can overcome the isolation and monadic autonomy of the older bourgeois subjects in such a way that individual consciousness can be lived—and not merely theorized—as an "effect of structure" (Lacan).

How this historical perspective can be dialectically related to the problems of narrative analysis in such a way as to produce a more reflexive view of the operation of "characters" in a narrative structure we will try to show in the next chapter. For the moment, we must return to Greimas in order to underscore a certain gap between his narrative theory, as we have criticized it here, and his concrete practice of narrative analysis. We may now reformulate our earlier diagnosis of the semiotic ideal of formalization in the more practical terms of our objection to classificatory operations. From this point of view, what is problematical about Propp's character-functions (hero, donor, villain) or Greimas' more formalized *actants* emerges when it turns out that we are merely being asked to drop the various elements of the surface narrative into these various prepared slots. Thus, returning to Stendhal's narratives, we find that the functional or actantial reduction seems to involve little more than "deciding" that this novelist's secondary male figures—l'Abbé Pirard, l'Abbé Blanès, Mosca, the Marquis de la Mole,—as so many spiritual fathers of the protagonists of Stendhal's novels, are all to be classed as so many manifestations of the donor.

Yet this method celebrates its true triumphs, and proves to be a methodological improvement over Propp, precisely in those moments in which Greimas is able to show a disjunction between the narrative surface and the underlying actantial mechanisms. Actantial reduction is indeed particularly revealing in those instances in which the surface unity of "character" can be analytically dissolved, by showing, as Greimas does in certain of his readings, that a single character in reality conceals the operation of two distinct *actants*.[22] This x-ray process could obviously also work in the other direction; thus, our scattered remarks about Stendhal, above, suggest that in his narratives, the function of the donor finds manifestation in two distinct groups of characters, the supportive or maternal women figures and the spiritual fathers. Such surface or narrative reduplication will evidently not be without important consequences for the ultimate shape of the narrative as a whole. What we can at once suggest is that both the Propp model and Greimas' more complex narrative system become productive at the moment when the narrative text in one way or another *deviates* from its basic schema; far less so in those instances where, the narrative proving to be its simple replication, the analyst is reduced to noting the conformity of the manifest text to the underlying theoretical schema.

I have in another place maintained that the originality and usefulness of Propp's model from an interpretive standpoint lay in his conception of the donor, which I argued to be the central mechanism of his reading of fairy tales.[23] It is now time to reexamine this proposition from our present perspective, according to which the value of such narrative models lies in their capacity to register a given text's specific deviation from them, and thereby to raise the more dialectical and historical issue of this determinate formal difference. We can better appreciate the usefulness of actantial reduction, if we reflect, for instance, on the "character" of Heathcliff in *Wuthering Heights*, a figure whose ambiguous nature (romantic hero or tyrannical villain?) has remained an enigma for intuitive or impressionizing, essentially "representational," criticism, which can only seek to resolve the ambiguity in some way (for example, Heathcliff as "Byronic" hero). In terms of actantial reduc-

---

22. A. J. Greimas, "La Structure des actants du récit," in *Du Sens* (Paris: Seuil, 1970), pp. 249–270.
23. *Prison-House of Language*, pp. 65–69.

tion, however, the text would necessarily be read or rewritten, not as the story of "individuals," nor even as the chronicle of genera- tions and their destinies, but rather as an impersonal process, a semic transformation centering on the house, which moves from Lockwood's initial impressions of the Heights, and the archaic story of origins behind it, to that final ecstatic glimpse through the window, where, as in the final scene of Cocteau's *Orphée,* "le décor monte au ciel" and a new and idyllic family takes shape in the love of Hareton and the second Cathy. But if this is the central narrative line of the work, or what Greimas would call its principal *isotopie,* then Heathcliff can no longer be considered the hero or the pro- tagonist in any sense of the word. He is rather, from the very beginning—the abrupt introduction into the family of the orphan child, "as dark almost as if it came from the devil"—something like a mediator or a catalyst, designed to restore the fortunes and to rejuvenate the anemic temperament of the two families. What is this to say but that "Heathcliff" occupies in some complicated way the place of the donor in this narrative system: a donor who must wear the functional appearance of the protagonist in order to perform his quite different actantial function. The resolution of the narrative in fact undermines one's earlier impression that Heathcliff, by his pas- sion for the first Cathy and his matrimonial alliance with the Lin- tons, was to be read as the protagonist of the romance. This mis- reading, deliberately projected by the text, serves in fact to disguise his twofold mission as donor, to restore money to the family and to reinvent a new idea of passion, which will serve as the model—in the sense of a Girardian triangular mediation—for the later and conclusive passion.

Hence the complex semic confusion between good and evil, love and money, the role of the "jeune premier" and that of the pa- triarchal villain, which mark this "character" who is in reality a mechanism for mediating these semes. Such a view at once leads us away from the narrative model of which a conventional semiotic reading of Heathcliff would simply provide a validation, and to- ward a historical inquiry into the reasons for this complex and unique deviation from it. What we have said earlier about such oppositions now allows us to sketch out the historical ground on which such a deviation could be understood as a meaningful sym- bolic act.

What has been called Byronic about Heathcliff could indeed with as much justice be termed Nietzschean: this peculiar character or actantial locus exasperates just that system of ethical judgments which are as unavoidable for the reader as they are unsatisfactory and nonfunctional. But this is because Heathcliff is the locus of *history* in this romance: his mysterious fortune marks him as a protocapitalist, in some other place, absent from the narrative, which then recodes the new economic energies as sexual passion. The aging of Heathcliff then constitutes the narrative mechanism whereby the alien dynamism of capitalism is reconciled with the immemorial (and cyclical) time of the agricultural life of a country squiredom; and the salvational and wish-fulfilling Utopian conclusion is bought at the price of transforming such an alien dynamism into a benign force which, eclipsing itself, permits the vision of some revitalization of the ever more marginalized countryside. To see "Heathcliff" as a historical modification of the function of the donor thus allows us to glimpse the ideologeme—the conceptual antinomy but also the social contradiction—which generates the narrative, but which it is the latter's mission to "resolve."

Such a dialectical reappropriation of the semiotic model suggests that some more general sense of the historic adaptation of classical romance to nineteenth-century conditions—which include the new social content of nascent capitalism as well as its new forms, in particular the realistic novel—might be gained by further investigation of the role of the donor in these works. What we have said about Stendhal, in particular, leads to an unexpected view of the Utopian love-death which concludes *Le Rouge et le noir:* for Julien's discovery of his authentic self, his rediscovery of his "true" love for Mme de Renal, must now clearly be seen as a fundamental modification in the actantial role of the latter, who has been transformed from the donor into the object of the protagonist's quest.

This transformation suggests that Stendhal's narrative must be seen as something more complex than a mere appropriation or replication of that romance structure whose analysis gave us the preliminary instruments to read it or rewrite it in such terms. Indeed, it is as though the semiotic equipment, whose use was predicated on the assumption that Stendhal's novel is simply another manifestation of Propp's narrative structure, now completes its work by discrediting itself and betraying its own typologizing limits. The dialectical moment is upon us when, having first read Stendhal as an embodiment of the romance structure, we then find ourselves forced into the realization that what is historically specific about Stendhal's novel is precisely its deviation from that underlying structure which was the starting point of the analysis. Yet we would not have been able to detect this feature of the work—in which its historicity becomes accessible to us for the first time—had we not begun by respecting the working convention of first-level semiotics, namely that the text was at the start to be analyzed and laid out *as though* it were the mere replication of Propp's narrative line or "deep structure."

We may now, therefore, see *Le Rouge et le noir* less as an example than as a kind of immanent critique of romance in its restructuration of the form. As we observed in a somewhat different way in *Wuthering Heights,* the complex transformation and foregrounding of the original "function" of the donor amounts to something like a dialectical self-consciousness of romance itself. But whereas *Wuthering Heights* projected its "critique" of the donor into the whole realm of instrumental history, Stendhal's dissociation of this function into the "paternal" donor and the "maternal" object of desire has a somewhat different emphasis, and tends to foreground the phenomenon of desire itself, thereby reflecting the emergence of a new commodity object-world in which the "objects" of desire, necessarily degraded by their new status as commodities, tend to call the very authenticity of the quest-romance, organized around them, back into question. The later system of *La Chartreuse de Parme,* in which the figure of a more properly feminine donor, the Duchess Sanseverina, is gradually disjoined in a more explicit way from that of a more properly "desirable" quest-object, in the person of Clélia, may then be seen as something like a second-degree re-containment of the earlier contradiction—one which, returning nostalgically to the original romance paradigm, releases that more archaic fairy-tale atmosphere which is so striking in the later work.

IV

With these twin reopenings upon history of our two approaches to genre, we are now in a better position to evaluate Frye's notion of generic history, which he describes in terms of the displacement of romance from one mimetic level or "style" (high, low, mixed) to another. Transformations in the status of the hero ("superior in *kind* both to other men and to the environment of other men," "superior in *degree* to other men and to his environment," "superior in degree to other men but not to his natural environment," "superior neither to other men nor to his environment," "inferior in power or intelligence to ourselves"[24]) signal a modulation from some "original" solar myth, through the levels of romance, epic and tragedy, comedy and realism, to that of the demonic and ironic, of the contemporary antihero, whence, as at the end of Vico or of the *Inferno* ("lasciò qui loco vòto / quella ch'appar di qua, e sù ricorse") the whole storytelling system rotates on its axis and the original solar myth reappears. In this sense, *The Secular Scripture* is itself the strongest contemporary renewal of romance, and may be added into its own corpus in much the same way that Lévi-Strauss has suggested that all later interpretations of the Oedipus myth (including Freud's) be understood as variants on the basic text.

I have suggested elsewhere[25] that, despite the use of the Freudian concept of displacement, with its negative implications (repression, distortion, negation, and the like), the driving force of Frye's system is the idea of historical *identity:* his identification of mythic patterns in modern texts aims at reinforcing our sense of the affinity between the cultural present of capitalism and the distant mythical past of tribal societies, and at awakening a sense of the continuity between our psychic life and that of primitive peoples. Frye's is in this sense a "positive" hermeneutic, which tends to filter out historical difference and the radical discontinuity of modes of production and of their cultural expressions. A negative hermeneutic, then, would on the contrary wish to use the narrative raw material shared by myth and "historical" literatures to sharpen our sense of historical difference, and to stimulate an increasingly vivid apprehension of what happens when plot falls into history, so to speak, and enters the force fields of the modern societies.

From this point of view, then, the problem raised by the persistence of romance as a mode is that of substitutions, adaptations, and appropriations, and raises the question of what, under wholly altered historical circumstances, can have been found to replace the raw materials of magic and Otherness which medieval romance found ready to hand in its socioeconomic environment. A history of romance as a mode becomes possible, in other words, when we explore the substitute codes and raw materials, which, in the increasingly secularized and rationalized world that emerges from the collapse of feudalism, are pressed into service to replace the older magical categories of Otherness which have now become so many dead languages.

An instructive example of this process of secularization and renewal by substitution may be observed in one of the earliest nineteenth-century reinventions of the genre, Manzoni's *I Promessi Sposi,* surely, along with Dostoyevsky's *Brothers Karamazov,* one of the few persuasive post-revolutionary attempts to express a religious vision through the novel form. In our present context, it is immediately clear that Manzoni's sophisticated theology—a post-Jansenist preoccupation with states of sin and grace, a post-Calvinist fascination with the workings of Providence—marks a beginning secularization of romance as a form, not merely in its substitution of religious for magical categories, but above all in the way in which an older sense of animistic powers is rationalized into the far more "realistic" and psychological "miracle" of conversion.

The plot of *I Promessi Sposi,* indeed, charts an ever-widening conflict between forces of good and evil, which, still clearly linked to older categories of white and black magic, are here rewritten as charismatic forces that radiate outward from historic individuals. Here one does more than suffer evil, one is contaminated by it. On learning of Don Rodrigo's plot to stop his marriage, Renzo is possessed by "a mad longing to do something strange and awful," a reaction which Manzoni glosses as follows:

Those who provoke or oppress, all those who do any wrong to others, are guilty not only of the harm they do, but also of the twists they arouse in the minds of those they have injured. Renzo was a peaceable young man and averse to bloodshed—an open youth who hated deceit of any kind; but at that moment his heart only beat to kill, and his mind turned only on thoughts of treachery. He would have liked to rush to Don Rodrigo's house, seize him by the throat, and. . . .[26]

The passage is significant, not because it expresses Manzoni's personal opinion on the subject, but rather because it projects and blocks out a *world* of a determinate structure, a world in which moral essences exercise an active power at distance, in which character-emanation becomes a causal convention as plausible in this narrative as the magical curse or supernatural possession of oral tales. In such a world, we come to admit the baleful spell exuded by the Gothic fortress of l'Innominato, which broods over the landscape like the very promise of evil, and to believe in the healing power of Archbishop Federigo as he moves through an anarchic and plague-ridden countryside progressively touched by the grace that radiates from his person. In such a world, the climactic event is then conversion, and the old physical *agon* of the romances of chivalry is transformed into the struggle of Good and Evil for the individual soul.

In the Italian society of the period, strongly marked by the new Enlightenment values but far less secularized than the more advanced post-revolutionary states, the concept of Providence still provides an adequate theoretical mediation between the salvational logic of the romance narrative and the nascent sense of historicity imposed by the social dynamic of capitalism. Where, in other situations, such as that of Stendhal, this compromise concept is unavailable, we observe a curious oscillation and hesitation between the archaic and the secular; episodes such as Julien's discovery of a scrap of newsprint that prefigures his future death on the scaffold, or the various astrological predictions and omens of *La Chartreuse de Parme,* may be read as magical survivals of the older form which have found themselves, in secular society, degraded to the status of private superstitions.

In Stendhal, the principal narrative function of magic is, however, rationalized far more completely than in Manzoni and finds itself oddly reinscribed in the realm of psychology. Now the "higher" and "lower" worlds of white and black magic have been

26. Alessandro Manzoni, *I Promessi Sposi,* chap. 2 (translated as *The Betrothed,* by A. Colquhoun [New York: Dutton, 1968], p. 25).

rewritten as two independent and irreconcilable psychological "instances": on the one hand a realm of spontaneity and sensibility, the place of the erotic, but also of political, passion, of *bonheur* and Rousseauean "natural man"; on the other a source of vanity and ambition, hypocrisy and calculation, the locus of all those ego activities which, based on deferred gratification, find their fulfillment in commerce and in the obsession with status. Nothing else in Stendhal is quite so striking as the language in which the mutual interference of these two systems and the mechanisms by which they short-circuit each other are registered:

> Grace is perfect when it is natural and unselfconscious: Julien, who had distinct ideas about feminine beauty, would have sworn at that moment that she was only twenty years old. All of a sudden the wild idea occurred to him of kissing her hand. At first he was afraid of his own idea: an instant later he said to himself: It will be cowardice on my part not to carry out a scheme that may be useful to me, and cut down this fine lady's contempt for a laborer just liberated from his sawmill.[27]

The resultant transformation in Julien is the psychological equivalent of that physical and natural desolation which in the older Grail romances is visited on the waste land. Indeed, the older magical landscape, weakened into figures of speech, still clings to the wondrous sentences with which Stendhal notes the process, as in a similar situation in *La Chartreuse:* "La pensée du privilège avait desséché cette plante toujours si délicate qu'on nomme le bonheur." Such passages do not so much document the originality of the contribution Stendhal felt he was making to the nascent "science" of psychology (or of *idéologie,* as his master Destutt de Tracy called it), but rather mark the rationalizing interiorization of the form by way of the assimilation of historically new types of content.

Quite different replacement strategies, however, are observable in the same historical situation. In Eichendorff's *Aus dem Leben eines Taugenichts,* for example, in many ways a purer specimen of the romantic art-romance than Stendhal's eclectic narratives, a well-nigh Shakespearean dramatic metaphor presides over the "re-

27. Stendhal, *Le Rouge et le noir,* Book I, chap. 6 (translated as *Red and Black,* by R. M. Adams [New York: Norton, 1969], p. 24).

motivation" of the older structure, whose explainable mysteries are then reinforced by the point of view of the Candide-like *naïf* or inverted picaro, the "good-for-nothing" himself, his adventures, like Bottom's dream, persisting in memory after "reality" has laid them to rest. Rationalization can then be grasped as something like the "reality principle," the censorship, of the new bourgeois social order, from which the longing for magic and providential mystery must be smuggled in order to find symbolic appeasement.

Thus, in the first great period of bourgeois hegemony, the reinvention of romance finds its strategy in the substitution of new positivities (theology, psychology, the dramatic metaphor) for the older magical content. When, at the end of the nineteenth century, the search for secular equivalents seems exhausted, the characteristic indirection of a nascent modernism, from Kafka to Cortázar, circumscribes the place of the fantastic as a determinate, marked *absence* at the heart of the secular world:

> Andreas turned away from the house Zorzi had vanished into, and strolled to the other end of the rather narrow street. It ended in an archway; but oddly, on the other side, a little bridge over the canal led to a small oval plaza with a chapel. Andreas turned back, and was annoyed to find that after so short a time he could no longer recognize the house among so many others of similar construction. One door, dark green, with a bronze knocker in the form of a dolphin, looked like the right one; but it was closed, and Andreas thought he could remember seeing Zorzi in the hall through an open doorway. Still, there was little chance of their missing one another if Andreas went back to the bridge, and took a look at the little square with the church on it. Street and square were utterly deserted; he would have heard footsteps, let alone a cry or repeated calls if Zorzi were looking for him. So he crossed the bridge; below, a little boat hung moored on the dark water, not another human being to be seen or heard: the whole square had something lost and forsaken about it.[28]

The unnatural neutrality of this vacant cityscape may stand as an emblem of the contemporary fantastic in general, its expectant hush revealing an object world forever suspended on the brink of mean-

---

28. Hugo von Hofmannsthal, *Erzählungen* (Tübingen: Niemeyer, 1945), p. 176, my translation.

ing, forever disposed to receive a revelation of evil or of grace that never comes. The unpeopled streets, the oppressive silence, convey this absent presence like a word on the tip of your tongue or a dream not quite remembered, while for the subject himself, a succession of trivial and apparently insignificant feelings (the *seltsamerweise* that nags at Andreas' attention, the sudden bursts of inexplicable humor—"Andreas war *ärgerlich*") records the internal activity of a psyche buffeted by forebodings, and confirms Heidegger's account of *Stimmung* as the privileged medium through which the worldness of world manifests itself.[29]

Stimmung—much stronger than the English "mood" in its designation of moments when a landscape seems charged with alien meaning (Julien Gracq), when a glimpse of sordid wallpaper chokes us with anxiety or a framed and distant vista fills us with an equally unaccountable elation—is the very element of what Frye, following Joyce, terms the romance "epiphany." The latter term, however, is misleading, precisely to the degree to which it suggests that in the secularized and reified world of modern capitalism, epiphany is possible as a positive event, as the revelation of presence.[30] But if epiphany itself is a mirage, then the most authentic vocation of romance in our time would not be that reinvention of the providential vision invoked and foretold by Frye, but rather its capacity, by absence and by the silence of the form itself, to express that ideology of desacralization by which modern thinkers from Weber to the Frankfurt School have sought to convey their sense of the radical impoverishment and constriction of modern life. So the great expressions of the modern fantastic, the last unrecognizable avatars of romance as a mode, draw their magical power from an unsentimental loyalty to those henceforth abandoned clearings across which higher and lower worlds once passed.

29. Heidegger, *Sein und Zeit,* pp. 131–140.

30. "Las cosas que le occurian a Dante en un claustro de convento o a orillas del Arno han cambiado de localizacion, las epifanias pasan de otra manera . . ." (Julio Cortázar, *El Libro de Manuel* [Buenos Aires: Sudamericana, 1973], p. 279). Indeed, the dream-fable at the heart of this novel is something like a repudiation of traditional epiphanies, or an autocritique of the storyteller's earlier work: the darkened movie theater, the dream as discontinuous and edited as a Fritz Lang film, the message from the Cuban, whose repressed kerygma, from the first liberated territory of the Western hemisphere, slowly rises to the surface in the course of events: Wake up!

V

In the preceding section we have told a historical narrative about the destinies of romance as a form; and it will be said that such a narrative (what I have elsewhere called a "diachronic construct") is for all its emphasis on the reappropriation of romance in discontinuous historical situations, no less "linear" than the historical continuities affirmed by Frye. To write either kind of "history" of romance is thus apparently to construct a narrative in which a recognizable protagonist—some "full" romance form realized, say, in the *romans* of Chrestien de Troyes—evolves into the elaborate Italian and Spenserian poems and knows its brief moment on the stage in the twilight of Shakespearean spectacle before being revived in romanticism, where under the guise of the novel it leads a new existence in the art-romances of Stendhal and Manzoni, of Scott and Emily Bronte, only to outlive itself in modern times under the unexpected formal mutations of the fantastic on one hand (Cortázar, Kafka) and of fantasy (Alain-Fournier, Julien Gracq) on the other. This, it will be said, is surely a fiction on the order of Virginia Woolf's *Orlando,* and merits the most withering contemporary Althusserian or Nietzschean denunciations of Hegelian idealistic historiography, of evolutionism, or of "old-fashioned linear history."

As these frequent reproaches tend to project a kind of "thought of the Other" (a reverse image of nonthinking always attributed to *other people*), it is worth examining in more detail the mental operations involved in the construction of such apparently inadmissible diachronic series. When, for instance, Frye describes one of the "functions" of his master tale, the *eiron,* as the "man who deprecates himself, as opposed to the *alazon,*" or boastful imposter, it is evident that we are still in a synchronic system, where functions are understood as logical inversions of one another. But then he goes on to observe:

> Another central *eiron* figure is the type entrusted with hatching the schemes which bring about the hero's victory. This character in Roman comedy is always a tricky slave (*dolosus servus*), and in Renaissance comedy he becomes the scheming valet who is so frequent in Continental plays, and in Spanish drama is called the *gracioso.* Modern audiences are most familiar with him in Figaro and in the

Leporello of *Don Giovanni*. Through such intermediate nineteenth-century figures as Micawber and the Touchwood of Scott's *St. Ronan's Well*, who, like the gracioso, have buffoon affiliations, he evolves into the amateur detective of modern fiction. The Jeeves of P. G. Wodehouse is a more direct descendant.[31]

The evolutionary language Frye uses here clearly allows this series of identifications to be constructed and represented in the form of a micronarrative. What is less obvious is that this micronarrative has a synchronic function, and that it must be completed by a return to any single one of the texts in question. These two movements are usefully reidentified in the current concept of intertextuality, in which a diachronic sequence finds its proper use in the projection of a stereoptic vision of an individual text. So in Frye's passage, the function of the micronarrative is not to use the figure of Micawber as evidence for some "evolutionary" theory, but rather to permit a return to Micawber himself in such a way that we rewrite this character together with all his predecessors and descendants in the form of a new composite and multidimensional entity. The purpose is not to replace Micawber with his "original" in the *dolosus servus,* nor to dissolve him into Jeeves, but to produce a new narrative component which may be defined as a Micawber-considered-as-a *dolosus-servus.*

But, as we have already observed, this intertextual construction, based on identity and persistence, is not the only form that can be taken by the diachronic construct, which can also be used to register a determinate and signifying *absence* in the text, an absence that becomes visible only when we reestablish the series that should have generated the missing term. Eichendorff's novella can again offer a demonstration of such negative intertextuality.

As we have already noted, the theatricality of the novella—stylistically, the text may be read as the virtual transcription of a theatrical performance—inscribes it in that long tradition of the comedy of errors (doubles, disguises, sexual confusion, ritual unmasking) from the Roman tradition to Shakespeare. Such formal affinities suggest the additional affiliation with the theatrical double plot, as William Empson has described it in *Some Versions of*

31. Frye, *Anatomy*, p. 173.

Pastoral, and in which an aristocratic plot line is reduplicated (and sometimes inverted) in the subplot of a low-born protagonist. Yet to set *Aus dem Leben eines Taugenichts* in this generic series allows us to note a marked or signifying absence: Eichendorff's novella can be grasped as a double plot system of which we have been given only the secondary line, the comic, or low-class subplot. As for the aristocratic component (the background situation of the elopement and so forth), it is evidently too well known and stereotypical to need representation, and functions as a mere overtone. At the moment of explanations, the bewildered hero is simply asked whether he has never read any novels! We must therefore conclude that in *Taugenichts* the aristocratic main plot has been structurally repressed, for the strategic reason that its manifest presence would serve as an unavoidable reminder, for a new post-revolutionary readership, of the survival in Germany of a quasi-feudal power structure.

But now the insertion of *Taugenichts* into the principal generic sequence, the "tradition" of the comedy of errors, can also be read in a different way, in order to register a decisive change in function. On the surface, this material has remained the same: Shakespearean quid-pro-quos, which, flirting with scandal, end in laughter, the play with homosexual overtones, forbidden encounters between apparent male figures which are returned to safety when one is unmasked as a girl. But in Eichendorff, this flirtation with taboo and transgression may now be grasped as a displacement that performs an indispensable diversionary function and is meant to draw off the power of a far more dangerous and explosive taboo, namely the anxieties of something like miscegenation aroused by the scandal of a peasant youth courting an aristocratic woman. The homosexual comedy distracts us from this more disturbing sociological anxiety, and is dismissed back into mere appearance when it comes time for us to learn, to our class relief, that the girl in question, far from being a noblewoman, was in reality merely the porter's niece! These two related diachronic or intertextual constructs, then, allow us to reread the text, synchronically, as the coexistence, contradiction, structural hierarchy, or uneven development of a number of distinct narrative systems; and it is the possibility of such a reading which in turn allows us to grasp the text as a socially symbolic act, as the ideological—but formal and immanent—response to a historical dilemma.

I would not, however, want to be understood as having conceded to the critique of linear history in advance, or as having acknowledged that the diachronic moment of this process of intertextual construction was some mere "necessary fiction" or operational myth. The critique of linear or evolutionary history can be dramatized by the paradox of Raymond Roussel's anecdote about the traveler who claimed to have seen, under glass in a provincial museum, "le crâne de Voltaire enfant." The logical fallacy is that of anachronistically designating a term of one system as the "precursor" of a term in a system that does not yet exist. So it is said that Marxism mythically transforms elements of a precapitalist system (for example, commerce or merchant capital) into evolutionary forerunners of a more properly capitalist system which has not yet come into being and with which such elements have nothing whatsoever to do, either causally or functionally. But this is not at all what happens in *Capital* (nor in the works of Darwin, either, for whom a similar rectification ought to be undertaken some day). Diachronic representation in Marx is not constructed along those principles of continuity which have been stigmatized as Hegelian or evolutionary. Rather, the constructional model is quite different one, which Nietzsche was the first to identify and to designate as the *genealogy*. In genealogical construction, we begin with a full-blown system (capitalism in Marx, and in the present book, reification) in terms of which elements of the past can "artificially" be isolated as objective preconditions: genealogy is not a historical *narrative*, but has the essential function of renewing our perception of the synchronic system as in an x-ray, its diachronic perspectives serving to make perceptible the articulation of the functional elements of a given system in the present.

It will be observed, however, that not all the diachronic constructs we have mentioned operate in this way, and in particular that we have sometimes seemed to begin a diachronic sequence with a strong term (Frye's *dolosus servus*, for example) of which the later versions are, on the contrary, something like a dissolution. Thus, even if we grant the conceptual respectability of the genealogy, this second sequence would seem fatally to project some "myth

of origins." Let us now look more closely at this type of construction, which we will designate as a model of formal *sedimentation,*
and whose essential theory we owe to Edmund Husserl.[32] To limit
ourselves to generic problems, what this model implies is that in its

32. Husserl's principal illustration of this process—the constitution of Galilean
science by way of a repression of praxis—is worth quoting at some length: "Now we
must note something of the highest importance that occurred even as early as
Galileo: the surreptitious substitution of the mathematically substructed world of
idealities for the only real world, the one that is actually given through perception,
that is ever experienced and experienceable—our everyday life-world. This substitution was promptly passed on to his successors, the physicists of all the succeeding
centuries.

"Galileo was himself an heir in respect to pure geometry. The inherited geometry,
the inherited manner of 'intuitive' conceptualizing, proving, constructing, was no
longer original geometry: in this sort of 'intuitiveness' it was already empty of
meaning. Even ancient geometry was, in its way, *techne,* removed from the sources of
truly immediate intuition and originally intuitive thinking, sources from which the
so-called geometrical intuition, i.e., that which operates with idealities, had at first
derived its meaning. The geometry of idealities was preceded by the practical art of
surveying, which knew nothing of idealities. Yet such a pregeometrical achievement
was a meaning-fundament for geometry, a fundament for the great invention of
idealization; the latter encompassed the invention of the ideal world of geometry, or
rather the methodology of the objectifying determination of idealities through the
constructions which create 'mathematical existence.' It was a fateful omission that
Galileo did not inquire back into the original meaning-giving achievement which, as
idealization practiced on the original ground of all theoretical and practical life—the
immediately intuited world (and here especially the empirically intuited world of
bodies)—resulted in the geometrical ideal constructions. He did not reflect closely on
all this: on how the free, imaginative variation of this world and its shapes results
only in possible empirically intuitable shapes and not in exact shapes; on what sort
of motivation and what new achievement was required for genuinely geometric
idealization. For in the case of the inherited geometrical method, these functions
were no longer being *vitally* practiced; much less were they reflectively brought to
theoretical consciousness as methods which realize the meaning of exactness from
the inside. Thus it could appear that geometry, with its own immediately evident a
priori 'intuition' and the thinking which operates with it, produces a self-sufficient,
absolute truth which, as such—'obviously'—could be applied without further ado.
That this obviousness was an illusion . . ., that even the meaning of the application of
geometry has complicated sources: this remained hidden for Galileo and the ensuing
period. Immediately with Galileo, then, begins the surreptitious substitution of
idealized nature for prescientifically intuited nature" (Edmund Husserl, *The Crisis
of the European Sciences and Transcendental Phenomenology,* trans. David Carr
[Chicago: Northwestern University Press, 1970], pp. 48–49). Husserl's perception
has now been grounded on a historically materialist basis by a remarkable book by
Alfred Sohn-Rethel, *Intellectual and Manual Labour: A Critique of Epistemology*
(London: Macmillan, 1978). This work lays the philosophical basis for a theory of
scientific abstraction in much the same way that Lukács' *History and Class Consciousness* does for a theory of reification; its findings are here presupposed
throughout.

emergent, strong form a genre is essentially a socio-symbolic message, or in other terms, that form is immanently and intrinsically an ideology in its own right. When such forms are reappropriated and refashioned in quite different social and cultural contexts, this message persists and must be functionally reckoned into the new form. The history of music provides the most dramatic examples of this process, wherein folk dances are transformed into aristocratic forms like the minuet (as with the pastoral in literature), only then to be reappropriated for new ideological (and nationalizing) purposes in romantic music; or even more decisively when an older polyphony, now coded as archaic, breaks through the harmonic system of high romanticism. The ideology of the form itself, thus sedimented, persists into the later, more complex structure as a generic message which coexists—either as a contradiction or, on the other hand, as a mediatory or harmonizing mechanism—with elements from later stages.

This notion of the text as a synchronic unity of structurally contradictory or heterogeneous elements, generic patterns and discourses (what we may call, following Ernst Bloch, the *Ungleichzeitigkeit* or synchronic "uneven development" within a single textual structure[33]) now suggests that even Frye's notion of displacement can be rewritten as a conflict between the older deep-structural form and the contemporary materials and generic systems in which it seeks to inscribe and to reassert itself. Beyond this, it would seem to follow that, properly used, genre theory must always in one way or another project a model of the coexistence or tension between several generic modes or strands: and with this methodological axiom the typologizing abuses of traditional genre criticism are definitely laid to rest.

It has perhaps already become clear that traditional generic systems—tragedy and comedy, for instance, or lyric/epic/drama—which in earlier social formations have their own objectivity and constitute something like a formal environment or historical situation into which the individual work must emerge and against which it must define itself, are for the contemporary critic the occasion for the stimulation of essentially differential perceptions. On such oc-

33. Ernst Bloch, "Nonsynchronism and Dialectics," *New German Critique*, No.11 (Spring, 1977), pp. 22–38.

casions, even if the critic "classes" the text as a whole in this or that traditional genus, as a romance, say, rather than a comedy, the thrust of such a decision is to define the specificity of this text and mode *against* the other genre, now grasped in dialectical opposition to it. So to define romance in terms of wish-fulfillment, as Frye does, is already implicitly or explicitly to stage a comparative analysis in which this form is systematically differentiated from comedy, which is clearly also a wish-fulfilling narrative structure. The materials of comedy, however, are not the ethical oppositions and magical forces of its generic opposite, but rather those of the Oedipal situation, with its tyrannical fathers, its rebellious younger generation, and its renewal of the social order by marriage and sexual fulfillment. Comedy is active and articulates the play of desire and of the obstacles to it, whereas romance develops, as we have seen, under the sign of destiny and providence, and takes as its outer horizon the transformation of a whole world, ultimately sealed by those revelations of which the enigmatic Grail is itself the emblem. Comedy is social in its ultimate perspective, whereas romance remains metaphysical; and the wish-fulfillments of comedy may be identified as those of the genital stage, whereas romance would seem to betray older, more archaic fantasy material and to reenact the oral stage, its anxieties (the baleful spell of the intruding father-magician-villain) and its appeasement (the providential vision), reawakening the more passive and symbiotic relationship of infant to mother. Yet such psychoanalytic readings, although perfectly appropriate, should not be understood as diagnoses of these modes, but rather as new motifs and pretexts for a more thoroughgoing differential description of the two forms. In particular, the archaic fantasy material that psychoanalytic criticism feels able to detect in such forms can never be imagined as emerging in any pure state, but must always pass through a determinate social and historical situation, in which it is both universalized and reappropriated by "adult" ideology. The fantasy level of a text would then be something like the primal motor force which gives any cultural artifact its resonance, but which must always find itself diverted to the service of other, ideological functions, and reinvested by what we have called the political unconscious. We have indeed already observed such a process of ideological reappropriation at work in Eichendorff's novella, whatever its instinctual sources. In

Taugenichts, the comic mode—the place of the father, of the obstacle to desire, but also of social contradiction—is systematically effaced by the generic discourse of magical phantasmagoria, with its quite different perspective of a providential or maternal harmony. But in the Germany of the Holy Alliance this instinctual compromise is also an ideologically symbolic act.

When we have to do, however, with those eclectic, omnibus forms which are the monuments of nineteenth-century novelistic production, global classifications of a work in this or that traditional generic category at once become problematical. Is not, for instance, Manzoni's great work, far from being a romance, rather one of the supreme embodiments of what we call the historical novel? Or should it be seen as a late and unexpected avatar of the Byzantine novel, in which, as in the *Ethiopica* of Heliodorus, lovers are torn asunder by labyrinthine adventures and coincidences which ultimately reunite them? And are not Stendhal's novels far more easily ranged under the more traditional notion of the *Bildungsroman?* All these uncertainties and false problems are evidently generated by a "form"—the novel—which is not assimilable to either of the critical options of mode or of narrative structure.

Yet the eclecticism of the novel can itself become the occasion for a different type of generic analysis. In *I Promessi Sposi,* for instance, the separation of the lovers allows Manzoni to write two very distinct narrative lines which can be read as two different generic modes. The plight of Lucia, for instance, gives him the material for a Gothic novel, in which the feminine victim eludes one trap only to fall into a more agonizing one, confronting villains of ever blacker nature, and providing the narrative apparatus for the development of a semic system of evil and redemption, and for a religious and psychological vision of the fate of the soul.

Meanwhile, Renzo wanders through the *grosse Welt* of history and of the displacement of vast armed populations, the realm of the destiny of peoples and the vicissitudes of their governments. His own episodic experiences, formally something like a *roman d'aventures,* the misadventures of a peasant Candide, thus provide a quite different narrative register from that, inward and psychologizing, of the Lucia narrative: the experience of social life as it comes to its moment of truth in the bread riots and the economic depression of Milan, the anarchy of the *bravi* and the incompetence of the state, and ultimately—going beyond history to those "acts of God" which govern it—the supreme event of the plague, and the rejuvenation of the land that follows. On this reading, then, the "novel" as an apparently unified form is subjected to a kind of x-ray technique designed to reveal the layered or marbled structure of the text according to what we will call *generic discontinuities.* The novel is then not so much an organic unity as a symbolic act that must reunite or harmonize hetereogeneous narrative paradigms which have their own specific and contradictory ideological meaning. It is at any rate the systematic interweaving of these two distinct generic modes—in later bourgeois society they will be definitively sundered from each other in the sealed compartments of the private and the public, the psychological and the social—which lends Manzoni's book an appearance of breadth and variety, and a totalizing "completeness," scarcely equaled elsewhere in world literature.

In Stendhal, such layering and internal discontinuity can more immediately be traced back to the coexistence of distinct and sedimented types of generic discourse, which are the "raw material" on which the novel as a process must work. The court material of *La Chartreuse,* centering around the principality of Parma and the personal power of the Duchess, derives from that literature of *mémoires* and political gossip which has nourished the French tradition from Balzac to Proust and of which Saint-Simon remains the fountainhead and the monument. This is a generic discourse whose privileged content is the gesture, and more particular its verbal manifestation in the *trait d'esprit,* and whose privileged form is the anecdote.

The story of Fabrice is, on the other hand, the exercise of a quite different generic or discursive register, which we have already characterized as that of introspection or of psychology in the specialized sense of the *idéologues* or of Stendhal's own book *De l'amour:* the articulation of the associative processes of the mind in what are essentially allegorical micronarratives. The Enlightenment rationality of this mode is itself a variant on the older analytic tradition of the seventeenth-century French *moralistes,* so that Stendhal's books—*mémoires* plus moral epigrams—prove to reunite two relatively conventional strains and impulses in French classicism.

Such generic analysis thus tends to prolong its operations to the point at which the generic categories themselves—Gothic and picaresque, *mémoire* and associative psychology—are once more dissolved into the historical contradictions or the sedimented ideologemes in terms of which alone they are comprehensible. This final moment of the generic operation, in which the working categories of genre are themselves historically deconstructed and abandoned, suggests a final axiom, according to which *all* generic categories, even the most time-hallowed and traditional, are ultimately to be understood (or "estranged") as mere ad hoc, experimental constructs, devised for a specific textual occasion and abandoned like so much scaffolding when the analysis has done its work. This is in fact already obviously the case with the various generic classifications which people have invented for the novel (and of which we have given a few above: the *Bildungsroman,* the historical novel, the *roman d'aventures,* and the rest). Such classifications in fact prove rewarding only as long as they are felt to be relatively arbitrary critical acts, and lose their vitality when, as with the category of the *Bildungsroman,* they come to be thought of as "natural" forms. Genre criticism thereby recovers its freedom and opens up a new space for the creative construction of experimental entities, such as Lukács' reading of Solzhenitsyn in terms of an invented "genre" that might be termed the "closed laboratory situation,"[34] which project their "diachronic constructs" only the more surely to return to the synchronic historical situation in which such novels can be read as symbolic acts.

VI

The structural approach also knows its own specific opening onto history, which must now be described. We have already observed the play of structural norm and textual deviation which characterizes such analysis at its best; but we have not yet observed that this analytical operation is not a two- but rather a three-term process, and that its greater complexity makes of structural analysis something quite different from the conventional systems of norm and deviation (as, for instance, in a host of theories of poetic language, or, in the area of the psychic, in theories of transgression).

34. Georg Lukács, *Solzhenitsyn,* trans. W. D. Graf (Boston: MIT Press, 1969), pp. 35–46.

What is dialectical about this more complete structural model is that the third term is always absent, or, more properly, that it is nonrepresentable. Neither the manifest text, nor the deep structure tangibly mapped out before us in a spatial hieroglyph, the third variable in such analysis is necessarily history itself, as an absent cause.

The relationship between these three variables may be formulated as a permutational scheme or *combinatoire,* in which the systematic modification or commutation of any single term—by generating determinate variations in the other two—allows us to read the articulate relationships that make up the whole system. Thus, the deviation of the individual text from some deeper narrative structure directs our attention to those determinate changes in the historical situation which block a full manifestation or replication of the structure on the discursive level. On the other hand, the failure of a particular generic structure, such as epic, to reproduce itself not only encourages a search for those substitute textual formations that appear in its wake, but more particularly alerts us to the historical ground, now no longer existent, in which the original structure was meaningful. Finally, an a priori and experimental commutation of the historical term may stimulate our perceptions of the constitutive relationship of forms and texts to their historical preconditions by producing artificial laboratory situations in which such forms or texts are rigorously inconceivable. Thus, paradoxically, the ultimate model of such a *combinatoire* recalls the form of Hegel's reflections on epic ("our present-day machinery and factories together with the products they turn out . . . would . . . be out of tune with the background of life which the original epic requires");[35] save for the absence in Hegel's thought of the fundamental structural discovery, namely the twin variables of a deep structure and a manifest text.

What is paradoxical, of course, is that structural analysis should

---

35. "What man requires for his external life, house and home, tent, chair, bed, sword and spear, the ship with which he crosses the ocean, the chariot which carries him into battle, boiling and roasting, slaughtering, drinking and eating,—nothing of this must have become merely a dead means to an end for him; he must still feel alive in all these with his whole sense and self in order that what is in itself merely external be given a humanly inspired individual character by such close connection with the human individual" (G. W. F. Hegel, *Aesthetik* [Frankfurt: Europäische Verlagsanstalt, 1955], II, 414, my translation).

thus finally open out onto the third term of what I have elsewhere called "the logic of content"[36]: the semantic raw materials of social life and language, the constraints of determinate social contradictions, the conjunctures of social class, the historicity of structures of feeling and perception and ultimately of bodily experience, the constitution of the psyche or subject, and the dynamics and specific temporal rhythms of historicity. Where the interpretation of genre in terms of mode led us ultimately to the ideologeme, to the narrative paradigm, and to the sedimentation of various generic discourses—all essentially cultural or superstructural phenomena—structural analysis demands as its completion a kind of negative reconstruction, a postulation by implication and presupposition, of an absent or unrepresentable infrastructual limiting system. Now ultimately perhaps we may return to linguistics for a working projection of these discontinuities which is more productive and less paralyzing and absolute than the distinction between semantics and structure from which we started; here, as so often, Hjelmselv's four-part mapping of the expression and the content of what he sees as the twin dimensions of the form and the substance of speech[37] is suggestive, and may be adapted to genre theory as follows:

FORM	*expression:*	the narrative structure of a genre
	content:	the semantic "meaning" of a generic mode
SUBSTANCE	*expression:*	ideologemes, narrative paradigms
	content:	social and historical raw material

It will be noted that each method, as it moves from the "form" of a text to the latter's relationship to "substance," completes itself with the complementary term. Thus, the semantic reading of genre ultimately grounds itself in expressive materials, while structural analysis, through the *combinatoire,* finds its ground in the text's "logic of content."

Still, some final word must be added about the nature of the relationship between text and context projected by the structural

---

36. In *Marxism and Form*, pp. 327–359.
37. Louis Hjelmslev, *Prolegomena to a Theory of Language,* trans. F. J. Whitfield (Madison: University of Wisconsin Press, 1961), chap. 13.

combinatoire, if only because some readers may overhastily assimilate this scheme to the mechanical Marxist notion of a determination of superstructure by base (where "determination" is read as simple causality). In the generic model outlined here, the relationship of the "third term" or historical situation to the text is not construed as causal (however that might be imagined) but rather as one of a limiting situation; the historical moment is here understood to block off or shut down a certain number of formal possibilities available before, and to open up determinate new ones, which may or may not ever be realized in artistic practice. Thus, the *combinatoire* aims not at enumerating the "causes" of a given text or form, but rather at mapping out its objective, a priori conditions of possibility, which is quite a different matter.

As for romance, it would seem that its ultimate condition of figuration, on which the other preconditions we have already mentioned are dependent—the category of worldness, the ideologeme of good and evil felt as magical forces, a salvational historicity—is to be found in a transitional moment in which two distinct modes of production, or moments of socioeconomic development, coexist. Their antagonism is not yet articulated in terms of the struggle of social classes, so that its resolution can be projected in the form of a nostalgic (or less often, a Utopian) harmony. Our principal experience of such transitional moments is evidently that of an organic social order in the process of penetration and subversion, reorganization and rationalization, by nascent capitalism, yet still, for another long moment, coexisting with the latter. So Shakespearean romance (like its falling cadence in Eichendorff) opposes the phantasmagoria of "imagination" to the bustling commercial activity at work all around it, while the great art-romances of the early nineteenth century take their variously reactive stances against the new and unglamorous social institutions emerging from the political triumph of the bourgeoisie and the setting in place of the market system. Late variants of romance like that of Alain-Fournier may be understood as symbolic reactions to the stepped-up pace of social change in the late nineteenth-century French countryside (laicization and the *loi Combes,* electrification, industrialization), while the production of Julien Gracq presupposes the regressive situation of Brittany within an otherwise "modernized" state.

Yet the point of such correlations is not simply to establish something like Plekhanov's "social equivalent" for a given form, but rather to restore our sense of the concrete situation in which such forms can be seized as original and meaningful protopolitical acts. This is the sense in which we have used the model of the *combinatoire* to locate marked or charged absences in Eichendorff's *Taugenichts,* and in particular the repression of comedy structure by way of the attenuation of authority figures (in this novella, indeed, authority is personified only by an older woman briefly glimpsed, the single villainous character being that secondary and grotesque Italian spy, who, galloping across the field in moonlight, "looked like a ghost riding on a three-legged horse"). We might also have shown this text's repression of other basic functions in the romance structure as well: most notably the omission of what we have called the transformation scene, and the substitution for the basic conflict between Eichendorff's two worlds—the humdrum workaday world of the village and the enchanted space of the chateau, with its music and candelabra, its gardens and eys twinkling through half-opened shutters—of compromise formations and mediatory combinations in which the two codes are playfully recombined (the flute-playing porter as a bourgeois with an aristocratic hobby, the old peasant with silver buckles, and so forth). On a narrative level, indeed, the two realms swap functions: that of work borrows its magic and its phantasmagorical elements from the aristocratic realm of leisure, while it proves to be in the latter that the various illusory plot complications—what in classic romance would be the force of evil and the malignant spell—originate. The resolution of the narrative thus cannot dramatize the triumph of either force over the other one, or enact any genuine ritual purification, but must produce a compromise in which everything finds its proper place again, in which the Taugenichts is reconciled through marriage to the world of work, while at the same time finding himself endowed with a miniature chateau of his own within the enchanted grounds of the aristocratic estate. It is because Eichendorff's opposition between good and evil threatens so closely to approximate the incompatibility between the older aristocratic traditions and the new middle-class life situation that the narrative must not be allowed to press on to any decisive conclusion. Its historical reality must rather be disguised and defused by the sense of moonlit revels dissolving into thin air, and conceal a perception of class realities behind the phantasmagoria of *Schein* and *Spiel*. But romance does its work well; under the spell of this wondrous text, the French Revolution proves to be an illusion, and the grisly class conflict of decades of Napoleonic world war fades into the mere stuff of bad dreams.

3

REALISM AND DESIRE:
Balzac and the Problem of the Subject

The novel is the end of genre in the sense in which it has been defined in the previous chapter: a narrative ideologeme whose outer form, secreted like a shell or exoskeleton, continues to emit its ideological message long after the extinction of its host. For the novel, as it explores its mature and original possibilities in the nineteenth century, is not an outer, conventional form of that kind. Rather, such forms, and their remains—inherited narrative paradigms, conventional actantial or proairetic schemata[1]—are the raw material on which the novel works, transforming their "telling" into its "showing," estranging commonplaces against the freshness of some unexpected "real," foregrounding convention itself as that through which readers have hitherto received their notions of events, psychology, experience, space, and time.

The "novel" as process rather than as form: such is the intuition to which apologists of this narrative structure have found themselves driven again and again, in an effort to characterize it as something that happens to its primary materials, as a specific but quite properly interminable set of operations and programming

---

1. On the term *actant* see above, Chapter 2, note 21. The "proairetic code" is Roland Barthes's designation for the terms or names of the conventional unities and actions of everyday life: "What is a series of actions? the unfolding of a name. To *enter*? I can unfold it into 'to appear' and 'to penetrate.' To *leave*? I can unfold it into 'to want to,' 'to stop,' 'to leave again.' To *give*?: 'to incite,' 'to return,' 'to accept.' Inversely, to establish the sequence is to find the name." *S/Z*, trans. R. Miller (New York: Hill and Wang, 1974), p. 82.

procedures, rather than a finished object whose "structure" one might model and contemplate. This process can be evaluated in a twofold way, as the transformation of the reader's subjective attitudes which is at one and the same time the production of a new kind of objectivity.

Indeed, as any number of "definitions" of realism assert, and as the totemic ancestor of the novel, *Don Quixote*, emblematically demonstrates, that processing operation variously called narrative mimesis or realistic representation has as its historic function the systematic undermining and demystification, the secular "decoding," of those preexisting inherited traditional or sacred narrative paradigms which are its initial givens.[2] In this sense, the novel plays a significant role in what can be called a properly bourgeois cultural revolution—that immense process of transformation whereby populations whose life habits were formed by other, now archaic, modes of production are effectively reprogrammed for life and work in the new world of market capitalism. The "objective" function of the novel is thereby also implied: to its subjective and critical, analytic, corrosive mission must now be added the task of producing as though for the first time that very life world, that very "referent"—the newly quantifiable space of extension and market equivalence, the new rhythms of measurable time, the new secular and "disenchanted" object world of the commodity system, with its post-traditional daily life and its bewilderingly empirical, "meaningless," and contingent *Umwelt*—of which this new narrative discourse will then claim to be the "realistic" reflection.

The problem of the subject is clearly a strategic one for both dimensions of the novelistic process, particularly if one holds, as Marxists do, that the forms of human consciousness and the mechanisms of human psychology are not timeless and everywhere essentially the same, but rather situation-specific and historically produced. It follows, then, that neither the reader's reception of a particular narrative, nor the actantial representation of human figures or agents, can be taken to be constants of narrative analysis but must themselves ruthlessly be historicized. The Lacanian terminol-

2. See in particular Roman Jakobson, "On Realism in Art," in K. Pomorska and L. Matejka, eds., *Readings in Russian Formalist Poetics* (Cambridge: MIT Press, 1971), pp. 38–46. "Decoding" is a term of Deleuze and Guattari: see the *Anti-Oedipus*, pp. 222–228.

ogy and thematics in which much of the present chapter has been cast offer a tactical advantage here.[3] Lacan's work, with its emphasis on the "constitution of the subject," displaces the problematic of orthodox Freudianism from models of unconscious processes or blockages toward an account of the formation of the subject and its constitutive illusions which, though still genetic in Lacan himself and couched in terms of the individual biological subject, is not incompatible with a broader historical framework. Furthermore, the polemic thrust of Lacanian theory, with its decentering of the ego, the conscious subject of activity, the personality, or the "subject" of the Cartesian cogito—all now grasped as something like an "effect" of subjectivity—and its repudiation of the various ideals of the unification of the personality or the mythic conquest of personal identity, poses useful new problems for any narrative analysis which still works with naive, common-sense categories of "character," "protagonist," or "hero," and with psychological "concepts" like those of identification, sympathy, or empathy.

We have already touched, in the first chapter, on the ways in which the Althusserian attack on "humanism"—on the categories of bourgeois individualism, and its anthropological myths of human nature—may be read as one powerful way of historicizing the Lacanian critique of the "centered subject." What becomes interesting in the present context is not the denunciation of the centered subject and its ideologies, but rather the study of its historical emergence, its constitution or virtual construction as a mirage which is also evidently in some fashion an objective reality. For the lived experience of individual consciousness as a monadic and autonomous center of activity is not some mere conceptual error, which can be dispelled by the taking of thought and by scientific rectification: it has a quasi-institutional status, performs ideological functions, and is susceptible to historical causation and produced and reinforced by other objective instances, determinants, and mechanisms. The concept of reification which has been developed in these pages conveys the historical situation in which the

3. For a fuller account of my own understanding and use, here and later on in this chapter, of Lacanian terminology, see my "Imaginary and Symbolic in Lacan," *Yale French Studies*, Nos. 55–56 (1977), pp. 338–395. The accredited exposition of the Lacanian "system" is Anika Rifflet-Lemaire, *Jacques Lacan* (Brussels: Dessart, 1970).

emergence of the ego or centered subject can be understood: the dissolution of the older organic or hierarchical social groups, the universal commodification of the labor-power of individuals and their confrontation as equivalent units within the framework of the market, the *anomie* of these now "free" and isolated individual subjects to which the protective development of a monadic armature alone comes as something of a compensation.

Cultural study allows us to isolate a certain number of specific instances and mechanisms which provide concrete mediations between the "superstructures" of psychological or lived experience and the "infrastructures" of juridical relations and production process. These may be termed *textual determinants* and constitute quasi-material transmission points which produce and institutionalize the new subjectivity of the bourgeois individual at the same time that they themselves replicate and reproduce purely infrastructural requirements. Among such textual determinants in high realism are surely to be numbered narrative categories such as Jamesian point of view or Flaubertian *style indirect libre*, which are thus strategic loci for the fully constituted or centered bourgeois subject or monadic ego.

I

This is the context in which a crucial feature of an earlier "realism"—what is often designated as the "omniscient narrator" in Balzac—may usefully be reexamined. Omniscience is, however, the least significant thing about such authorial intervention, and may be said to be the aftereffect of the closure of classical *récit*, in which the events are over and done with before their narrative begins. This closure itself projects something like an ideological mirage in the form of notions of fortune, destiny, and providence or predestination which these *récits* seem to "illustrate," their reception amounting, in Walter Benjamin's words, to "warming our lives upon a death about which we read." Such *récits*—closed adventures, *unerhörte Begebenheiten*, the very idea of strokes of fortune and destinies touched off by chance—are among the raw materials upon which the Balzacian narrative process works, and with whose inherited forms it sometimes uneasily coexists. At the same time the gestures and signals of the storyteller (perpetuated in the English novel well beyond 1857, the year Flaubert abolishes them with a single stroke in France) symbolically attempt to restore the coordinates of a face-to-face storytelling institution which has been effectively disintegrated by the printed book and even more definitively by the commodification of literature and culture.

The constitutive feature of the Balzacian narrative apparatus, however, is something more fundamental than either authorial omniscience or authorial intervention, something that may be designated as libidinal investment or authorial wish-fulfillment, a form of symbolic satisfaction in which the working distinction between biographical subject, Implied Author, reader, and characters is virtually effaced. Description is one privileged moment in which such investments may be detected and studied, particularly when the object of the description, as in the following evocation of a provincial townhouse, is contested, and focuses antagonistic ambitions within the narrative itself:

> On the balustrade of the terrace, imagine great blue and white pots filled with wallflowers; envision right and left, along the neighboring walls, two rows of square-trimmed lime-trees; you will form an idea of this landscape filled with demure good humor, with tranquil chastity, and with modest homely [bourgeois] vistas offered by the other bank and its quaint houses, the trickling waters of the Brillante, the garden, two rows of trees lining its walls, and the venerable edifice of the Cormon family. What peace! what calm! nothing pretentious, but nothing transitory: here everything seems eternal. The ground-floor, then, was given over to reception rooms for visitors. Here everything breathed the Provincial, ancient but unalterable.[4]

The familiar mechanisms and characteristic rhetoric of Balzacian description are here reappropriated by a less characteristic function, or, to use a term which will be further developed in this chapter, are

---

4. "Sur la balustrade de la terrasse imaginez de grands vases en faïence bleue et blanche d'où s'elevent des giroflées; à droite et à gauche, le long des murs voisins, voyez deux couverts de tilleuls carrément taillés; vous aurez une idée du paysage plein de bonhomie pudique, de chasteté tranquille, de vues modestes et bourgeoises qu'offraient la rive opposée et ses naïves maisons, les eaux rares de la Brillante, le jardin, ses deux couverts collés contre les murs voisins, et le vénérable édifice des Cormon. Quelle paix! quel calme! rien de pompeux, mais rien de transitoire: là, tout semble éternel. Le rez-de-chaussée appartenait donc à la réception. Là tout respirait la vieille, l'inaltérable province" (Honoré de Balzac, *La Comédie humaine* [Paris: La Pléiade, 1952], 11 vols., "La Vieille Fille," IV, 247).

projected through a rather different *register* than the metonymic and connotative one of normal Balzacian exposition. The Cormon townhouse, along with its unwed heiress, is indeed the prize on which the narrative struggle or *agon* of *La Vieille Fille* turns. It is therefore quintessentially an object of desire; but we will not have begun to grasp its historical specificity until we sense the structural difference between this object and all those equally desirable goals, aims, or ends around which classical *récits* or quest narratives of the type studied by Propp are organized. The content, indifferently substitutable, of these last—gold, princess, crown or palace— suggests that the signifying value of such objects is determined by their narrative position: a narrative element becomes desirable whenever a character is observed to desire it.

In Balzac, as the heavily persuasive nature of the passage in question testifies, it has for whatever historical reason become necessary to secure the reader's consent, and to validate or accredit the object as desirable, before the narrative process can function properly. The priorities are therefore here reversed, and this narrative apparatus depends on the "desirability" of an object whose narrative function would have been a relatively automatic and unproblematical secondary effect of a more traditional narrative structure.

But the historical originality of the Balzacian object needs to be specified, not merely against the mechanisms of classical storytelling, but against the psychological and interpretive habits of our own period as well. For us, wishes and desires have become the traits or psychological properties of human monads; but more is at stake in this description than the simple "identification" with a plausible desire that we do not ourselves share, as when our films or bestsellers offer the proxy spectacles of a whole range of commodified passions. For one thing, we cannot attribute this particular desire (for the Cormon townhouse) to any individual subject. Biographical Balzac, Implied Author, this or that desiring protagonist: none of these unities are (yet) present, and desire here comes before us in a peculiarly anonymous state which makes a strangely absolute claim on us.

Such an evocation—in which the desire for a particular object is at one and the same time allegorical of all desire in general and of Desire as such, in which the pretext or theme of such desire has not yet been relativized and privatized by the ego-barriers that jealously confirm the personal and purely subjective experience of the monadized subjects they thus separate—may be said to reenact the Utopian impulse in the sense in which Ernst Bloch has redefined this term.[5] It solicits the reader not merely to reconstruct this building and grounds in some inner eye, but to reinvent it as Idea and as heart's desire. To juxtapose the depersonalized and retextualized provincial houses of Flaubert with this one is to become perhaps uncomfortably aware of the degree to which the Balzacian dwelling invites the awakening of a longing for possession, of the mild and warming fantasy of landed property as the tangible figure of a Utopian wish-fulfillment. A peace released from the competitive dynamism of Paris and of metropolitan business struggles, yet still imaginable in some existent backwater of concrete social history; a well-nigh Benjaminian preservation of the storehouse of the past, and of its quintessential experience, within the narrative present; a "chaste" diminution of the libidinal to its mildest and least afflictive murmur; a Utopia of the household, in whose courtyards, hallways, and garden paths the immemorial routines of daily life, of husbandry and domestic economy, are traced in advance, projecting the eternal cycle of meals and walks, marketing and high tea, the game of whist, the preparation of the daily menu and the commerce with faithful servants and with habitual visitors—this mesmerizing image is the "still point" around which the disorder and urgency of a properly novelistic time will turn. It is the modulation into Biedermeier of that more properly "sublime" wish-fulfillment of the magnificent opening description of the chateau of Les Aigues in *Les Paysans,* where this milder longing for landed property is magnified into the fantasy of feudal lordship and of the return of the great estate. Nor are the ideological conflicts of the later, more openly historical and political, master novel alien to this relatively minor comic *fabliau:* indeed, Mademoiselle Cormon's townhouse—an architectural monument to the splendor of an ancient patrician *Bürgertum* or merchant aristocracy—already "resolves" in advance, and in the recollected vividness of a tangible image, by its combination of the twin "semes" of bourgeois commercial activity and aristocratic tradition, the social and ideological contradiction around which the novel will turn.

The peculiarity of a Utopian libidinal investment of this kind can

---

5. In *Das Prinzip Hoffnung* (Frankfurt: Suhrkamp, 1959), 2 vols.; for a brief account, see *Marxism and Form,* pp. 116–158.

be underscored by shifting from the landed manifestation of this desire to its actantial personification in the figure of Mademoiselle Cormon herself, the old maid of the title. What is significant here is that, as with the house itself, no reconstruction of this character in a properly ironic perspective is possible. Mademoiselle Cormon is comic, grotesque, and desirable all at once (or in succession): her big feet, the "beauty" of her "force and abundance," her "embonpoint," her massive hips, "which made her seem cast in a single mould," her triple chin, with its "folds" rather than "wrinkles"— none of these features is inconsistent with the Utopian desire that takes her person as its focus. Nor is anything to be gained by referring the bewildered reader back to the documented peculiarities of Balzac's own sexual tastes, here reinscribed in the narrative in the passion of the unhappy young poet Athanase Granson for this corpulent older woman ("this ample person offered attributes capable of seducing a young man full of desires and longing, such as Athanase"). To be sure, La Vieille Fille is a comic novel, heavily and insistently punctuated by sexual innuendo and by undertones of the type of gross physical farce Balzac himself rehearsed in his Contes drolatiques; this essentially comic register of the narrative, is, then, presumably enough to account for a perspective in which the vicissitudes of carnal desire are observed with sympathetic detachment and malicious empathy.

Yet to insist on the Utopian dimension of this particular desire is evidently to imply that this particular comic narrative is also an allegorical structure, in which the sexual "letter" of the farce must itself be read as a figure for the longing for landed retreat and personal fulfillment as well as for the resolution of social and historical contradiction. The Silenus box—a grotesque and comical exterior which contains a wondrous balm—is, of course, the very emblem of the hermeneutic object;[6] but the relationship between

---

6. "Sileni of old were little boxes, like those we now may see in the shops of apothecaries, painted on the outside with wanton toyish figures, as harpies, satyrs, bridled geese, horned hares, saddled ducks, flying goats, thiller harts, and other such counterfeited pictures, at pleasure, to excite people unto laughter, as Silenus himself, who was the foster-father of good Bacchus, was wont to do; but within those capricious caskets called Sileni were carefully preserved and kept many rich and fine drugs, such as balm, ambergreese, amomon, musk, civet, with several kinds of precious stones, and other things of great price" (Author's Prologue, Gargantua [the Urquhart-Mortteux translation]).

farce and the Utopian impulse is not particularly clarified by this image.

Paradoxically, however, it is this very tension or inconsistency between levels which will vanish from expressions of the Utopian impulse in a later age of high reification. A passage from the American writer whose commodity lust and authorial investments and attitudinizing are most reminiscent of Balzac may give some sense of the transformation:

> At this time of the year the days are still comparatively short, and the shadows of the evening were beginning to settle down upon the great city. Lamps were beginning to burn with that mellow radiance which seems almost watery and translucent to the eye. There was a softness in the air which speaks with an infinite delicacy of feeling to the flesh as well as to the soul. Carrie felt that it was a lovely day. She was ripened by it in spirit for many suggestions. As they drove along the smooth pavement an occasional carriage passed. She saw one stop and the footman dismount, opening the door for a gentleman who seemed to be leisurely returning from some afternoon pleasure. Across the broad lawns, now first freshening into green, she saw lamps faintly glowing upon rich interiors. Now it was but a chair, now a table, now an ornate corner which met her eye, but it appealed to her as almost nothing else could. Such childish fancies as she had had of fairy palaces and kingly quarters now came back. She imagined that across these richly carved entrance-ways, where the globed and crystalled lamps shone upon panelled doors set with stained and designed panes of glass, was neither care nor unsatisfied desire. She was perfectly certain that here was happiness.[7]

Between the moment of Balzac and the moment of Dreiser, *bovarysme* has fallen, and the congealment of language, fantasy, and desire into Flaubertian *bêtise* and Flaubertian cliché transmutes Balzacian longing into the tawdriness of Carrie's hunger for trinkets, a tawdriness that Dreiser's language ambiguously represents and reflects all at once.[8]

7. Theodore Dreiser, *Sister Carrie* (New York: Norton, 1970), p. 86.
8. The axiological paradox about Dreiser—he is best at his worst—is peculiarly intensified by the problem of his style, which must be studied in terms of alienation and reification, rather than according to the usual positivist categories; see Sandy Petrey, "Language of Realism, Language of False Consciousness: A Reading of *Sister Carrie*," *Novel* 10 (1977), 101–113.

Commodification is not the only "event" which separates Dreiser's text from Balzac's: the charges it has wrought in the object world of late capitalism have evidently been accompanied by a decisive development in the construction of the subject as well, by the constitution of the latter into a closed monad, henceforth governed by the laws of "psychology." Indeed, for all the caressing solicitations of this text, it clearly positions us outside Carrie's desire, which is represented as a private wish or longing to which we relate ourselves as readers by the mechanisms of identification and projection, and to which we may also adopt a moralizing stance, or what amounts to the same thing, an ironic one. What has happened is that "Carrie" has become a "point of view": this is in effect, as we have already suggested, the textual institution or determinant that expresses and reproduces the newly centered subject of the age of reification. Not coincidentally, the emergence of such narrative centers is then at once accompanied by the verbal or narrative equivalents of techniques characterstic of film (the tracking shot, the panning of the camera from Carrie's position as observer to that telescopic or keyhole glimpse of the ultimate interior, with its enclosed warmth and light)—that medium which will shortly become the hegemonic formal expression of late capitalist society. With this virtually fullblown appearance of filmic point of view, however, the Utopian overtones and intensities of desire are ever more faintly registered by the text; and the Utopian impulse itself, now reified, is driven back inside the monad, where it assumes the status of some merely psychological experience, private feeling, or relativized value.

It should not overhastily be concluded, however, that Dreiser's situation is only one of loss and constraint; as we will have occasion to observe in a later chapter, on Joseph Conrad, the effects of reification—the sealing off of the psyche, the division of labor of the mental faculties, the fragmentation of the bodily and perceptual sensorium—also determine the opening up of whole new zones of experience and the production of new types of linguistic content. In Dreiser, indeed, we witness the emergence of an incomparable sensory intensity, "that infinite delicacy of feeling to the flesh as well as to the soul," which marks the passage from Balzacian rhetoric to a more properly modern practice of *style* in Dreiser, a strange and alien bodily speech which, interwoven with the linguistic junk of commodified language, has perplexed readers of our greatest novelist down to the present day.[9]

Now it is time to examine the operation of a narrative apparatus about which we have implied that, antedating the emergence of the centered subject, it has not yet developed the latter's textual determinants, such as point of view or protagonists with whom the reader sympathizes in some more modern psychological sense. Yet it is evident that *La Vieille Fille* is by no stretch of the imagination a post-modern or "schizophrenic" text, in which traditional categories of character and narrative time are dissolved altogether. We will indeed want to suggest that the "decentering" of Balzacian narrative, if that is not an anachronistic term for it, is to be found in a rotation of character centers which deprives each of them in turn of any privileged status. This rotation is evidently a small-scale model of the decentered organization of the *Comédie humaine* itself. What interests us in the present context, however, is the glimpse this turning movement gives us into the semic production of characters, or in other words into what we will call a *character system*.

We have already mentioned the least important of the suitors for Mademoiselle Cormon's hand, the poet Athanase, who, unlike his more celebrated counterpart Lucien de Rubempré, finds no Vautrin to dissuade him from the suicide that removes him from this competition. Alongside this pitiable romantic, two more powerful but more grotesque figures emerge as the principal candidates for a prize that, as we have seen, is not merely matrimonial (or financial) but also Utopian: an elderly and penniless nobleman, who claims descent from the (extinct) House of Valois and worthily upholds the traditions of elegance of the *ancien régime;* and a bourgeois "Farnese Hercules," former profiteer of the Revolutionary armies and victim of Napoleon's animosity, who, as head of the liberal opposition to the Bourbon restoration, counts on the marriage with Mademoiselle Cormon not merely to reestablish his finances, but

9. On the use of the distinction between rhetoric and style as a historical and periodizing concept, see Roland Barthes, *Writing Degree Zero*, trans. A. Lavers and C. Smith (London: Cape, 1967), pp. 10–13, 41–52. The distinction is that evoked by Genette, following Lubbock's differentiation of *picture* (or "report") from *scene*, as "the opposition between classical *abstraction* . . . and 'modern' *expressivity*" (Gérard Genette, *Figures III* [Paris: Seuil, 1972], p. 131); and see Percy Lubbock, *The Craft of Fiction* (New York: Viking, 1957), esp. pp. 251–254.

above all to carry him back to political power (he wants to be appointed Prefect of Alençon).

The reader does not need to wait for Lukács' theory of typification to grasp the social and historical figuration of these characters, since Balzac underscores it heavily and explicitly himself:

> The one [the Liberal Du Bousquier], abrupt, energetic, with loud and demonstrative manners, and brusque and rude of speech, dark in complexion, hair and look, terrible in appearance, in reality as impotent as an insurrection, might quite adequately be said to represent the Republic. The other [the Chevalier de Valois], mild and polished, elegant, carefully dressed, reaching his ends by the slow but infallible methods of diplomacy, and upholding good taste to the end, offered the very image of the old court aristocracy.[10]

Lukács' theory of typification, while confirmed by such a passage, can nonetheless be said to be incomplete on two counts; on the one hand, it fails to identify the typifying of characters as an essentially allegorical phenomenon, and thus does not furnish any adequate account of the process whereby a narrative becomes endowed with allegorical meanings or levels. On the other, it implies an essentially one-to-one relationship between individual characters and their social or historical reference, so that the possibility of something like a *system* of characters remains unexplored.

In fact, the reader's initial attentions are less absorbed by matters of social status here taken for granted, or by the struggle for Mademoiselle Cormon's hand, which will set in only later on, than directed to the solution of a group of puzzles and enigmas. Du Bousquier's secret is indeed no secret for the reader, since it is quickly made apparent to us that he is sexually impotent. What this revelation does to our reading, however, is to generate a systematic movement back and forth between what we know (and what poor Mademoiselle Cormon has to marry him to find out) and that external appearance by which the other characters are deceived: not merely his physical strength and his powerful deportment, but also his association with new industrial wealth and with the Jacobin traditions of the bourgeois political system. The "secret" no doubt underscores Balzac's own opinion of these ideals and traditions in a crude but effective manner; yet, unlike Poe's story, "The Man That

10. *La Vieille Fille*, p. 228.

Was Used Up," this "reality" never undermines the power and the objectivity of an "appearance" in which Du Bousquier has very real social and political importance, and which is indeed consecrated by his ultimate triumph over his rival.

As for the latter, the various enigmas that center on the Chevalier (those, in particular, of the legitimacy of his title and the true sources of his income) tend to be displaced in the direction of the sexual code. Thus, a series of gross allusions (the size of the Chevalier's nose, for instance) begin to make it clear that his "secret" is on the contrary one of unexpected potency and of a properly aristocratic capacity for gallant adventures.

The point to be made about this whole initial narrative movement—the operation of what Barthes somewhat improperly calls the "hermeneutic code" of a play of appearance and reality and a search for withheld secrets—is that, itself a preparation for the principal narrative, it is never fully resolved: the revelation of the sexual secret does not, in other words, spell a conclusion to the comedy, as it would in Boccaccio or in the *Contes drolatiques*, but is a means to a more unexpected end.[11] The function of the sexual comedy is essentially to direct our reading attention toward the relationship between sexual potency and class affiliation. Our assumption that it is the former which is the object of this particular game of narrative hide-and-seek is in fact the blind or subterfuge behind which the otherwise banal and empirical facts of social status and political prehistory are transformed into the fundamental categories in terms of which the narrative is interpreted. Our reading "set" toward the social and historical interpretations which can be allegorically derived from the narrative is thus something like a lateral by-product of our initial attention to the sexual comedy; but this allegorical by-product, once established, reorients the narrative around its new interpretive center, retroactively returning upon the sexual farce to assign it a henceforth marginalized place in the narrative structure, where it comes to seem a relatively inessential or arbitrary "bonus of pleasure."

Thus established, the allegorical reading becomes the dominant one, and the struggle for Mademoiselle Cormon's hand becomes the unavoidable figure not merely for the struggle for power over

11. See, for a more detailed reading of the opening section of the novel, the first version of the present chapter, "The Ideology of Form: Partial Systems in *La Vieille Fille*," *Sub-stance*, No. 15 (Winter, 1976).

France, but also the conquest of legitimation and the appropriation of everything in the post-revolutionary state which remains the most authentically and quintessentially "French" by tradition and by inheritance: the old patrician values of a provincial merchant aristocracy with the slow eternity of its custom, as embodied in the houses and gardens of Alençon. But if this were all that was at stake, then the conclusion of the drama—Du Bousquier's triumph over his rival, precipitated by his Napoleonic decisiveness and by the Chevalier's complacent confidence in his own preponderancies— would amount to little more than a punctual allusion to an empirical event, namely, the failure of the restoration with the overthrow of the Bourbons, in 1830, by liberal middle-class forces. This would certainly be a reflection of historical reality in Lukács' sense, even though scarcely a prophetic one (the novel, whose action takes place in 1816, was written in 1836). Lukács' general point about Balzac is, of course, that this novelist's sense of historical realities inflects his own personal wishes (presumably they accompany the Chevalier) in the direction of social and historical verisimilitude (it is after all Du Bousquier who wins out).

The novel is, however, more complicated than this, and if it inscribes the irrevocable brute facts of empirical history—the July Revolution, for Balzac a fall into the secular corruption of a middle-class age—it does so in order the more surely to "manage" those facts and to open up a space in which they are no longer quite so irreparable, no longer quite so definitive. *La Vieille Fille* is indeed not merely a matrimonial farce, nor even only a social commentary on provincial life; it is above all a didactic work and a political object-lesson that seeks to transform the events of empirical history into an optional trial run against which the strategies of the various social classes can be tested. This peculiar shift in registers, in which the events of the narrative remain the same but yet somehow are emptied of their finality, is perhaps best conveyed by way of Todorov's conception of a "modal" poetics, and of a variety of modal realizations of narrative content in the surface of a narrative text.[12] If, as Greimas suggests, we suppose that a narrative can be modeled like an individual sentence, then it

---

12. Tzvetan Todorov, "Poétique," in F. Wahl, ed., *Qu'est-ce que le structuralisme?* (Paris: Seuil, 1968), pp. 142–145. And see the special number of *Lan-*

might well follow that, as with sentences themselves, each deep narrative structure could be actualized according to a number of different modes, of which the indicative, governing conventional narrative realism, is only the most familiar. Yet other possible narrative modalizations—the subjunctive, the optative, the imperative, and the like—suggest a heterogeneous play of narrative registers which will gradually, as we shall see in our next chapter, be recontained and reunified under the massive homogenization of a later high realism. On this view, the didactic status of *La Vieille Fille* can be accounted for by a modalization in terms of the *conditional* (if this . . . then this), whose content must now be determined.

Now the entire sequence of our reading frameworks must be reversed. The earlier frameworks—the initial sexual "hermeneutic code" and the subsequent reading of the primary *agon* (who will finally win out?)—are now retroactively restructured in terms of a new kind of reading interest, namely the effort to assign responsibilities, and to determine what as yet undetermined advantage Du Bousquier (= impotent) can have had over his aristocratic rival (= potent). The establishment of these causes and responsibilities will ultimately make up the content of what has now become a history lesson.

This restructuration, however, confronts us not with answers or immediate ideological solutions, but rather with a set of determinate contradictions. What began by being a simple judgment—that the Revolution and its bourgeois values are essentially sterile, that is to say, *impotent,* but also, in Edmund Burke's sense artificial and non-organic—now turns into a problem or an antinomy. The *ancien régime,* coded as sexual gallantry through its stereotypical representations as Regency, Deer Park, Watteau, Fragonard, Louis

---

gages devoted to "modalités" (No. 43, September 1976). The ultimate philosophical underpinnings are to be found in modal logic: see Georg Henrik von Wright, *An Essay in Modal Logic* (Amsterdam: North Holland Publishing Co., 1951), and *An Essay in Deontic Logic* (Amsterdam: North Holland Publishing Co., 1968). Properly formalized, the model of an ideological axiomatic proposed here may be described as a projection onto narrative and macrostructure of Oswald Ducros' account of presuppositions in individual propositions or sentences: Ducros expands the notion of the performative or speech act into what he calls "the juridical act" in which, as in Mauss's conception of the gift, the act of reception structurally entails the receiver's consent to the ideological content presupposed by a given utterance (Oswald Ducros, *Dire et ne pas dire* [Paris: Hermann, 1972], pp. 69–80).

XV, and the like, lends its positive sexual seme to the portrait of the Chevalier; yet even before the failure of his matrimonial attempt, the combination of semes which make up his portrait can be shown to be contradictory, and the reading mind must on some level worry the question: how is it possible for the graceful, effeminate, elderly Chevalier to be more "potent" than the rough-and-ready bourgeois speculator Du Bousquier? Meanwhile, the latter offers no less of a paradox, namely the relation to his sexual impotence of that principle of quasi-military initiative and decisiveness to which he owes his triumph and about whose historical reference the text leaves us in no doubt: it is the energy Balzac associates with Napoleon and with the whole history of the Revolutionary armies from Valmy to the anticlimax at Waterloo. Yet this seme is already historically ambiguous, for if such martial initiative is sharply dissociated from the culture, values, and practices of the *ancien régime*, neither can it be wholly identified with the business society that will come into its own after 1830.

Following the program we outlined in our initial chapter, we will wish to distinguish between the reconstruction of this particular inconsistency as a *contradiction* and its formulation in terms of an *antinomy* for the reading mind. We there suggested that whereas the former is governed by a properly dialectical thinking, the latter may be most appropriately mapped out by semiotic method, which is in this sense the privileged instrument of analysis of ideological closure. Greimas' semiotic rectangle[13] suggests an initial formulation of this antinomy or double bind as follows: sexual potency + languour versus energy + impotence. The underlying ideological contradiction here can evidently be expressed in the form of a meditation on history: Balzac as a royalist and an apologist for the essentially organic and decentered *ancien régime* must nonetheless

13. Briefly, the semiotic rectangle or "elementary structure of signification" is the representation of a binary opposition or of two contraries (S and −S), along with the simple negations or contradictories of both terms (the so-called subcontraries −S̄ and S̄): significant slots are constituted by the various possible combinations of these terms, most notably the "complex" term (or ideal synthesis of the two contraries) and the "neutral" term (or ideal synthesis of the two subcontraries). See A. J. Greimas and François Rastier, "The Interaction of Semiotic Constraints," *Yale French Studies*, No. 41 (1968), pp. 86–105; and F. Nef, ed., *Structures élémentaires de la signification* (Brussels: Complexe, 1976). See also my *Prison-House*, pp. 162–168.

confront the latter's palpable military failures and administrative inefficiencies, which are underscored by the inevitable juxtaposition with the power of the Napoleonic period, although that period itself, a kind of hybridization of Jacobin values and monarchic trappings, proved to be a dead end.

Faced with a contradiction of this kind—which it cannot think except in terms of a stark antinomy, an insoluble logical paradox—the historical *pensée sauvage,* or what we have called the political unconscious, nonetheless seeks by logical permutations and combinations to find a way out of its intolerable closure and to produce a "solution," something it can begin to do owing to the semic dissociations already implicit in the initial opposition formulated above. Thus, it would seem possible to disjoin the seme of "energy" from that of "impotence" or "sterility" (part of a larger ideologeme that denotes the world of bourgeois materialism and business generally); and, on the other side of this opposition, to disjoin the valorized seme of the *"ancien régime"* from its general debility which may perhaps be resumed under the theme of "culture" (manners, traditions, forms, aristocratic values, and the like). At this point, we can map these terms, and the possibilities of new combinations they suggest, as follows.

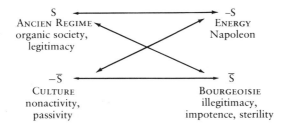

It now becomes clear that of the four chief logical combinations available here, we so far have only identified two. From this perspective, then, we can observe the way in which a semic system generates those anthropomorphic combinations that are narrative characters, and in particular, in the present instance, how the semes S and −S̄ produce the representation of the "Chevalier," while the combination −S and S̄ gives anthropomorphic content to that other proper name, "Du Bousquier." What is so far missing are the two combinations designated by Greimas as the complex and the neutral term respectively: the ideal synthesis which would "resolve" the initial binary opposition by subsuming it under a single unity, and that union of purely negative or privative terms which would subsume the simple contradictories of the two terms of the initial binary opposition. Our methodological hypothesis would be validated, and our demonstration of a character system fulfilled, if it could be shown that these two additional logical possibilities have their equivalent in the Balzacian text.

But we have already mentioned a likely candidate for the neutral or neuter term. Its apparently inconsistent synthesis of bourgeois origins and cultural values is indeed realized in the sorry young would-be poet Athanase, and beyond him by Romanticism itself: a movement of which Balzac's work, like that of Hegel, stands as a thoroughgoing critique.[14]

As for the complex term or ideal synthesis, we have omitted to mention until now the retarding episode that precipitates the crisis of the novel and impels Du Bousquier on to his climactic decision. This is the arrival, at Mademoiselle Cormon's house, of an exiled aristocratic officer, the Comte de Troisville, who, returning from Russia to reestablish himself in the region, is for a fond moment imagined by Mademoiselle Cormon to be the "solution" to her problems and a more appropriate match than either of the other contenders. Unfortunately, the Count is already married; this "solution," which would satisfactorily combine undoubted aristocratic "legitimacy" with documented military prowess of the Napoleonic type, is thus explicitly marked by the narrative as a merely "ideal" one, as a Utopian resolution in the narrower and empirically unrealizable sense.

The "Count de Troisville" thus figures as what we will call a horizon-figure in this narrative. He blocks out a place which is not that of empirical history but of a possible alternate one: a history in which some genuine Restoration would still be possible, provided the aristocracy could learn this particular object-lesson, namely that it needs a strong man who combines aristocratic values with Napoleonic energy (at some wish-fulfilling or fantasy level, Balzac

---

14. On Balzac's antiromanticism, see Pierre Barbéris, *Balzac et le mal du siècle* (Paris: Gallimard, 1970), especially chap. 7.

obviously has himself in mind). This is then the ultimate sense in which the novel's comic yet rueful ending—the ultimate fate of Mademoiselle Cormon, married, *and* an old maid all at once! the very caricature of a dialectical resolution—is not truly a definitive one, but merely a horrible object-lesson.

In this light, *Les Paysans*—which is something like a transposition of these materials into a more somber and tragic register—can also be reread, and its well-known interpretation by Lukács shown to be a premature finalization.[15] For the doomed hero of *Les Paysans*, Count Montcornet, is, like Valois here, only ambiguously aristocratic; his title is in reality a Napoleonic one, and the doubtful legitimacy of his "feudal" authority over the chateau is underscored by the existence at the margins of the narrative of two other great estates, Ronquerolles and Soulanges, still in the possession of authentic noblemen. The implication is that where Montcornet failed, owing to the imperfection of his origins, these neighboring horizon-figures, the representatives of a more authentic nobility, have some chance of succeeding—provided they heed Balzac's narrative warning! The disaster of *Les Paysans* (like that of *La Vieille Fille*, a reflection of a certain empirical history) is thus emptied of its finality, its irreversibility, its historical inevitability, by a narrative register which offers it to us as merely conditional history, and transforms the indicative mode of historical "fact" into the less binding one of the cautionary tale and the didactic lesson.

II

The preceding demonstration posited a constitutive relationship between three distinct features of *La Vieille Fille:* a wish-fulfilling or fantasy investment that dissolved the biographical into the Utopian; a narrative without a hero (in the sense of a privileged "point of view" or centered subject), whose characters were seen to be generated by a deeper semic system; and finally, the possibility of a certain *dérive* or drift in narrative registers, such that a still apparently "realistic" representation is no longer binding in the fashion of empirical history. What was to have been shown was evidently the historical specificity of Balzac's "moment" and of a

15. In his essay on "Balzac: *The Peasants*," in *Studies in European Realism*, pp. 21–46.

situation—before the full constitution of the bourgeois subject and the omnipresent effects of massive reification—in which desire, the decentering of the subject, and a kind of open history are still conjoined. It would seem sufficient response, however, to point to the many novels of Balzac which, prefiguring the *Bildungsroman,* "point of view" and irony, undoubtedly contain protagonists; nor does their equally undoubted autobiographical content imply a Utopian investment but rather precisely that later monadic bourgeois subjectivity whose absence from Balzac has been affirmed above. It will also be observed that it is on the face of it rather perverse to seek to deny the commodification of desire in a work such as Balzac's, which is so saturated with object-hunger of all kinds.

We therefore need to look at a second text whose narrative is more conventional than *La Vieille Fille* and more consonant with the received idea of Balzacian realism. *La Rabouilleuse* undoubtedly has a "hero"—indeed, it has two, the rival brothers Joseph and Philippe Bridau—and its quintessentially Balzacian *agon* turns on the struggle for that quintessentially Balzacian object of desire, money—in this case a provincial inheritance. Yet in late Balzac, a prodigious expansion of the narrative frame, as well as a profound historicization of its raw materials, tends to displace the older static desires and manias of the conventional Balzacian protagonists and to shift the focus of the narrative to something like an etiology of desire, on the one hand (what is its origin and prehistory, into what can it be transformed or sublimated?), and on the other to a construction of the various means, strategies, and instruments which can lead to the desired end, itself now conventionally bracketed.

La Rabouilleuse is a prototypical embodiment of the Balzacian *agon,* in which little by little two primal enemies or adversaries are constructed, each with his network of allies and his own specific weapons and advantages, until at length a headlong collision brings the *dénouement* and leaves one of the rivals in a precarious and historically provisional possession of the object of the duel. In this novel, the twin protagonists come to represent and to champion the two rival branches of the Rouget family in their struggle for its inheritance. Yet a lengthy opening account of the misfortunes of the younger branch, in Paris—the death of the husband, a Napoleonic administrator, in his prime, a subsequent life of straitened circumstances and self-sacrifice—constructs an initial, anticipatory rivalry within this line itself, in the tension between its two brothers: the elder, a Napoleonic officer doted on by his mother, but adapting only with the greatest difficulty to peacetime life, while the younger, in all his unloved ugliness, shows promise of becoming a great painter. There thus emerges a secondary tension between this particular opposition and the major one which will absorb it when Philippe comes into collision with the challenger of the elder branch of the family in Issoudun—who is himself a former Napoleonic officer, and in background and ferocity virtually his enemy's mirror image.

Yet it is precisely this tension or inconsistency in narrative focus that gives *La Rabouilleuse* its unique power, since each of these axes or *agons* will stage its principal exhibit—the character of Philippe—in a different register and for quite different narrative ends. This figure, surely one of the most alarming in all Balzac, is anticipatory in a number of ways: one of the earliest literary representations of the "demi-solde" or demobilized soldier down on his luck, Philippe in his physical deterioration also prefigures a Victorian fantasy-image of the lumpenproletarian at his most threatening, and beyond that announces a whole renewal of melodrama as a narrative instrument for managing social tensions and conflicts. Philippe is not yet, however, a melodramatic figure in that sense: he is not a villain in the twin sense of reinforcing our essentially ideological conception of evil on the one hand, and of "explaining" the existence of social disorder on the other. He is obviously a principle of disorder and violence, but the narrative does not seek to hypostasize this dangerous energy into some ethical or mythic force. Rather it posits the emergence and perversion of that energy in such a way as to imply an essentially historical diagnosis of Philippe which is beyond mere ethical judgment.

Yet in fact *La Rabouilleuse* makes use of two distinct diagnoses, two independent and mutually exclusive explanatory systems or "psychologies," to account, in a curiously superimposed and overdetermined fashion, for one set of character traits; and with this curious reduplication—of an essentially objective or sociological diagnosis with an essentially subjective or protopsychoanalytic one—we are at the heart of the novel and the place from which its twin registers can be distinguished.

As the designation of "demi-solde" suggests, the first diagnosis is a historical and indeed a dialectical one. Whatever the general ideological status of the myth of energy in Balzac, its function here is to foreground the primacy of its social situation: the quality of Philippe's energy is thus here directly proportionate to the historical praxis and social role available to him. Under Napoleon he becomes a colonel; during the Restoration he is a threat to those around him and to society as a whole; readapted to the struggle for the Rouget inheritance, harnessed to the value of the family and recontained by its discipline, he once again offers a model of intuitive action, of strategy and tactics alike. Yet as we have already observed, in the lengthening and well-nigh interminable historical perspective of late Balzac, the objects and prizes of such struggles are insensibly bracketed or devalorized by the ruses of History. As victor, Philippe, well qualified to handle adversaries cast in his own image, finds himself disarmed by the impersonal institutions of nascent capitalism and destituted by the events of July 1830 as well as by the new banking forces of Louis-Philippe's bourgeois monarchy. He proves therefore to have been something of a "vanishing mediator" between an older provincial France and the market and financial dynamics of the metropolis, his "objective historical function" turning out to have been that of appropriating and transferring the accumulated wealth of the former into the speculative funds of the latter. Now thrown aside by History like an old shoe, his remaining qualities assign him to the very boundary of "civilized society," where, in the campaign to seize Algeria from the Bey, like Tête d'Or arriving at the limits of empire only to confront the faceless but absolute Otherness of an alien horde, he is overwhelmed by the earliest Third World guerrillas represented in modern literature.

Yet this representation of a historical dialectic is at one and the same time the locus of an essentially ideological reflection, or in our previous terminology, of the meditation on a conceptual antinomy. From this angle, the problem is one of the ideological category of "violence" and can perhaps best be conveyed in the following formulation: how is it conceivable for the family to generate a force explosive enough to wrest the fortune away from its other branch without itself being blown open and destroyed in the process?

When we understand that the family is here, according to the canonical logic of Balzac's conservatism, the figure of society, it will become evident that the "political unconscious" of this text is thereby raising, in symbolic form, issues of social change and counterrevolution, and asking itself how the force necessary to bring about a return to the old order can be imagined as doing so without at the same time being so powerful and disruptive as to destroy that order itself in the process.

Turning to the other diagnostic or explanatory system implicit in *La Rabouilleuse*, we find that it is a psychological one, still familiar today, in which Philippe's "egotism" is denounced as a result of excessive maternal indulgence, to which the responsibility for social and familial "permissiveness" and the resultant lawlessness and disrespect for authority is imputed. What is significant for us is not this rather banal ideologeme, but rather its structural consequences for a narrative which is at least in part conceived as an object-lesson to the overindulgent mother herself. The patient devotion of the younger brother underscores Agathe's well-nigh criminal blindness and partiality, while his nascent glory as a painter tangibly reveals everything she is unwilling or unable to see. In conventional critical terminology, Agathe is little more than a background figure, and belongs to a secondary plot at that; perhaps we need a different type of narrative theory to identify the psychic center of gravity of a narration whose surface categories and representational tactics are not demonstrably or symptomatically distorted by it; and to register the peculiarity of a situation in which a moral *blindness* witnessed indulgently by a *perceptive* son (who is in fact its victim) is then offered as a *spectacle* to a presumably supportive readership. Meanwhile, this representation, in which the mother is, as it were, a theme or an object of mimetic contemplation, is then curiously redoubled by a reception situation in which the ostensible reader senses a more fundamental gaze over his shoulder, in which it becomes clear that the spectacle has already been seen, or was destined for the edification of that far more essential, yet absent, *witness,* who is the biographical mother herself. But this category, the absent reader, the absent witness, is no longer another individuality, but rather something like a pole of intersubjectivity, a space or term in the communicational circuit, such that not merely the

character "Agathe," but Balzac's own mother is indistinctly included. This is indeed the point at which the obvious biographical
references become relevant: the rivalry between Balzac and his
younger brother (ages here strategically reversed), a good-for-
nothing manifestly preferred by Madame Balzac, the eclipse of the
(much older) father, the sense that he has been from childhood the
object of an incomprehensible maternal hostility (which, according
to the biographers, will receive its ultimate literary representation in
the character of Cousine Bette).[16] These details are less interesting
as sources than they are as coordinates in which the present narrative is produced and positioned. The object-lesson over the reader's
shoulder to some absent but crucial maternal witness is then yet a
further stage in the didactic register we have identified in *La Vieille
Fille:* the latter was also, but to a lesser degree, a lesson for its
female protagonist—a figure for France itself, whose mistaken decision (Du Bousquier = 1830) is herein censured. At this point, then,
it would seem that the subject is positioned outside the text as an
Other, a kind of Absolute Reader with whom the real or empirical
reader can never coincide. The latter is thus, to this representation,
something like a bystander or a chance observer, and no structural
position—no fourth wall—is opened for him or her in the narrative.

In effect, then, the section of the narrative that deals with the
Agathe subplot and the rivalry between the two brothers, has the
structure of a wish-fulfillment, or better still, of a daydream, a
daytime fantasy into which the subject projects his own image and
of which the reader or spectator does not occupy the empty slot of
mature universal representation (something on the order of the
shifter in language), but rather precisely the place of one of the
other characters in the daydream. This peculiar narrative logic not
only corresponds to an archaic stage in the development of the
mature subject (that stage which Lacan conveniently terms the Imaginary); it also presents, according to Freud, the fundamental
problem for aesthetic creation, which must somehow universalize,

16. On Balzac's parents and his relation to them, see Barbéris, *Balzac et le mal du
siècle,* chap. 2. On his brother Henry and the motif of fraternal rivalry in the
Comédie humaine, see M. Fargeaud and R. Pierrot, "Henry le trop aimé," *Année
balzacienne,* 1961, pp. 29–66; P. Citron, "Sur deux zones obscures de la psychologie
de Balzac," *Année balzacienne,* 1967, pp. 4–10; and P. Citron, "Introduction," *La
Rabouilleuse* (Paris: Garnier, 1966).

displace, and conceal the private wish-fulfilling elements of its content if it wants to make the latter receivable as art by other subjects who are "repelled" by the poet's own private wish-fulfillments.[17] Flaubert's program for the depersonalization of the literary text can thus in one way be seen as the recognition of the dilemma designated by Freud, and as the systematic attempt to remove all traces of wish-fulfillment from the narrative surface. What is striking in Balzac, on the other hand, is not merely the continuing presence of this psychic mechanism, but also and above all the absence of any shame or self-consciousness about the process.

From this Imaginary or wish-fulfilling register of the preparatory section, the novel moves to the quite different narrative dynamic of the main plot—the mission of the baleful Philippe to Issoudun and the climactic struggle for the inheritance. It would be tempting to characterize this second register in terms of what Lacan calls the Symbolic order: the emergence of the subject from the essentially "analog" or wish-fulfilling thought of the mirror stage, the accession into language, with its digital thinking, its proper names, negatives, and above all its "shifters" or empty pronominal slots in which transitory subjects can lodge in succession. But in that case we must add that it is a truncated or mutilated experience of the Symbolic, and that Balzac's novel is essentially characterized by the dissociation of these two orders, Imaginary and Symbolic, which are normally, in mature experience—and, presumably, in the "high realism" of the constituted subject—inseparable.

Indeed, if the first or Imaginary register of the narrative is characterized by the absent presence of the mother, the second or Symbolic development of the main plot is haunted by the dead father, the enigmatic Doctor Rouget, whose only appearance as a character in this text marks the crucial moment of origins: the oneiric, Faulknerian moment in which for the first time, in early morning, the aged physician, on horseback in the fields about his calls, meets the already ravishingly beautiful peasant child stirring for crayfish in a stream (hence her patois nickname, the *rabouilleuse*).

For Lacan, the passage from the Imaginary stage to the Symbolic Order is marked by the infant's experience of what he calls the

---

17. Sigmund Freud, "Creative Writers and Day-Dreaming," Standard Edition, IX (London: Hogarth, 1959), 143–153.

Name-of-the-Father, a formulation which unites the classical Freudian account of the Oedipus complex and the castration anxiety to
the essentially linguistic discovery of the distinction between the
paternal function itself—the term "father"—and that individual
biological parent to whom he has hitherto related in a more properly Imaginary mode. This is, then,

> the Oedipal moment, in which a ternary structure emerges against the
> background of the dual structure [of the Imaginary], when the Third
> (the father) intrudes on the imaginary satisfaction of dual fascination,
> overthrows its economy, destroys its fascinations, and introduces the
> child to what Lacan calls the Symbolic Order, the order of objectify-
> ing language that will finally allow him to say: I, you, he, she or it,
> that will therefore allow the small child to situate itself as a *human
> child* in the world of adult thirds.[18]

La Rabouilleuse, the third novel in a series Balzac called *Les
Célibataires* (the unwed), in this respect tells the story of a prolonged and unnatural vacancy of the paternal function; and the
struggle for the inheritance is less a matter of an object of desire—
either in the sense of Propp's quest or in that of the commodity
form—than it is a symptom of paternal absence. The "bachelor-
hood" of the series title might indeed designate any of the principal
actors in this complex *agon:* from Joseph (neglected by his mother),
or Philippe, whose menacing energy is significantly accompanied by
physical deterioration, to the latter's adversary Max (rumored, according to the classical Freudian mechanism of "family romance,"
to be Dr. Rouget's bastard son) and to the *rabouilleuse* herself,
Flore Brazier, whose ultimate passage beneath the conjugal yoke—
in Philippe's triumph—marks the beginning of a long degradation.

Yet the most striking of these casualties is surely the biological
son, the wealthy and debilitated Jean-Jacques, whose failure to occupy the paternal succession with the appropriate authority creates
the vacuum into which the other characters rush, and whose various clinical features—hereditary debility associated with venereal
disease, impotence, but also masochism and incest (his mistress,
Flore, also "lay with" his father)—entitle this work to take its place

---

18. Louis Althusser, "Freud and Lacan," in *Lenin and Philosophy,* trans. Ben
Brewster (New York: Monthly Review, 1971), p. 210.

alongside others whose tactful but explicit evocations of male homosexuality, Lesbianism, frigidity, bestiality, transvesticism and satyriasis range Balzac in the lineage of Sade and among the precursors of modern psychopathology, just as his interest in the determining influences of profession, social class, and region mark him as a forerunner of historical materialism (and of Taine's positivism as well).

If the Joseph narrative is distinguished by something like an overinvestment of the subject, in its wish-fulfilling and Imaginary function, the main plot of the novel, the Philippe narrative, would seem to be marked by something like an absence of psychic investment: its melodramatic excitement is characterized by a peculiarly unmelodramatic lack of side-taking, a kind of fascinated indifference to either of these maimed and repulsive groups of actors. The authorial diagnosis of Jean-Jacques provides the key to this strange vacancy at the heart of the Symbolic order:

> At his father's death, Jean-Jacques was aged thirty-seven, and as timid and submissive to paternal discipline as a child of twelve. For those who are not prepared to believe in his character, or in the facts of this story, this timidity is the key to his childhood, youth and indeed his entire life. . . . There are two kinds of timidity: timidity of mind and timidity of the nerves, physical and moral timidity. Each is independent of the other. The body can be afraid and tremble, whilst the mind remains calm and brave; the opposite is also true. This accounts for many strange acts of behaviour. When both kinds of timidity are found in one and the same individual, that man will be worthless throughout his life. *Complete* timidity of this kind is found in the people we call idiots.[19]

It is significant that, like the diagnosis of Philippe discussed earlier, this one is also fundamentally overdetermined, and provides two distinct explanations for Jean-Jacques' premature senility: heredity and environment, tainted blood and paternal oppression. The very inconsistency between the two accounts—in Philippe's case the family situation (in his case, the *absence* of a father) is doubled by a

---

19. Honoré de Balzac, *The Black Sheep*, trans. D. Adamson (London: Penguin, 1970), p. 171 (*La Rabouilleuse* [*La Comédie humaine*: Paris: La Pléiade, 1952, 11 vols.], III, 971).

world-historical one, the rise and fall of the Napoleonic empire, rather than by a physiological one, as in the case of Jean-Jacques— suggests that we have here to do with a single complex of ideas, in which themes of heredity, familial situation, and sociohistorical occasion are symbolically equivalent. In effect, both diagnoses of the strange case of Jean-Jacques Rouget lead back to the dead patriarch: the authoritarian father's crushing effect on the son's personality is here reduplicated by a biological mythology dear to Balzac (and significantly enough derived from thoughts cherished by his own father!), according to which human energy, and, in particular, human sexuality, is something like a fixed capital which can never be replaced once it has been spent. The father's excesses thus account only too "fatally" for the son's mysterious languour. At this point, then, the failure of the subject to constitute itself (or to assume the paternal name and function) is ultimately attributed to the dead father in a twofold thematization—authoritarianism and sexual excess—which will now allow us to identify the absent yet narratively determinant ideologeme.

Indeed, the historical message of this particular combination of semes—"tyranny" and "libertinage"—is quite unmistakable: only the *ancien régime* can be thereby designated, and the dead physician thus rises before us as the very prototype of the eighteenth-century libertine immortalized in the pages of Sade. His profession then underscores, or indeed restores, the close relationship, in the original seventeenth-century conception of *libertinage,* between scientific knowledge (materialism and atheism) and sexual license, both of which affirm the ultimate primacy of the body, whether as the horizon of all scientific inquiry or as that of the quest for *bonheur.*

In this sense, then, what Dr. Rouget was responsible for is a good deal more than the crippling of one son, or many, and far transcends even that brutal struggle for money which his disappearance authorized, extending to the whole fallen world of nascent capitalism, as it emerged from the destruction of the traditional monarchy by the twin agencies of Voltairean skepticism and the arbitrariness and excess of the state. This historical or allegorical significance of the orphaning of Jean-Jacques may, then, be seen to have its counterpart in the story of Philippe as well: son of one of the great imperial functionaries, whose health was broken by devotion and self-sacrifice, Philippe finds his spiritual progenitor in Napoleon himself, whose disappearance leaves another kind of hole against the sky. It is thus in a world which is the legacy of the bad Jacobin father, and in which the spurious benevolence of the paternal usurper (Napoleon) has been exposed, that the survivors—both of the Rouget family and of the Restoration—"red of tooth and claw," struggle for psychic and political mastery.

The heterogeneous narrative registers that allow Balzac's novel to record these social and historical overtones are thus dependent, as their condition of possibility, upon a psychic situation in which the centered subject has not yet emerged. Nor is this reading predicated on some ideal of the unification of the psyche, the conquest of identity, the triumph of the ego, against which such psychic fragmentation was measured. On the contrary, the final perspective of the novel, in which Joseph Bridau's ultimate artistic glory and social success are foretold, has already been marked as a purely Imaginary wish-fulfillment by the opening section of the text. The Symbolic once again relaxes into the Imaginary: so dreams of privilege console the imagination tormented by unresolvable contradictions.

III

We are now able to draw some provisional conclusions as to the relationship between desire, ideology, and the possibility for certain types of narrative apparatus to lay claim to a social and historical "realism." Before doing so, however, we must address a related issue and respond to the inevitable objection about the repeated and systematic violation, in the preceding pages, of the taboo against biographical criticism.

The earliest type of biographical criticism, that against which the older New Criticism very properly reacted, was essentially a genetic affair, whose object was the discovery in the appropriate archives of the source, model, or original of this or that character, event, or situation. In a second moment, that of existential psychoanalysis, psychobiography, and most of the great literary biographies of the present day, we find a significant modification in the way in which a "life" is related to a particular "work": at its best, in such criticism, the "life" itself becomes yet one more text by the same author, no more, but no less privileged than his other works, and to be added into the corpus of study along with them.

The position of biographical information in the present framework is somewhat different from either of these: in the preceding pages, the "life" of the historical individual Balzac has been used, neither as a set of empirical facts, nor as a textual system of characteristic behavior, but rather as the traces and symptoms of a fundamental family situation which is at one and the same time a fantasy master narrative. This unconscious master narrative—which we will call, following French usage, a *fantasm,* in order to distinguish it from the connotations of daydream or wish-fulfillment unavoidable in the English term "fantasy"—is an unstable or contradictory structure, whose persistent actantial functions and events (which are in life restaged again and again with different actors and on different levels) demand repetition, permutation, and the ceaseless generation of various structural "resolutions" which are never satisfactory, and whose initial, unreworked form is that of the Imaginary, or, in other words, of those waking fantasies, daydreams, and wish-fulfillments of which we have already spoken.

We have already sketched out some of the ways in which the "facts" of Balzac's life can be reconstructed in the form of a fantasmatic subtext of this kind: the child caught between an aging father with whom he can only imperfectly identify (Bernard-François Balzac was already fifty-three years old when his eldest son was born), and a mother not merely openly adulterous, but also distressingly attached to the pampered younger brother who was the product of this liaison. What needs to be stressed, however, is that this contradictory situation is a social as well as a private, familial, or "psychoanalytic" one: Sartre's *Search for a Method* has taught us to read the family situation as the mediation of class relationships in society at large, and to grasp the parental functions as socially coded or symbolic positions as well. Enlarged to include these meanings, a matrimonial tie between a former peasant, grown rich in land speculation during the Revolutionary and Napoleonic periods, and a representative of the older merchant aristocracy will obviously not be without some formative relationship to Balzac's mature ideological fantasy-solution of a monarchism and landed conservatism. Yet other mediations must also be inserted here; in particular, we have already noted the paternal origins of Balzac's economic myths—most notably the fantasmatic opposition of the hoarding of energy, either economic or sexual, and its vital expenditure in a squandering that ultimately leads (as in *La Peau de cha-grin*) to death. The passionate adoption of this paternal system of "hygiene" is, however, not inconsistent with the formative influence on Balzac's "mature" philosophy of his mother's passion for occult and religious literature; and indeed, Balzac's philosophy can in this sense be read as an original symbolic act, a kind of symbolic resolution, whereby a business ethic of delayed gratification (in Weber's sense of the "protestant ethic") is mythically projected through the medium of a Romantic and nostalgic Swedenborgianism. But this projection, which can rewrite Balzacian opinion in the form of a symbolic act or of the resolution of contradictions, at best accounts for only a very specific narrative production, that of the fantastic novels and stories (grouped in the *Etudes philosophiques*) of the 1830s.

We have, however, been able to isolate certain properly Imaginary or wish-fulfilling registers in the two works of Balzac's maturity studied here: the dream of landed establishment marked out but left narratively unfulfilled in the horizon-figure of Troisville (in *La Vieille Fille*), the fantasy of ultimate reinstatement in the mother's eyes, and ultimate triumph over the unworthy sibling rival, in the Joseph section of *La Rabouilleuse*. These Imaginary or wish-fulfilling texts are then the first stage or moment in the process whereby the original fantasm seeks an (impossible) resolution.

But this moment—the production of the wish-fulfilling text—is not yet, according to Freud, the moment of genuine literary or cultural production, let alone that of "realism" in any sense this word can have. What it allows us to account for is the production of that quite different thing called ideology, which Althusser defines as "the imaginary representation of the subject's relationship to his or her real conditions of existence."[20] We may now refine this "definition" by distinguishing between such an "imaginary representation" and its narrative conditions of possibility: the former is precisely the wish-fulfilling daydream or fantasy text of which *La Vieille Fille* and *La Rabouilleuse* gave us fragments, and which can be indefinitely enlarged to include Balzac's vision of himself as a great Tory landlord after the model of Sir Walter Scott, with local authority but also national influence, the head of a dynasty, but

---

20. Althusser, *Lenin and Philosophy,* p. 162.

also a peer and the member of a revitalized upper chamber, an ideological spokesman for the aristocratic elite, a statesman and a cabinet minister like Rastignac or De Marsay, and finally, perhaps, that Napoleonic "strong man" needed to achieve a triumphant, and this time definitive, counterrevolution.

Balzac's ideology may now be grasped as the *axiomatic* of this fantasy text: in other words, as those conceptual conditions of possibility or narrative presuppositions which one must "believe," those empirical preconditions which must have been secured, in order for the subject successfully to tell itself this particular day-dream. Primogeniture, for instance, becomes an essential prelimi-nary requirement for the reestablishment of the great landed estates on whose basis alone a revitalized aristocracy is conceivable: it thus at once becomes a significant political "principle," and the produc-tion of the fantasy-text knows a peculiar "unconscious" reflexivity, as, in the process of generating itself, it must simultaneously secure its own ideological preconditions.

However, daydreaming and wish-fulfilling fantasy are by no means a simple operation, available at any time or place for the taking of a thought. Rather, they involve mechanisms whose in-spection may have something further to tell us about the otherwise inconceivable link between wish-fulfillment and realism, between desire and history. It would seem, indeed, that the production of a whole ideology as a precondition for the indulgence of a specific daydream implies something like a reality principle or censorship within the latter. This peculiar dialectic, in which the desiring sub-ject is forced to enumerate the objections to his or her Imaginary gratification in order to realize the latter even on the level of a daydream, has nowhere so strikingly been described as in Proust, whose narrator finds that it is no easy matter to imagine receiving a love letter from the indifferent girl with whom he is infatuated:

> Every evening I indulged myself in imagining this letter, felt I could even read it before me, recited it line by line and sentence by sentence. But suddenly I would break off in terror. I understood that, were I ever to receive a letter from Gilberte, it could under no circumstances ever be this one, for I had just composed it myself. After that, I forced myself to look away in thought from the words I would have liked to have her address to me, for fear that, by pronouncing them, I would

thereby have banished precisely those words—the most cherished and desirable—from the field of possible realizations.[21]

The Proustian "solution," a kind of negation of the negation of desire, may be said to be a kind of modernizing formula in which the object to be fantasized is magically evoked by way of its very renunciation. Yet it allows us to glimpse other, "stronger" solutions which will be those of writers like Balzac. For the generation and adoption of ideological preconditions are still matters of what we may call the first level of the wish-fulfillment: the subject wishes for the realization of the ideological axiomatic in order to be able then to wish the fantasy narrative. But one can imagine a more consequent act of desire in which the wish-fulfilling mind sets out systematically to satisfy the objections of the nascent "reality principle" of capitalist society and of the bourgeois superego or censorship. Unlike the more degraded, and easily commodifiable, texts of the Imaginary level, these new, second-level narratives—we will call them, following our earlier distinction, "Symbolic texts"—entertain a far more difficult and implacable conception of the fully realized fantasy: one which is not to be satisfied by the easy solutions of an "unrealistic" omnipotence or the immediacy of a gratification that then needs no narrative trajectory in the first place, but which on the contrary seeks to endow itself with the utmost representable density and to posit the most elaborate and systematic difficulties and obstacles, in order the more surely to overcome them, just as a philosopher imagines in advance the objections his triumphant argumentation will be summoned up to confute.

It then sometimes happens that the objections are irrefutable, and that the wish-fulfilling imagination does its preparatory work so well that the wish, and desire itself, are confounded by the unanswerable resistance of the Real. This is the sense in which Lukács is right about Balzac, but for the wrong reasons: not Balzac's deeper sense of political and historical realities, but rather his incorrigible fantasy demands ultimately raise History itself over against him, as absent cause, as that on which desire must come to grief. The Real

21. Marcel Proust, *A la recherche du temps perdu* (Paris: La Pléiade, 1954), I, 409.

is thus—virtually by definition in the fallen world of capitalism—that which resists desire, that bedrock against which the desiring subject knows the breakup of hope and can finally measure everything that refuses its fulfillment. Yet it also follows that this Real—this absent cause, which is fundamentally unrepresentable and non-narrative, and detectable only in its effects—can be disclosed only by Desire itself, whose wish-fulfilling mechanisms are the instruments through which this resistant surface must be scanned. When, in Flaubert, Balzacian fantasy is effaced, its place taken by the twin phenomena of *bovarysme*, that "desire to desire" whose objects have become illusory images, and of the anorexia of the first antihero, Frédéric Moreau, who no longer has the force to desire anything, at that point the Real ceases to reply, for no further demands are being made on it.

This narrative process may now be schematically represented:

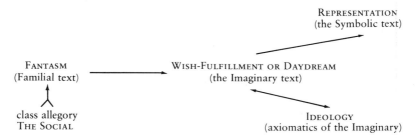

4

AUTHENTIC *RESSENTIMENT:*
Generic Discontinuities and Ideologemes in the "Experimental" Novels of George Gissing

Ideology necessarily implies the libidinal investment of the individual subject, but the narratives of ideology—even what we have called the Imaginary, daydreaming, or wish-fulfilling text—are equally necessarily collective in their materials and form. In this chapter, we will argue that the culture or "objective spirit" of a given period is an environment peopled not merely with inherited words and conceptual survivals, but also with those narrative unities of a socially symbolic type which we have designated as ideologemes.

Such ideologemes are the raw material, the inherited narrative paradigms, upon which the novel as a process works and which it transforms into texts of a different order. We must therefore learn to distinguish between the texts in which ideologemes have left their various traces, and the free-floating narrative objects themselves, which are never given directly in primary verbal form, but must always be reconstructed after the fact, as working hypothesis and subtext. It would be a mistake to conclude that the ideologemes of a given period are more directly accessible to us in so-called popular literature or mass culture (where they have presumably been less subject to the transformations of the more specifically "literary" text); on the other hand, it is evident that a certain derivate literature is a potential storehouse of such materials, provided they are not too rapidly resolved into matters of "influence."

A book such as Gissing's early *Nether World* is as Dickensian as one likes, provided it is understood that the hold of Dickensian paradigms over Gissing is not the result of some charismatic power of a temperamental or an artistic sort, but rather testimony for the fact that these paradigms offered objective "solutions" (or imaginary resolutions) to equally objective ideological problems confronted by the younger writer. In the case of Gissing, however, the most "French," it has been said, of British naturalists, and an incomparable writer whose unique novels have only begun to be rediscovered in the present decade, the early Dickensian "solutions" turn out to produce fresh problems and contradictions in their turn, for which a new and distinctive solution, that of Gissing's mature narrative apparatus, must be invented.

As for the Dickensian paradigms—and in particular, Dickensian sentimentality, the narrative paradigm of the Dickensian heroine, which Alexander Welsh has aptly termed the "angel of the hearth"[1]—it is perhaps best grasped as part of a larger system whose other narrative option, that of melodrama, is more tangibly realized in the work of Dickens' contemporary, Eugène Sue. These two paradigms, the sentimental and the melodramatic, which from the standpoint of ideology may be see as two distinct (but not mutually exclusive) narrative strategies, may be said to be the carrot and the stick of nineteenth-century middle-class moralizing about the lower classes. This is why a book like *The Nether World,* in which both have left their traces, is best read, not for its documentary information on the conditions of Victorian slum life, but as testimony about the narrative paradigms that organize middle-class fantasies about those slums and about "solutions" that might resolve, manage, or repress the evident class anxieties aroused by the existence of an industrial working class and an urban lumpenproletariat.

I have argued in previous chapters that in its generic form, a specific narrative paradigm continues to emit its ideological signals long after its original content has become historically obsolete: the transformation of a peasant dance into the aristocratic minuet, and the reappropriation of this now doubly sedimented form by the Jacobin and then nationalist impulses of bourgeois salon music (in the third movement of the classical sonata form) provide a dramatic locus classicus of this process, in which the most archaic layer of

---

1. Alexander Welsh, *The City of Dickens* (London: Oxford, 1971), chap. 9.

content continues to supply vitality and ideological legitimation to its later and quite different symbolic function.

With the ideologeme, a similar residual effectivity can be observed. The conventional binary juxtaposition, in *The Nether World,* of the haughty and beautiful Clara and the modest and Dickensian Jane positions the reader to receive these two narratives as so many tacitly grasped, preconsciously understood, signals and allusions to preexisting ideologemes. When it is a matter of stigmatizing Clara's social aspirations, her questionable status as an actress is evidently not enough to drive the point home; we must have vitriol dashed in her face by a jealous rival. The moral seems somewhat clearer and simpler than it really is, its ethical form concealing a social and more properly political fantasy. The stock gesture can only be fully read and decoded as an ideological "sign" by consulting more articulated expressions of an ideologeme which is here merely alluded to, in a kind of narrative shorthand. To gloss this text with Sue's *Mystères de Paris* is therefore not to assert any immediate literary influence, but rather to attempt to restore the larger collective fantasy activated here, a fantasy of which it was Sue's doubtful merit to have furnished the most glaring expression. We will thus take the hand that flings the fateful acid as the schematic stenographic representation of a narrative gesture and an ideological fantasy more accessibly revealed and betrayed in the vengeful and monitory figure of Sue's Parisian Harun-al-Rashid, Prince Rodolphe, whose mission in life is the scourging of criminals, evildoers, and villains mostly drawn from the poorer classes, as Marx observed in his lengthiest piece of literary criticism.[2] Indeed, a good deal of light is shed on the melodramatic impulse in nineteenth-century fiction by that archetypal scene in which the Schoolmaster (nickname of the most notorious villain in *Les Mystères de Paris*) has his eyes put out by the Prince's own hand, in an effective example of preventive justice. The historical significance of this lumpen-villain can be sharpened by juxtaposition with Balzac's Philippe, who for all his antisocial tendencies does not quite achieve actantial status of this type, or with Conrad's Gentleman Brown, in whom "villainy" no longer expresses the dark underside of industrial capitalism, but rather the strange no-man's-land between the

2. Karl Marx, *Die Heilige Familie,* chap. 8, in Werke (Berlin, 1962), II, 172–221.

core countries of the advanced capitalist world and those archaic social formations that they seek to penetrate. The anxiety which is crystallized in the person of the Schoolmaster is the primal nineteenth-century middle-class terror of the mob—chief actor of the various climactic "days" of the French Revolution, an object of physical terror for Manzoni, and the theme of those great riot scenes in Scott, Manzoni, and early Dickens which most openly and authentically express a social and historical fear that will be inauthentically recontained and only symbolically expressed in melodrama and its ethical binary. The punishment of the Schoolmaster thus serves as a grim "solution" to the anxieties released when the preindustrial urban mob becomes institutionalized as a permanent lumpenproletariat, and suggests the lengths to which a terrorized propertied class was willing to go (and went, in the massacres of June, 1848, and the bloody repression of the Commune). It is to this whole ideological and iconic complex that the Clara subplot is keyed, and whose overtones it still faintly continues to emit.

The Dickensian paradigm, meanwhile, is no less socially and politically symbolic, although the meaning it had for Dickens—the idyllic space of family and child-bride as a Utopian refuge from the nightmare of social class—has here been modified into that rather different and omnipresent late-Victorian "seme," renunciation. Indeed, the most golden and intolerably Dickensian of all Gissing's early heroines, the unhappy Thyrza, in the novel of the same name, demonstrates how the refuge of the "hearth" has in Gissing become a kind of ghetto: Thyrza's sweetness and simplicity are specifically and constitutively related to her poverty, her ignorance, and her class situation. By definition, then, she cannot be allowed to escape the limits of that situation without also losing her attributes as a Dickensian symbol. She must therefore—in order to prevent her from marrying a man triply superior to her in station, education, and wealth—be killed off;[3] but Gissing's other works and his biog-

---

3. Gissing's worst rhetoric—but he is speaking in a voice he believes to be Dickens'—is summoned up to help the reader over this gratuitous development: "Had she not herself desired it [i.e., death]? And what gift, more blessed, of all that man may pray for? She was at rest, the pure, the gentle, at rest in her maidenhood" [and later, when Thyrza's aristocratic patroness learns the news:] "It is seldom that we experience a simple emotion. When the words, incredible at first, had established their meaning in her mind, Mrs. Ormonde knew that with her human grief there blended an awestruck thankfulness" (*Thyrza* [Cranbury, N.J.: Fairleigh Dickinson University Press, 1974], pp. 473–475).

raphy suggest that this denouement is overdetermined, and is also motivated by what was for him the personal nightmare of a marriage across class borders: the proletarian woman tormented by a middle-class marriage and drinking herself to death, like his first wife. The use of the Dickensian paradigm in *The Nether World* is a good deal less drastic than this, but it has lost none of these ideological connotations. In that "novel of the people," indeed, Jane Snowdon finds her qualifications as an idyllic heroine sorely tested by social and class discomfort, in the career of philanthropy forced on her by her wealthy grandfather. Renunciation thus comes as a blessed relief, when the appropriation of the inheritance by a good-for-nothing father releases her from a mission for which she was temperamentally so unsuitable.

Both these ideologemes, then, drive home the same ultimate message for the lower classes: stay in your place! The threat of the Sue paradigm is merely reduplicated by the promise of the Dickensian one, in which a bonus of charm and fascination is bestowed on those who know how to renounce gracefully. These are, however, as we have said, merely the raw materials upon which *The Nether World's* transformational production begins its work: they are not the end result, but merely the starting point of what proves in this case to be an unsuccessful yet contradictory and revealing process. *The Nether World* cannot be said to be a proletarian novel, in spite of the nominal occupations—die-sinking, the manufacturing of jewelry or artificial flowers—of some of its characters. Its conceptual and organizational framework is not that of social class but rather that very different nineteenth-century ideological concept which is the notion of "the people," as a kind of general grouping of the poor and "underprivileged" of all kinds, from which one can recoil in revulsion, but to which one can also, as in some political populisms, nostalgically "return" as to some telluric source of strength.[4] Gissing's own relationship to "the people" is a unique combination of revulsion and fascination which we will examine later.

What must first be observed about the populism of *The Nether World* is that it represents the solution (or attempted solution) to a

---

4. The classical nineteenth-century expression of this ideological complex is Jules Michelet, *Du Peuple* (1846); see, for contemporary reflections on the analysis of populism, Ernesto Laclau, *Politics and Ideology in Marxist Theory* (London: New Left Books, 1977), chap. 4.

specifically formal and narrative problem, what the younger Lukács would have called the crisis of narrative *totality*. The prodigious, ever-widening *agons* of Balzacian narrative do not seem to meet this dilemma in their path; nor does the immense spatial network of late Dickens, which weaves a bewildering host of characters and their itineraries into the "untotalizable totality" of a sprawling London, ever seem to approach the limit at which its own organizational device might become dangerously conscious of itself, and thereby register some objective crisis in its own raw material or "social equivalent." In Gissing, however, the Dickensian city is little by little drained of its vitality and reduced to the empty grid of calls by one character to another, visits to oppressive rooms and apartments, and intervals of random strolls through the poorer quarters. The city therefore no longer functions as the molar unity of these narratives, as their outer emblem of "totality," as the external sign of the meaningful unity of their social content.[5] Naturalist narrative will substitute, for the older totalizing frameworks, a new classification of narrative material according to specialization, or the division of labor; witness Zola's systematic mapping out of the "topics" of the Rougon-Macquart series into the various themes of railroads, finance, peasantry, war, medicine, religion, urban proletariat, and the like. What needs to be stressed, however, is that this new "solution" is in reality part of the problem: the crisis of the social totality is the result of the same phenomena—reification, social fragmentation, the division of labor, Taylorization[6]—which dictate the terms of the naturalist organizational strategy.

Gissing's conception of a novel about "the people" is a form of high naturalist specialization that seeks to pass itself off as a map of the social totality. In effect, the attempt to endow this ideological concept with literary representation systematically reveals its own inner contradictions: if the "people" functions successfully as a

5. Gissing's is, as John Goode observes, both a post-Dickensian and a post-Baudelairean city; and see Raymond Williams' splendid pages on this moment of the modern city in *The Country and the City* (New York: Oxford University Press, 1973), pp. 215–247.

6. Here the essential reference is Harry Braverman, *Labor and Monopoly Capital* (New York: Monthly Review, 1974). Named after its inventor, Frederick Winslow Taylor, Taylorization seeks to rationalize the labor process by dividing production into its smallest and most efficient units, much as Descartes sought to do with concepts.

merely classificatory concept, the characters of the novel will be reduced to nothing more than illustrations of their preexistent essences, and the novel can at best merely repeat over and over again the class warnings described above—which, in the present context of the dynamics of narrative, can be rewritten as an actantial injunction: do not attempt to become another kind of character from the one you already are! If, on the other hand, the notion of the "people" begins to take on class connotations in spite of itself, then it must fatally become relational, and draw into its field of representation those other social classes against which it is necessarily defined and with which it is explicitly or implicitly locked in struggle. Yet this too would amount to a transcendence of the initial framework, and something like an autocritique of the very concept of the "people," as well as a bursting of the narrative seams. In particular, as we shall see shortly, such a development would make the "otherness" of the concept of "the people" unavoidable, and uncomfortably underscore its dependence on the privileged yet placeless observer who complacently yet dispassionately collects this narrative raw material.[7]

The originality of *The Nether World* lies in the way in which it registers this contradiction in its content and invents a unique and provisional solution to it; this is, indeed, the ultimate significance of the philanthropic mission which gives the plot its center. Old Snowdon's account of his great idea projects a curious conjunction between an individual act and an undifferentiated background object, between a narrative character and something little better than an abstract idea:

> Suppose when I die I could have the certainty that all this money was going to be used for the good of the poor by a woman who herself belonged to the poor? You understand me? It would have been easy

7. This is essentially what I take to be John Goode's point in his "George Gissing's *The Nether World*" (in David Howard et al., *Tradition and Tolerance in Nineteenth-century Fiction* [London: Routledge & Kegan Paul, 1966], pp. 207–241), that the "nether world" is not a social class but rather something like a "culture of poverty": "the only real villain in the book is the objective fact of scarcity. . . . [According to Gissing] the only hope for the amelioration of the working classes is an improvement in moral standards, and there can be no improvement, because the economic forces to which they are committed predetermines their low moral quality" (pp. 234, 236).

enough to leave it among charities in the ordinary way; but my idea went beyond that. I might have had Jane schooled and fashioned into a lady, and still have hoped that she would use the money well; but my idea went beyond *that*. There's plenty of ladies nowadays taking an interest in the miserable, and spending their means unselfishly. What I hoped was to raise up for the poor and the untaught a friend out of their own midst, someone who had gone through all that *they* suffer, who was accustomed to earn her own living by the work of her hands as *they* do, who had never thought herself their better, who saw the world as they see it and knew all their wants.[8]

The philanthropic motif is autoreferential to the degree to which old Snowdon's sudden revelation of his purpose in life is *the same* as Gissing's discovery of a way to organize his narrative (and to solve the crisis of narrative totality). That it is no mere fluke will be made plain shortly when we show that the "philanthropic experiment" becomes the key mechanism of Gissing's mature narrative apparatus.

There is no need to rehearse at length the ideological content of philanthropy, which seeks a nonpolitical and individualizing solution to the exploitation which is structurally inherent in the social system, and whose characteristic motifs of cultural improvement and education are only too familiar.[9] What is interesting about Gissing is that he is locked into this program at the same time that he sees through it and arraigns it violently, oscillating between an implacable denunciation of the reformist-philanthropists and an equally single-minded indictment of the "poor" who cannot thus be rescued or elevated.

Yet it is as a narrative phenomenon that the philanthropic mission is surely most revealing; to introduce this ameliorative project into the heart of realistic representation is to pass implicit judgment on the quality of empirical being, and its fitness as literary raw material. What we have called the modal heterogeneity of narrative registers in Balzac can now strikingly be juxtaposed with the new

8. *The Nether World* (Cranbury, N.J.: Fairleigh Dickinson University Press, 1974), p. 178.

9. See, on the historical specificity of philanthropy as a British institution, David Owen, *English Philanthropy, 1660–1960* (Cambridge: Harvard University Press, 1964); and for related studies, Welsh, *The City of Dickens*, pp. 86–100, and Norris Pope, *Dickens and Charity* (New York: Columbia, 1978).

motif: in Balzac the weight of empirical being, of history and accumulated event, is apparently still light enough for alternate histories to be imagined, and expressed in a variety of narrative modalities. We have suggested that in high realism, such alternative narrative registers begin to disappear and a massively homogeneous narrative apparatus—a kind of obligatory "indicative" register—to take their place. Beneath the stifling and definitive weight of empirical being, even alternative social worlds, such as they are, must find representational expression, and the result is the Utopian or science-fiction novel, of which Chernyshevsky's *What's to Be Done?* is the monument, the text into which old Snowdon's successful project might have rewritten life itself.[10]

This is the situation in which the great realistic novelists, "shepherds of Being" of a very special, ideological type, are forced, by their own narrative and aesthetic vested interests, into a repudiation of revolutionary change and an ultimate stake in the status quo. Their evocation of the solidity of their object of representation—the social world grasped as an organic, natural, Burkean permanence—is necessarily threatened by any suggestion that that world is not natural, but historical, and subject to radical change. Indeed, a curious subform of realism, the proletarian novel, demonstrates what happens when the representational apparatus is confronted by that supreme event, the strike as the figure for social revolution, which calls social "being" and the social totality itself into question, thereby undermining that totality's basic preconditions: whence the scandal of this form, which fails when it succeeds and succeeds when it fails, thereby evading categories of literary evaluation inherited from "great realism." Meanwhile, the realists themselves are necessarily engaged in a host of containment strategies, which seek to fold everything which is not-being, desire, hope, and transformational praxis, back into the status of nature; these impulses toward the future and toward radical change must

10. The other appropriate reference is, of course, Morris' *News from Nowhere* (1891). In his "Gissing Morris, and English Socialism" (*Victorian Studies,* 12 [December, 1968], 201–226), John Goode suggests that the defects of *Demos* spring from its structural incapacity to register the future, and that they are therefore at one with the situation which dictates Morris' reinvention of a Utopian or science-fiction form—the insufficiency of an empirical present for the representation of socialist forces which aim at the transformation of that present.

systematically be reified, transformed into "feelings" and psychological attributes, the properties and accidents of "characters" now grasped as organisms and forms of being. As for the conscious political revolutionary, he or she must be the object of a very special kind of naturalizing operation, which we will examine shortly.

The philanthropic project stands at the very fault line of such narrative strategies, and is best renaturalized as quixotic altruism, eccentricity, or harmless mania. Thus read, as the attempt to resolve the dilemmas of totality, the philanthropic mission intersects with one of the great themes of dialectical philosophy, the Hegelian denunciation of the ethical imperative, taken up again by Lukács in his *Theory of the Novel*. On this diagnosis, the *Sollen*, the mesmerization of duty and ethical obligation, necessarily perpetuates a cult of failure and a fetishization of pure, unrealized intention.[11] For moral obligation presupposes a gap between being and duty, and cannot be satisfied with the accomplishment of a single duty and the latter's consequent transformation into being. In order to retain its own characteristic satisfactions, ethics must constantly propose the unrealizable and the unattainable to itself. But narrative, according to Lukács, can take only the empirical as its raw material; a character driven by ethical abstraction can thus be adequately represented only by a certain "narrowing of the soul," by endowing it with a "demonic obsession with an existing idea which it posits as the only and the most ordinary reality."[12] Lukács' model here is obviously *Don Quixote;* if he did not anticipate the peculiar flowering of the philanthropic novel in the nineteenth century, it was because he saw the ethical drive in the traditional sense, as the confrontation between an ethical individual and an individual *casus*. The philanthropic project, however, taking as its object not a single individual but a whole class or collectivity, expands the ethical act to its ultimate limit, that is, to that point beyond which it must necessarily become political.

The Nether World, however, deconstructs its narrative fabric in a second way, which will also be strategic for later Gissing. Here the narrative symptom may be detected in the imbalance of a single

11. Georg Lukács, *The Theory of the Novel*, trans. A. Bostock (Cambridge: MIT Press, 1971), pp. 65–66.
12. Ibid., pp. 97–111.

character, the putative hero of *The Nether World,* Sidney Kirkwood, whose contemplative passivity and lugubrious melancholy seem to mark him off from the rest and to endow him with an peculiar self-consciousness. It is indeed difficult to escape the impression that from this ostensible proletarian a different kind of character altogether is attempting to emerge, and that the narrative blur surrounding him is less a matter of technical incompetence than of the superposition upon this particular narrative pretext of what will shortly develop into that *alienated intellectual* so characteristic of Gissing's later work. It is as though the narrative substance itself—the reified and abstract material of "the people"—thereby attempted to remedy its own structural deficiencies and to reorganize itself around a privileged center or witness, who had, by definition, to belong to another class. Yet he must also remain an actor and a participant in the realities of this social world. Once again, the problem dictates its own solution, and the protagonist in question will be one who is alienated in a very special way, namely by *déclassement* and by that form of class treason which is fascination with or aspiration to the status of those on the other side of the class line.

Two other early novels of Gissing, indeed, *Demos* and *Thyrza,* suggest the basic structural variants of this narrative solution: the latter tracing the difficulties of an idealistic young gentleman intent on bringing culture to Lambeth, while the former recounts the destiny of a gifted young proletarian who, upon the unexpected inheritance of a fortune, finds himself thrust into the ownership of a factory. These plots solve the problem of the philanthropic "modality" in an original way which will provide Gissing with his mature narrative apparatus as it is most richly realized in *The Odd Women* and *New Grub Street.* This solution confirms our historical interpretation of the possibilities of narrative modalization in Balzac's novels outlined in the previous chapter;[13] indeed, it is as though in Gissing's "moment," the relative freedom of Balzacian modalization is no longer available. It is, in other words, as if in a universe of high reification and increasingly massive commodification, the "being" of things and institutions and the increasingly reified place and role of human subjects within them weigh so

13. See above, Chapter 3, note 12.

heavily upon the narrative imagination that shifts in register and the modal variation of destinies are no longer linguistic possibilities for the serious artist. The philanthropic strategy was empty of content and never a true narrative solution in this sense: it now—in this moment which is also that of the twin emergence of modernism and of mass culture—throws off a new (or reinvented) subgenre, the Utopian novel, which displays renewed vitality throughout this period. Likewise, the modalities of the Imaginary and of wish-fulfillment or desire find new institutionalization in the subgenres produced by emergent mass culture: gothics, adventure and myth, science fiction, and detective stories.

Gissing thus finds himself limited to something like an indicative mode; the "deontic" narrative registers available to Balzac are no longer functional. Yet something of the Balzacian character system survives here in a greatly modified form: for one of the structures by which Gissing can seek at least partially to relativize the finality of individual destinies is a use of echoing subplots in which the protagonists of each offer a *combinatoire* of the objective variants still possible in this increasingly closed universe. But these possibilities are no longer related, as in the Balzacian system, by the investment of a single wish-fulfilling impulse. They are now, as it were, merely empirical variants, and their relationship is determined by Gissing's appropriation of the naturalist paradigm discussed earlier: a kind of specialized division of official "subjects," such as feminism or free-lance journalism (in the two novels referred to above), which nonetheless here become a kind of lens or refracting medium through which a group of destinies are linked, whereas in French naturalism the organization by topics was a means of differentiating the content of various narratives. Gissing's use of high naturalist specialization is, however, ultimately merely a ruse: in the work of his maturity, indeed, the two great subjects of marriage and literary production, along with the third "topic" related to both, the problem of an independent income, are profoundly interconnected, in a way which remains to be specified below.

Yet this structural possibility of varying the finality of individual destinies is itself dependent on the more radical and ingenious "solution" already evolved in the earlier novels: a solution that marks Gissing's narratives as "experimental novels" in a far stricter sense than those of Zola. In Gissing's maturity the novel comes to be considered as something like a laboratory space, where given characters can be submitted to experiments in a controlled environment in which the modification of variables is systematically tested, and in which—unlike the novelistic experiments foreseen by Zola—a given experimental trajectory can be repeated and indeed reversed, and the experiment in question can be replayed in accordance with the variables to be tested.

That this is no mere neutral process, however, may be judged from the "experiment" of which *Demos* offers the narrative realization, in which the young working-class militant, Richard Mutimer, is given a chance at running his uncle's factory. This unexpected and properly "experimental" modification in Richard's destiny would normally generate a properly Utopian narrative, in which the possibility of some Owenite cooperative enclave would be explored (the generally negative conclusions of such Utopian narratives amount, in our terms here, to the attempt to reanchor a Utopian register back in the empirical realities of an existing "indicative" universe in which no such enclaves exist). But this is not at all what interests Gissing.

Indeed, we have already shown that Gissing's conception of class material is a relational or, better still, a conflictual one: the working-class novels are only in appearance "documents" about a proletarian way of life, nor are there any corresponding narrative representations of bourgeois or upper-class existence, in isolation. Rather, these seemingly separate and homogeneous zones of social space become interesting for the novelist only when they are intersected by characters from the other class, by class interlopers or refugees, defectors or missionaries. The very spirit of the narrative experiment of *Demos* is fundamentally altered by such an intersection, and what we are meant "scientifically" to observe is less the administrative and technological transformation of Wanley than the properly social and class transformation of Richard himself, when thrust into an essentially bourgeois situation. The factory, indeed, a complex of iron-foundries and mines, had been the property of an estranged uncle, a Tory ex-proletarian who had planned to leave it to a young aristocratic protégé. Ugly rumors about the young man's dissolute love affairs suddenly cause a change in plan, and the elder Mutimer's sudden death intestate gives Richard his opportunity, which results in an unfortunate marriage to a young woman "above his station." *Demos* thus becomes a virtual object lesson in snobbery, setting out systematically to show how irredeemable a working-class character is, and how unsuitable for the social and cultural conditions of a different class situation. The ugliness of these class attitudes is reconfirmed by the brutality and gratuitousness with which the experiment is reversed and terminated: seated in the pew in which the elder Mutimer was stricken, Richard's unhappy aristocratic bride suddenly finds a piece of paper which is none other than the missing testament; the original heir inherits after all (in fact he had not been as unworthy as rumor had it), and Richard must abandon, along with his new way of life, his whole Utopian project, which the new owner razes to the ground in order to restore the natural beauty of the spot.

The "experiment" in *Thyrza* would seem to be somewhat less drastic, and to have less shocking consequences: but this is only because the consequences have been displaced, and because such experiments in Gissing are never symmetrical. Thus, Egremont's abortive attempt to bring culture to the working classes recoils, not on himself, but on his putative wards and victims. Here a perfectly proper critique of the illusions of reformist educational strategy— and in particular of the lecture series and lending library whereby Egremont proposes to achieve the regeneration and the "aesthetic education" of working-class Lambeth—is inflected into a potentially even more damaging critique of the possibility of interclass relations by Egremont's involuntary passion for the eponymous proletarian heroine. Yet neither the latter's death (which is, as we have seen, so stylized and perfumed as to suggest all the ornamental unreality of a Preraphaelite angel), nor Egremont's own temporary depression (although an anticipation of the far more powerful representations of melancholy and spiritual death in the later novels) is really the appropriate reference here.

The principal "subject" of this particular experiment is, in fact, neither of these characters, but an apparently more minor figure, one of Egremont's initial working-class listeners, Gilbert Grail, who, passionately devoted to reading and culture, finds a place in the reformer's master scheme as librarian and chief mediator between the working-class readers and the middle-class experimenter. Egremont's plan, indeed, enters the older man's life like a thunderclap, transforming it from top to bottom and arousing expectations of a sort that would be unthinkable under the virtual caste system in which Grail's destiny has hitherto been confined. Grail's marriage proposal to Thyrza is only the most dramatic expression of this experimental change in status, which is then reversed and destroyed by the (mutually unwelcome) love between Egremont and Thyrza. Meanwhile, the new passion has the result of undermining Egremont's own project and of discrediting him more effectively than any working-class recalcitrance would have done, while the victimization of Grail himself—whose marriage and new profession are alike at one stroke undone—is rendered more objective by the absence of anything particularly likable about its victim (the prototype, indeed, of the later Gissing figures of the rancid fathers and doomed husbands, victims of irredeemable hard luck and malignant fortune, such as Mr. Yule or Widderson). Again, the abrupt termination of the narrative experiment has something so arbitrary about it as to suggest a deliberate affective logic.

The fate of Grail, indeed, enacts what might be called the Bathsheba archetype, and the figural fulfillment of the saying, "From him that hath not shall be taken away even that which he hath" (Matthew 25:29). The theft of Bathsheba from the unhappy Uriah and the latter's virtual murder by the king is the vehicle for a moral lesson which is also a class warning: "The rich man had exceeding many flocks and herds: but the poor man had nothing, save one little ewe lamb, which he had brought and nourished up: and it grew up together with him, and with his children; it did eat of his own meat," and so on to the predictable conclusion (2 Samuel 12:2–3). It is indeed hard to escape the feeling that Egremont, who already has everything that Grail lacks—birth, money, status, education, leisure, youth, ideas—is nonetheless intent on robbing the latter of even that "ewe lamb" which is his modest treasure; hard to escape the feeling that what is at work here is some primal *envy* at the heart of Egremont's interest in the poor, a longing to appropriate that class solidarity from which he must himself eternally remain excluded. The catastrophe of *Thyrza* may be read as a grim diagnosis and commentary on the unconscious meaning of Egremont's philanthropic altruism, a virtually Nietzschean unmasking of the gesture of hostility concealed within the charitable impulse.

On the other hand, the full ambivalence of Gissing's work cannot be measured unless we understand that from another point of view

Grail has no one but himself to blame, and that his ultimate misery is simply the result of his own desire to rise above his station, his own impulse to leave his appropriate class, which in that sense perfectly complements Egremont's. From this perspective, the narrative "experiment"—which ought to have opened up a space unrealizable in the asphyxiating conditions of a reified existence and of an empirically unchangeable destiny—brings its own retribution with it, and may be grasped as something like a grisly ritual in which *déclassement* is fittingly and emblematically punished.

In this light, it seems clear that the new narrative apparatus— what we have called the "experimental situation"—has been motivated or, if you prefer, overmotivated or overdetermined, by a more properly ideological motif. The protagonists of these early "experimental" novels, Richard Mutimer, Egremont, and even Gilbert Grail, are all in one way or another figures for that alienated intellectual whose presence we have detected in *The Nether World*. Now we must specify this motif still further, for it is clear that the author of *New Grub Street* does not understand the "alienation" of such intellectuals in the Romantic terms of the *poète maudit* struggling against the philistine masters of a business society, nor even in the Mallarmean terms of the structural alienation inherent in writing and linguistic production. On the contrary, alienation here designates class alienation and the "objective treason" of intellectuals perpetually suspended between two social worlds and two sets of class values and obligations. And evidently Gissing's own personal "wound"—like Dickens' early trauma, it involved scandal and ostracism, an accusation of theft, along with expulsion from the public school that might have led to a secure middle-class position in life—condemned him to a peculiarly social form of Hegelian Unhappy Consciousness which forebade any successful and definitive class identification.

But the theme of the alienated intellectual cannot properly be understood until it has been semantically restored to its full expressive value as an ideologeme. As with some of the earlier materials of the present chapter, indeed, I will argue that this particular "theme" and the characters who seem to dramatize it are themselves simply so many allusions to a more basic ideological "sign" which would have been grasped instinctively by any contemporary reader but from which we are culturally and historically somewhat distanced.

This sign or ideologeme, it is true, exists nowhere as such: part of the "objective spirit" or the cultural Symbolic order of its period, it vanishes into the past along with the latter, leaving only its traces—material signifiers, lexemes, enigmatic words and phrases—behind it. And just as our reconstruction of the texts of the past must necessarily be rerouted through the work of the reconstruction of such vanished lexical meanings and connotations and of the semantic systems that generate them, so also our reconstruction of the past's narrative texts presupposes a work that is at present less advanced than the lexicological research on their vocabulary: namely the reconstruction and inventory of the ideologemes of the historical period in question.

In the present instance, we may identify this particular ideologeme as that of *ressentiment,* of which Nietzsche was the primary theorist, if not, indeed, the metaphysician: "The slave uprising in ethics begins when *ressentiment* becomes creative and brings forth its own values: the ressentiment of those to whom the only authentic way of reaction—that of deeds—is unavailable, and who preserve themselves from harm through the exercise of imaginary vengeance."[14] Nietzsche's whole vision of history, his historical master narrative, is organized around this proposition, which diagnoses ethics in general and the Judeo-Christian tradition in particular as a revenge of the slaves upon the masters and an ideological ruse whereby the former infect the latter with a slave mentality—the ethos of charity—in order to rob them of their natural vitality and aggressive, properly aristocratic insolence.

Nietzsche's narrative or myth is ostensibly proposed as a kind of psychological mechanism in the service of a critique of Victorian moralism and hypocrisy. But its secondary adaptations show that it has a more fundamentally political function: thus in his *Origines de la France contemporaine,* Taine follows Michelet's lead in using the motif of *ressentiment* to "explain" the phenomenon of revolution, which it does in a twofold way. First, in a kind of exoteric and vulgar sense, the ideologeme of *ressentiment* can seem to account in a "psychological" and nonmaterialistic sense for the destructive envy the have-nots feel for the haves, and thus account for the otherwise inexplicable fact of a popular mass uprising against a

14. Friedrich Nietzsche, *The Geneaology of Morals,* i, 10.

hierarchical system of which the historian is concerned to demonstrate the essential wholesomeness and organic or communitarian virtue. Meanwhile, in a secondary and more esoteric, "overdetermined" use, *ressentiment* can also explain the conduct of those who incited an otherwise essentially satisfied popular mass to such "unnatural" disorders: the ideologeme thus designates Nietzsche's "ascetic priests," the intellectuals par excellence—unsuccessful writers and poets, bad philosophers, bilious journalists, and failures of all kinds—whose private dissatisfactions lead them to their vocations as political and revolutionary militants. This diagnostic double standard, which will furnish the inner dynamic for a whole tradition of counterrevolutionary propaganda from Dostoyevsky and Conrad to Orwell, is thus immediately relevant to the doubly ominous status of Richard Mutimer as proletarian intellectual, and serves as a legitimation for the gratuitous cruelty with which this character is structurally punished.

What is most striking about the theory of *ressentiment* is its unavoidably autoreferential structure. In *Demos,* certainly, the conclusion is inescapable: Gissing resents Richard, and what he resents most is the latter's *ressentiment.* We are perhaps now far enough distant from this particular ideologeme to draw a corollary: namely, that this ostensible "theory" is itself little more than an expression of annoyance at seemingly gratuitous lower-class agitation, at the apparently quite unnecessary rocking of the social boat. It may therefore be concluded that the theory of *ressentiment,* wherever it appears, will always itself be the expression and the production of *ressentiment.*

We cannot, however, leave the case of Gissing at this. Unlike Balzacian intervention, indeed, unlike Balzacian snobbery—which remains a vehicle for libidinal investment and Utopian wish-fulfillment—the frequent authorial expression of outrageous class positions and opinions in early Gissing has something profoundly unconvincing about it. It is as though, in a world of reified language, even the author's own personal language cannot be genuine any longer, and comes before us as a virtually Flaubertian mimicry of received ideas of a disembodied, floating sort. We need, indeed, a more complex model of what Bakhtin called "dialogical speech"[15]

15. See Chapter 1, note 63.

to understand a situation in which such expression can be grasped as something like a language of the Other, in which its own motivation, far from being *only* that of an identification with the attitudes of the upper classes, is *also,* given the system of Gissing's own ambivalence, a conduct of *ressentiment* against them, tending to embarrass and to compromise even those on whose behalf it seemed to testify.[16]

Such language disappears from the novels of Gissing's maturity, novels whose stylistic qualities have not been sufficiently celebrated. Indeed, it is to begin with difficult enough to understand how the electrical dryness of Gissing's later style, and what can only be called the wit of these novels' dialogue, are consistent with the unrelieved desolation of their psychic and material content. Yet wit is not necessarily incompatible with tension; on the contrary, its effects generally imply strong feelings deliberately unexpressed and affective silences that lend its apparently disinterested formulations their own secret intensity and urgencies.

As for Gissing's narrative style, its constituent features, such as the well-nigh rhetorical deployment of its adjectives, suggest something like a rigorous and depersonalized use of an inherited instrument, and in particular of the great analytic movement of the eighteenth-century adjective, with its triplication, its analysis into qualifying phrases, its elaborate flexing of syntax as the very armature of Reason itself. Still, when one contrasts this instrument with George Eliot's late and florid, supremely affective reinvention of the rhetorical apparatus, when one recalls Gissing's own past as the bursary classicist, suffering all his life from that incurable wound of social and class humiliation already alluded to, then it becomes difficult to escape the conclusion that Gissing is in reality working with linguistic material that is extinct, and that the secret of his style is to be found in the hypothesis that his "English" is a dead language like Latin. Better still, Gissing's language offers perhaps an

16. "Almost in spite of himself, the mirror which [the writer] modestly offers to his readers is magical: it enthralls and compromises. Even though everything has been done to offer them only a flattering and complacent image . . . aesthetic distance puts it out of reach. Impossible to be delighted with it, to find any comfortable warmth in it, any discrete indulgence. . . . Spontaneous behavior, passing to the reflective state, loses its innocence and the excuse of immediacy: it must be assumed or changed." J.-P. Sartre, *What Is Literature?,* trans. Bernard Frechtman (New York: Harper & Row, 1965), pp. 89–90.

early example of what Roland Barthes has called *écriture blanche,*[17] white or bleached writing, and for much the same reason as those later diagnosed by Barthes: this linguistic practice seeks through radical depersonalization—as though through a kind of preventive suicide—to neutralize the social conflicts immediately evoked and regenerated by any living use of speech.

From this linguistic perspective we may now better characterize the narrative apparatus and character system to which Gissing came in his later works. Two strategic displacements were necessary to convert the earlier narrative machinery which has been described here into that of Gissing's greatest novels: the alienated intellectual becomes more locally specified as the writer, so that the problems of *déclassement* raised above are immediately linked to the issue of earning money. Meanwhile, the class conflict evoked in the earlier works is here largely rewritten in terms of sexual differentiation and the "woman question": this allows the "experimental" situation we described to be staged within the more conventional novelistic framework of marriage, which thereby gains an unaccustomed class resonance.

The familiar character system of the later works—the aging masculine failure, in whom bitterness and ill temper transform the ancient icon of Melancholy into the ugliest and most incurable sickness of the soul; the languid young man of means, a kind of frivolous avatar of the Flaubertian antihero, in whom even the latter's vague and nagging "desire to desire" has been forgotten; the struggling young woman, whose independence must be bought with renunciation—this system can be understood only in terms of desire. But unlike Balzac, Gissing faces a situation in which the universal commodification of desire stamps any achieved desire or wish as inauthentic, while an authenticity at best pathetic clings to images of failure. The exclusive preoccupation in Gissing with the anxieties of money, the misery of hand-to-mouth survival, the absence of independent means or a fixed income, is a way of short-circuiting this intolerable alternative, for it positions the realization of genuine desire in the future, in that Utopian fantasy of a life situation in which one would finally have the leisure necessary to write.

17. Barthes, "Writing and Silence," *Writing Zero Degree.*

The quest for an income is therefore never commodity desire in Gissing, but something like a pre-desire, a precondition for desiring which has been systematically devalued in advance, so that neither success (marriage with a wealthy woman) nor failure casts the melodramatic shadows of high naturalism. In his later work the inevitability of frustration has been secretly bracketed and suspended by the essential pettiness and worthlessness of what could never be any more than a means to an end in the first place: the indispensable prerequisite to a self-realization that never comes, fatally condemning all these characters to preoccupations and anxieties which are distractions from and substitutes for some true and ideal (private) life. The dialectic of desire is thus in Gissing something like the negation of a negation. Since his characters never reach the point of being in a position to desire, it is as though the whole system of success and failure has been undermined from the outset by a narrative strategy which may thus be read as something like the final form of *ressentiment* itself. From that point of view, renunciation becomes dialectically transformed. No longer a response and an adaptation to the constricting situation of the petty bourgeoisie and the objective contraction of possibilities, it is now generalized into a global refusal of commodity desire itself.

Thus extended to a universal principle and absolutized as the very motor force of Gissing's narratives, *ressentiment* ceases to generate sheerly ideological images and becomes the guarantor of a divisiveness beyond ideological commitment. An Unhappy Consciousness too absolute to find any rest in conventional snobbery is now called on to register historical and social reality, its profound "mixed feelings" generating an omnipresent class consciousness in which it is intolerable for the bourgeois reader to dwell for any length of time. This is indeed the sense in which the oxymoron of our initial characterization of Gissing may be justified, and in which alone the phenomenon of *ressentiment*—surely, among all human passions, the most deeply driven by bad faith of the Sartrean type—may be said to have a certain authenticity.

5

ROMANCE AND REIFICATION:
Plot Construction and Ideological Closure in Joseph Conrad

Nothing is more alien to the windless closure of high naturalism than the works of Joseph Conrad. Perhaps for that very reason, even after eighty years, his place is still unstable, undecidable, and his work unclassifiable, spilling out of high literature into light reading and romance, reclaiming great areas of diversion and distraction by the most demanding practice of style and *écriture* alike, floating uncertainly somewhere in between Proust and Robert Louis Stevenson. Conrad marks, indeed, a strategic fault line in the emergence of contemporary narrative, a place from which the structure of twentieth-century literary and cultural *institutions* becomes visible as it could not be in the heterogeneity of Balzacian registers, nor even in the discontinuities of the paradigms which furnish materials for what is an increasingly unified narrative apparatus in Gissing. In Conrad we can sense the emergence not merely of what will be contemporary modernism (itself now become a literary institution), but also, still tangibly juxtaposed with it, of what will variously be called popular culture or mass culture, the commercialized cultural discourse of what, in late capitalism, is often described as a media society. This emergence is most dramatically registered by what most readers have felt as a tangible "break" in the narrative of *Lord Jim*,[1] a qualitative shift and diminution of

---

1. "The presentment of Lord Jim in the first part of the book, the account of the inquiry and of the desertion of the *Patna*, the talk with the French lieutenant—these are good Conrad. But the romance that follows, though plausibly offered as a

narrative intensity as we pass from the story of the *Patna* and the intricate and prototextual search for the "truth" of the scandal of the abandoned ship, to that more linear account of Jim's later career in Patusan, which, a virtual paradigm of romance as such, comes before us as the prototype of the various "degraded" sub-genres into which mass culture will be articulated (adventure story, gothic, science fiction, bestseller, detective story, and the like). But this institutional heterogeneity—not merely a shift between two narrative paradigms, nor even a disparity between two types of narration or narrative organization, but a shift between two distinct cultural spaces, that of "high" culture and that of mass culture—is not the only gap or discontinuity that *Lord Jim* symptomatically betrays. Indeed, we will have occasion to isolate the stylistic practice of this work as a virtually autonomous "instance" in its own right, standing in tension or contradiction with the book's various narrative instances or levels—just as we will insist on the repressed space of a world of work and history and of protopolitical conflict which may in this respect be seen as the trace and the remnant of the content of an older realism, now displaced and effectively marginalized by the emergent modernist discourse. The paradigm of formal history which must now be presupposed is thus evidently more complex than the framework of a movement from Balzacian realism to high realism with which we have previously worked. Schematically, it may be described as a structural breakdown of the older realisms, from which emerges not modernism alone, but rather two literary and cultural structures, dialectically interrelated and necessarily presupposing each other for any adequate analysis: these now find themselves positioned in the distinct and generally incompatible spaces of the institutions of high literature and what the Frankfurt School conveniently termed the "culture industry," that is, the apparatuses for the production of "popular" or mass culture.[2] That this last is a new term may be dramatically demon-

---

continued exhibition of Jim's case, has no inevitability as that; nor does it develop or enrich the central interest, which consequently, eked out to provide the substance of a novel, comes to seem decidedly thin" (F. R. Leavis, *The Great Tradition* [New York: New York University Press, 1969], p. 190).

2. T. W. Adorno and Max Horkheimer, "The Culture Industry," in *Dialectic of Enlightenment*, trans. J. Cumming (New York: Herder & Herder, 1972). pp. 120–167. and see my "Reification and Utopia in Mass Culture," *Social Text*, No. 1 (Winter, 1979), pp. 130–148.

strated by the situation of Balzac, a writer, if one likes, of "best sellers," but for whom this designation is anachronistic insofar as no contradiction is yet felt in his time between the production of best sellers and the production of what will later come to be thought of as "high" literature.

The coexistence of all these distinct but as yet imperfectly differentiated cultural "spaces" in Conrad marks his work as a unique occasion for the historical analysis of broadly cultural as well as more narrowly literary forms. It also offers a no less unique occasion for the type of investigation around which this book has been organized, namely the "metacommentary," or the historical and dialectical reevaluation of conflicting interpretive methods.[3] For the discontinuities objectively present in Conrad's narratives have, as with few other modern writers, projected a bewildering variety of competing and incommensurable interpretive options, which it will be our task to assess in what follows. We have already implicitly touched on two of these: the "romance" or mass-cultural reading of Conrad as a writer of adventure tales, sea narratives, and "popular" yarns; and the stylistic analysis of Conrad as a practitioner of what we will shortly term a properly "impressionistic" will to style.[4] Alongside these, however, and not related to them in any immediately evident way, we can distinguish other influential kinds of readings: the myth-critical, for instance, in which *Nostromo* is seen as the articulation of the archetype of buried treasure;[5] the Freudian, in which the failure of Oedipal resolution is ratified by the grisly ritual execution of Conrad's two son-heroes (Jim and Nostromo) by their spiritual fathers;[6] the ethical, in which Con-

---

3. See my "Metacommentary," *PMLA*, 86 (1971), 9–18.

4. See for example the remarks on "qualities" in J. Hillis Miller, *Poets of Reality* (Cambridge: Harvard University Press, 1965), pp. 24–29, 46–51; and see also Norman Holland, *Dynamics,* pp. 226–237. The "impressionism" debate of course greatly transcends the work of Conrad; for a critical evaluation see Ian Watt, *Conrad in the Nineteenth Century* (Berkeley: University of California Press, 1980), pp. 169–200.

5. Dorothy Van Ghent, "Introduction," to Joseph Conrad, *Nostromo* (New York: Holt, Rinehart, & Winston, 1961), pp. vii–xxv.

6. Bernard Meyer's *Joseph Conrad: A Psychoanalytic Biography* (Princeton: Princeton University Press, 1967) overstresses the maternal pole of Conrad's work; perhaps this is the place to suggest that the classical Freudian complex of familial relationships often functions as a free form of closure, emptied of its psychoanalytic

rad's texts are taken literally as books which raise the "issues" of heroism and courage, of honor and cowardice;[7] the ego-psychological, in which the story of Jim is interpreted as the search for identity or psychic unity;[8] the existential, in which the omnipresent themes of the meaninglessness and absurdity of human existence are foregrounded as "message" and as "world-view";[9] and finally, more formidable than any of these, the Nietzschean reading of Conrad's political vision as a struggle against *ressentiment,* and the structuralist-textual reading of Conrad's form as an immanent dramatization of the impossibility of narrative beginnings and as the increasing reflexivity and problematization of linear narrative itself.[10]

The competing claims and conflicts of these various interpretations constitute a network of leitmotifs within the reading of *Lord Jim* and *Nostromo* that will now, in the form of a kind of gradual reconstruction of formal levels, be presented. Here, as nowhere else in the present work, the double focus of the metacommentary must be apparent: we seek to construct a model of Conrad's text for its own sake, presupposing the intrinsic interest of this project; yet at the same time, this model, from another perspective, will serve as something like a pretext for a commentary on other critical methods. It is appropriate, however, that our reading draw on

content (see, for instance, Edward Said, *Beginnings* [New York: Basic Books, 1975], pp. 137–152). The Freudian acts which close *Nostromo* and *Lord Jim* may thus be seen as arabesques which seal these two narrative discourses, rather than as genuine symptoms.

7. Tony Tanner, *Conrad: Lord Jim* (London: Arnold, 1963).

8. The canonical reading, symptomatically based on "The Secret Sharer," is that of Albert J. Guérard, *Conrad the Novelist* (Cambridge: Harvard University Press, 1958); but see also Dorothy Van Ghent, *The English Novel* (New York: Rinehart, 1953), pp. 229–244: "the story of Lord Jim is a spiritually fertilizing experience, enlightening the soul as to its own meaning in a time of disorganization and drought." Van Ghent's elaborate parallels with Sophocles necessarily lean on the second part of the novel for their evidence.

9. See for example Murray Krieger, *The Tragic Vision* (New York: Holt, Rinehart, & Winston, 1960).

10. Indeed, Conrad's work has been the occasion for major statements in two significant and specifically American forms of post-structuralism: *Nostromo* for Said's *Beginnings,* pp. 100–137; and *Lord Jim* for J. Hillis Miller's "The Interpretation of *Lord Jim,*" in Morton W. Bloomfield, *The Interpretation of Narrative* (Cambridge: Harvard University Press, 1970), pp. 211–228.

momentum already acquired, and that we should initially return to the problem of narrative totality and framing devices or strategies of containment developed in previous chapters, which may be expected to take on new and original forms in Conrad's work.

I

The privileged place of the strategy of containment in Conrad is the sea; yet the fact of the sea also allows us to weigh and appreciate the relative structural difference between the "nascent modernism" that we will observe in these texts and the more fully achieved and institutionalized modernisms of the canon. For the sea is both a strategy of containment and a place of real business: it is a border and a decorative limit, but it is also a highway, out of the world and in it at once, the repression of work—on the order of the classic English novel of the country-house weekend, in which human relations can be presented in all their ideal formal purity precisely because concrete content is relegated to the rest of the week—as well as the absent work-place itself.

So the sea is the place from which Jim can contemplate that dreary prose of the world which is daily life in the universal factory called capitalism:

> His station was in the fore-top, and often from there he looked down, with the contempt of a man destined to shine in the midst of dangers, at the peaceful multitude of roofs cut in two by the brown tide of the stream, while scattered on the outskirts of the surrounding plain the factory chimneys rose perpendicular against a grimy sky, each slender like a pencil, and belching out smoke like a volcano. [5] [11]

Jim's externality to this world, his absolute structural distance from it, can be measured by a process to which we will shortly return, namely the impulse of Conrad's sentences to transform such realities into impressions. These distant factory spires may be considered the equivalent for Jim and, in this novelistic project, for

11. Page references are given in the text to the following editions: *Lord Jim*, ed. T. Moser (New York: Norton, 1968); and *Nostromo* (Harmondsworth: Penguin, 1963).

Conrad, of the great Proustian glimpses of the steeples of Martin-
ville (with the one obvious qualification that the latter are already
sheer impression and need neither aesthetic transformation, nor the
Archimedean point of a structural externality, all the energy of
Proustian style now being invested in the meditation on the object
itself).

Two comments on this geographical strategy of containment
need to be made before we do justice to its historical ambiguity.
First of all, in a certain sense Jim tries to reverse one of Marx's
classical ideological models (the repetition in pure thought of concrete social situations) and to reenact in reality what his father
achieves symbolically, in speech and idea. His father's vocation, as
ideologue in the characteristic British class system (he is an Angli-
can parson), is carefully underscored in the paragraph that precedes
the one quoted above:

> Jim's father possessed such certain knowledge of the Unknowable as
> made for the righteousness of people in cottages without disturbing
> the ease of mind of those whom an unerring Providence enables to live
> in mansions. [4]

From our point of view, and from the logic of its insertion in
Conrad's text, this ideological function of religion is also to be
grasped in terms of containment and totality; the geographical vision of cottage, mansion, and "little church" (the place of the production of the ideology that harmonizes them) requires that neither
class position be able to focus or indeed to see the other. Jim's
method for living this geography, harmonized by ideological blindness, is an uncommon one: choosing a vocation such that he can
step completely outside all three class terrains and see them all
equally, from over a great distance, as so much picturesque landscape.

Yet if Jim's choice of the sea as space and as vocation is a kind of
unconscious denunciation of ideology by way of its enactment and
its reversal, it is no less dependent for its realization on a rather
different level of ideological production, namely, that of the aesthetic. We must, indeed, carefully stress, as does Conrad in these
preparatory pages, Jim's *bovarysme,* the relationship between

his work and the "course of light holiday literature" that first suggests it to him:

> On the lower deck in the babel of two hundred voices he would forget himself, and beforehand live in his mind the sea-life of light literature. He saw himself saving people from sinking ships, cutting away masts in a hurricane, swimming through a surf with a line; or as a lonely castaway, barefooted and half-naked, walking on uncovered reefs in search of shell-fish to stave off starvation. He confronted savages on tropical shores, quelled mutinies on the high seas, and in a small boat upon the ocean kept up the hearts of despairing men—always an example of devotion to duty, and as unflinching as a hero in a book. [5]

Nowhere in Conrad are the Flaubertian accents stronger than in such a passage, which reproduces at a lower level of verbal intensity the great cadences of the Flaubertian lyric illusion, as in Emma's youthful dreams of romance, or even Félicité's musings about the outside world. We must indeed take Conrad seriously when he tells us that the only thing that interested him in Flaubert was the latter's style.[12] Yet precisely here we have not only the transition from the naive naming of the outside world in realism to the presentation of the image, a transition to modernism and impressionism which is itself dependent on the very ideology of the image and sense perception and the whole positivist pseudo-scientific myth of the functioning of the mind and the senses; we also have a preselection of narrative material such that thought can be fully realized in images, that is to say, a rejection of the conceptual in favor of the two great naturalist psychic and narrative texts of daydreaming and hallucination. Where Conrad marks an "advance," if that is the right term

12. "You say that I have been under the formative influence of *Madame Bovary.* In fact, I read it only after finishing *Almayer's Folly,* as I did all the other works of Flaubert, and anyhow, my Flaubert is the Flaubert of *St. Antoine* and *Education sentimentale,* and that only from the point of view of the rendering of concrete things and visual impressions. I thought him marvelous in that respect. I don't think I learned anything from him. What he did for me was to open my eyes and arouse my emulation. One can learn from Balzac, but what could one learn from Flaubert? He compels admiration—about the greatest service one artist can render to another." Letter to H. Walpole, June 7, 1918, in G. Jean-Aubry, *Joseph Conrad. Life and Letters* (New York: Doubleday, Page, 1927), II, 206.

to use about this historical process, is in his own mesmerization by such images and such daydreaming. *Madame Bovary* invented a register of impressionistic daydreaming in order then sharply to differentiate its own "realistic" language from the other, to use the first register of language as the object to be demystified by the second, to create a decoding machinery which does not have its object external to itself but present within the system—and a presence which is no longer merely abstract, in the form of the "illusions" and ideals of the Balzacian or Stendhalian heroes, but stylistic and molecular, of a piece with the text and the life of the individual sentences. The force of Flaubert lies in the nonrealization of the image—and this most poignantly at those moments, the endings of *La Tentation de Saint Antoine* and the various tales of the *Trois Contes,* when a regression to religious ideology seems to permit us to posit a *parole pleine* or full mystical and visionary experience. But the point we wish to develop about *Lord Jim* is that in the second half of the novel Conrad goes on to write precisely the romance here caricatured both by himself and, implicitly, by way of stylistic pastiche, by his great predecessor.

Thus the non-place of the sea is also the space of the degraded language of romance and daydream, of narrative commodity and the sheer distraction of "light literature." This is, however, only half the story, one pole of an ambiguity to whose objective tension we must now do justice. For the sea is the empty space between the concrete places of work and life; but it is also, just as surely, itself a place of work and the very element by which an imperial capitalism draws its scattered beachheads and outposts together, through which it slowly realizes its sometimes violent, sometimes silent and corrosive, penetration of the outlying precapitalist zones of the globe. Nor is the sea merely a place of business; it is also a place of labor, and clearly we will say nothing of consequence about the author of *The Nigger of the "Narcissus," Typhoon,* and *The End of the Tether* if we overlook the "realistic" presentation of working life at sea, of which all these narratives give a characteristic glimpse. Yet strategies of containment are not only modes of exclusion; they can also take the form of repression in some stricter Hegelian sense of the persistence of the older repressed content beneath the later formalized surface. Indeed, I have argued elsewhere that such vertical repression and layering or sedimentation is the dominant structure of the classical modernistic text.[13] In this respect, too, Conrad, as a merely emergent moment in such a strategy, has suggestive and emblematic things to show us, as witness the following supremely self-conscious art-sentence, whose Flaubertian triplication is a virtual allegory of manifest and latent levels in the text:

> Above the mass of sleepers, a faint and patient sigh at times floated, the exhalation of a troubled dream; and short metallic clangs bursting out suddenly in the depths of the ship, the harsh scrape of a shovel, the violent slam of a furnace-door, exploded brutally, as if the men handling the mysterious things below had their breasts full of fierce anger: while the slim high hull of the steamer went on evenly ahead, without a sway of her bare masts, cleaving continuously the great calm of the waters under the inaccessible serenity of the sky. [12]

Ideology, production, style: on the one hand the manifest level of the content of *Lord Jim*—the moral problem of the "sleepers"—which gives us to believe that the "subject" of this book is courage and cowardice, and which we are meant to interpret in ethical and existentializing terms; on the other, the final consumable verbal commodity—the vision of the ship—the transformation of all these realities into style and the work of what we will call the impressionistic strategy of modernism whose function is to derealize the content and make it available for consumption on some purely aesthetic level; while in between these two, the brief clang from the boiler room that drives the ship marking the presence beneath ideology and appearance of that labor which produces and reproduces the world itself, and which, like the attention of God in Berkeleyan idealism, sustains the whole fabric of reality continuously in being, as Marx reminded Feuerbach in one of the most dramatic perorations of *The German Ideology:*

> So it happens that in Manchester, for instance, Feuerbach sees only factories and machines, where a hundred years ago only spinning-wheels and weaving looms were to be seen, or in the Campagna di Roma he finds only pasture lands and swamps, where in the time of

13. "Modernism and Its Repressed: Robbe-Grillet as Anti-Colonialist," *Diacritics,* VI, No. 2 (Summer, 1976), pp. 7–14.

Augustus he would have found nothing but the vineyards and villas of Roman capitalists. Feuerbach speaks in particular of the perception of natural science; he mentions secrets which are disclosed only to the eye of the physicist and chemist; but where would natural science be without industry and commerce? Even this "pure" natural science is provided with an aim, as with its material, only through trade and industry, through the sensuous activity of men. So much is this activity, this unceasing sensuous labor and creation, this production, the foundation of the whole sensuous world as it now exists that, were it interrupted only for a year, Feuerbach would not only find an enormous change in the natural world, he would very soon find that the whole world of men and his own perceptive faculty, nay his own existence, were missing.[14]

So this ground bass of material production continues underneath the new formal structures of the modernist text, as indeed it could not but continue to do, yet conveniently muffled and intermittent, easy to ignore (or to rewrite in terms of the aesthetic, of sense perception, as here of the sounds and sonorous inscription of a reality you prefer not to conceptualize), its permanencies ultimately detectable only to the elaborate hermeneutic geiger counters of the political unconscious and the ideology of form.

This reality of production is, of course, at one with the intermittent vision of the sea's economic function, and with Conrad's unquestionable and acute sense of the nature and dynamics of imperialist penetration. We will shortly see how even awareness of this latter historical and economic type is "managed" in the text itself. As for the productive relationship of human beings to nature, I will argue that Conrad's consciousness of this ultimate building block of social reality (as well as of its class content under capitalism—the "fierce anger" of the muffled sounds) is systematically displaced in two different ways. The first is by a recoding of the human pole of the labor process in terms of the whole ideological myth of *ressentiment* outlined in our previous chapter. Indeed the narrative of *The Nigger of the "Narcissus,"* with its driving power and ideological passion, may in this respect be characterized as one long tirade against *ressentiment;* the work concludes with the

14. Karl Marx and Friedrich Engels, *The German Ideology* (Moscow: Progress, 1976), p. 46.

transformation of its villain, Donkin, the epitome of the *homme de ressentiment,* into a labor organizer (who "no doubt earns his living by discussing with filthy eloquence upon the right of labour to live"[15]). The other pole of the labor process, that nature which is its material object and substratum, is then strategically reorganized around one of great conceptual containment strategies of the day, one which we have come to call existentialism, and becomes the pretext for the production of a new metaphysic—a new myth about the "meaning" of life and the absurdity of human existence in the face of a malevolent Nature. These two strategies—*ressentiment* and existentializing metaphysics—allow Conrad to recontain his narrative and to rework it in melodramatic terms, in a subsystem of good and evil which now once again has villains and heroes. So it is no accident that Jim's first experience of the violence of the sea is at once coded for us in existential terms, the sea, the source of this mindless violence, becoming the great adversary of Man, in much the same way that Camus' vision of absurdity rewrites an essentially nonhuman nature into an anthropomorphic character, a vengeful God ("the first assassin, because he made us mortal"):

> Only once in all that time he had again the glimpse of the earnestness in the anger of the sea. That truth is not so often made apparent as people might think. There are many shades in the danger of adventures and gales, and it is only now and then that there appears on the face of facts a sinister violence of intention—that indefinable something which forces it upon the mind and the heart of a man, that this complication of accidents or these elemental furies are coming at him with a purpose of malice, with a strength beyond control, with an unbridled cruelty that means to tear out of him his hope and his fear, the pain of his fatigue and his longing for rest: which means to smash, to destroy, to annihilate all he has seen, known, loved, enjoyed, or hated; all that is priceless and necessary—the sunshine, the memories, the future,—which means to sweep the whole precious world utterly away from his sight by the simple and apalling act of taking his life. [7]

But if you believe this version of the text, this particular rewriting strategy by which Conrad means to seal off the textual process, then all the rest follows, and *Lord Jim* really becomes what it keeps

---

15. Joseph Conrad, *The Nigger of the "Narcissus," Typhoon and Other Stories* (Harmondsworth: Penguin, 1963), p. 143.

telling us it is, namely a tale of courage and cowardice, a moral story, and an object-lesson in the difficulties of constructing an existential hero. I will argue that this ostensible or manifest "theme" of the novel is no more to be taken at face value than is the dreamer's immediate waking sense of what the dream was about. Yet as this is a complex argument, which will ultimately be validated only by the rest of the present chapter, I will simply suggest, at this point, that our business as readers and critics of culture is to "estrange" this overt theme in a Brechtian way, and to ask ourselves why we should be expected to assume, in the midst of capitalism, that the aesthetic rehearsal of the problematics of a social value from a quite different mode of production—the feudal ideology of honor—should need no justification and should be expected to be of interest to us. Such a theme must mean *something else:* and this even if we choose to interpret its survival as an "uneven development," a nonsynchronous overlap in Conrad's own values and experience (feudal Poland, capitalist England).

At any rate, with the problematic of existentialism and the heroic confrontation with the malignant absurdity of Nature, we are obviously very far from that productive process with which we began; the capacity of the new strategy to displace unwanted realities thereby becomes clear. We will return to the strategic function of the ideology of *ressentiment* later on; for the moment one reflection may be in order about the paradoxical relationship between labor and that non-space, those places of strategic narrative containment (such as the sea) which are so essential in what the Frankfurt School called the "degradation" of mass culture (that is, the transformation of formerly realistic materials into repetitive diversions which offer no particular danger or resistance to the dominant system). The paradox lies in the relationship between the peculiarly unpleasant narrative raw materials of the sea—not only that of sheer physical exertion and exposure to the elements, but also that of isolation, sexual privation, and the like—and the daydreaming fantasies of the mass public, for whom such "diversions" are destined. Such paradoxes are not new in aesthetic theory (think, for instance, of the classic problem of the aesthetic pleasurability of tragedy, that is, of the starkest contemplation of death and of what crushes human life), but in consumer culture they take on a heightened significance. I think, for example, of that relatively late mass-cultural genre, the "space opera"; we would understand a great deal about the mechanics of mass culture and the ideological operation of this particular narrative form, if we could grasp the dynamics of that purely imaginative excitement and sense of adventure which readers derive from the contemplation of one of the most physically restrictive situations into which human beings can be thrust—if we could sense the intimate relationship between the libidinally gratifying experience of the reading of such texts and the unimaginably barren sensory privation which is their content and the "lived truth" of the experience of space flight. The intergalactic spaceship is, at any rate, an avatar of Conrad's merchant vessels, projected into a world that has long since been reorganized into a capitalist world system without empty places.

Analogous problems arise, therefore, wherever we choose to articulate the generic discontinuities in the text of *Lord Jim:* whether we understand its stylistic modernism as the repression of a more totalizing realism both expressed and recontained or managed within the narrative as a whole; or, on the contrary, register the emergence of something like the nascent mass-cultural discourse of a degraded romance from that quite different high-cultural or textual discourse of the *Patna* episode. As has been suggested in our discussion of genre in Chapter 2, the categories of periodization employed in such readings—troublesome indeed if we take them as exercises in linear diachrony where they seem to generate the usual unanswerable questions about the chronological establishment of this or that "break," this or that "emergence"—are meaningful only on condition we understand that they draw on a linear fiction or diachronic construct solely for the purpose of constructing a synchronic model of coexistence, nonsynchronous development, temporal overlay, the simultaneous presence within a concrete textual structure of what Raymond Williams calls "residual" and "emergent" or anticipatory discourses.[16]

Ultimately, however, the justification for this kind of deconstruction and reconstruction of the text of *Lord Jim* cannot be an immanent one, but derives from juxtaposition with the more fully achieved possibilities of *Nostromo* as a companion text: it is the new collective framework of this second novel, the explicitly socioeconomic terms of its narrative vision, and above all, the

16. Raymond Williams, *Marxism and Literature* (Oxford: Oxford University Press, 1977), pp. 121–127.

transformation of its strategies of containment from those still narrowly physical ones of the sea and its enclosed vessels to the later novel's national and political geography, which by contrast allow us, as we shall see, to formulate the structural limits of the earlier narrative experiment more concretely.

II

A case could be made for reading Conrad not as an early modernist, but rather an anticipation of that later and quite different thing we have come to call variously textuality, *écriture*, post-modernism, or schizophrenic writing. Certainly the first half of *Lord Jim* is one of the most breathtaking exercises in nonstop textual production that our literature has to show, a self-generating sequence of sentences for which narrative and narrator are mere pretexts, the realization of a mechanism of well-nigh random narrative free association, in which the aleatory and seemingly uncontrollable, unverifiable generation of new detail and new anecdotal material out of the old—all the while filling in the exposition, so that it ends up presenting the narrative content as exhaustively as any representational aesthetic—obeys a logic of its own, as yet unidentified in this text taken by itself, but which in the hindsight of the emergent textual aesthetic of our own time we can clearly see to be textuality born fully grown. On this view, then, Conrad would be so archaic, so regressive and old-fashioned, as to be at one and the same time post-modern, and more modern than any of his contemporaries. It is clear that to return from the primacy of the Jamesian narrative category of point of view to the older fiction of the storyteller and the storytelling situation is to express impatience with the objective yet ever intensifying alienation of the printed book, those bound and portable novels which "when they have been once written down ... are tumbled about anywhere among those who may or may not understand them, and know not to whom they should reply, to whom not: and, if they are maltreated or abused, they have no parent to protect them; and they cannot protect or defend themselves."[17] The representational fiction of a

17. Plato, *Phaedrus,* paragraph 275, trans. Benjamin Jowett, in *Dialogues* (New York: Random House, 1937). The most influential contemporary exegesis of this passage is that of Jacques Derrida, "La Pharmacie de Platon," in *La Dissémination* (Paris: Seuil, 1972), esp. pp. 164–179.

storytelling situation organized around Marlow marks the vain attempt to conjure back the older unity of the literary institution, to return to that older concrete social situation of which narrative transmission was but a part, and of which public and bard or storyteller are intrinsic (although not necessarily visible or immediately present) components: such literary institutions, once genuine or concrete forms of social relationships, have long since been blasted by the corrosive effects of market relations, and, like so many other traditional, organic, precapitalist institutions, systematically fragmented by that characteristic reorganizational process of capitalism which Weber described under the term *rationalization*. [18] The older, inherited ways of doing things are broken into their component parts and reorganized with a view to greater efficiency according to the instrumental dialectic of means and ends, a process that amounts to a virtual bracketing or suspension of the ends themselves and thus opens up the unlimited perspective of a complete instrumentalization of the world: cultural institutions could scarcely hope to resist this universal process, which sunders subject from object and structurally colonizes each separately, producing hierarchies of functions according to their technical use (thus, the quantifying, "rational" parts of the psyche are to be developed, indeed, overdeveloped, while the more archaic functions—the senses, or certain types of thinking—are allowed to vegetate in a kind of psychic backwater).

So the book or printed text is wrenched from its concrete position within a functioning social and communicational situation, and becomes a free-floating object, which, as Plato observes, "has the attitude of life, and yet if you ask it a question it preserves a solemn silence. . . . You would imagine that [such printed texts] had intelligence, but if you want to know anything and put a question to one of them, the speaker always gives one unvarying answer." [19] Flaubert is the privileged locus of this development, which the term

18. See, for instance, Max Weber, *The Theory of Social and Economic Organization*, trans. A. M. Henderson and Talcott Parsons (New York: Free Press, 1947). We have already noted the relationship between this concept and Lukács' notion of reification, which includes it (*History and Class Consciousness*, esp. pp. 83–110). The only properly materialistic regrounding of the phenomenon of rationalization, however, is that which reveals its functional relationship to the labor process (see Braverman, *Labor and Monopoly Capital*).

19. Plato, *Phaedrus*, paragraph 275.

reification in its strictest sense designates; and the depersonalization of the text, the laundering of authorial intervention, but also the disappearance from the horizon of its readership, which will become the *public introuvable* of modernism, are all so many features on which the process of reification feeds, using Flaubert's aesthetic vocation as its vehicle and mode of realization.

In such a situation, it is abundantly clear that the Jamesian invention of point of view (or better still, Henry James's codification of this already existing technique, his transformation of it into the most fundamental of narrative categories, and the development around it of a whole aesthetic) is a genuinely historical act. The subject having been by the logic of social development stripped from its textual object, the latter must now be constructed in such a way as to bear the place of the former within itself: the narrative becomes a tree-crashing sound that will remain *heard* even when the forest is empty, since its subject-pole, its organization by reception, is built into it. What is perhaps less well understood, even today, about the Jamesian aesthetic is the degree to which point of view is also part and parcel of a whole ideology. The current polemics about ego psychology, the various philosophies of the subject, the rising countervalue of psychic fragmentation with its counteraesthetic in the schizophrenic text, all these straws in the wind suggest a perspective from which the Jamesian operation, on the level of the construction of aesthetic discourse, may be grasped as part of the more general containment strategy of a late nineteenth-century bourgeoisie suffering from the aftereffects of reification. The fiction of the individual subject—so-called bourgeois individualism—had of course, always been a key functional element in the bourgeois cultural revolution, the reprogramming of individuals to the "freedom" and equality of sheer market equivalence. As this fiction becomes ever more difficult to sustain (or, to use the somewhat mythic terminology of the Frankfurt School, as the old "autonomy" of the bourgeois subject is increasingly lost under the effects of disintegration and fetishization), more desperate myths of the self are generated, many of which are still with us today. Jamesian point of view, which comes into being as a protest and a defense against reification, ends up furnishing a powerful ideological instrument in the perpetuation of an increasingly subjectivized and psychologized world, a world whose social vision is one of a thoroughgoing relativity of monads in coexistence and whose *ethos* is irony and neo-Freudian projection theory and adaptation-to-reality therapy. This is the context in which the remarkable transformation of Henry James from a minor nineteenth-century man of letters into the greatest American novelist of the 1950s may best be appreciated.

Now it may also be clearer why Conrad's historical place in this development is an unsettled one: to revive the old-fashioned presence of authorial intervention, even *within* the text, as nostalgic representation rather than Victorian mannerism is to propose an impossible solution, whose enabling condition is the ambiguous situation of merchant service and the profession of the sea. Meanwhile, Conrad's elaborate narrative hermeneutic—what really did happen? who knows it all? what impressions do people have who possess only this piece of the puzzle, or that one?—tends to reinforce and supply powerful narrative demonstrations of just that ideology of the relativity of the individual monads evoked above (indeed, when, as in *Chance,* Conrad tries for a "mainstream" subject, the result is a mediocre imitation of James, just as Conrad's women tend to reproduce everything that is unsatisfactory about James's "female eunuchs" without any of the more splendid intensities of the latter's narrative discourse).

So there is a modernist Conrad who, far more easily than Ford, may be rewritten as second-rate Henry James. But there were also other objective tendencies in the great narrative and aesthetic dilemmas of high capitalism which do not develop in the direction of the Jamesian solution: indeed, point of view is not nearly so stable a part of Flaubert's narrative practice as has been supposed, while even the uses of classical point of view in Flaubert sometimes generate a quite different problematic from what we find in James. I am thinking particularly of Jean Rousset's comment about Flaubert's art as one of transitions:[20] here there is a fundamental displacement, and what is essential to the production of the text is not, as in James, the construction of a central observational and psychic perspective within which one may for a time remain, but rather the quite different matter of inventing modulations, chromatic bridge-passages, cinematographic fadeouts or montages, which allow us to

20. Jean Rousset, *Forme et signification* (Paris: Corti, 1963), pp. 117–122.

slip from one point of view to another. Take this tendency of Flaubertian narrative and enlarge it photographically until its grain
becomes visible; a wholly new narrative texture appears, and you
have that new surface which is the first half of *Lord Jim, écriture*
that, approaching its narrative presence, its anecdotal center, at
once denies the possibility of such presence and spills us over into
yet further sentence production and the further frustration of presence affirmed and denied. Yet this texture is not post-modern
either, insofar as the content projected by this free play of sentences
on the ideological level turns out, as we shall see, to be the now
more traditional existential one: to search for narrative plenitude,
narrative presence, is essentially to seek the unity of the act, or
analytically to call it into question.

   The mechanics of this particular process of textualization (there
are many other kinds) can perhaps best be described in terms of that
narrative logic of the aleatory and the accidental which, in this
respect at least, Conrad shares with the Bloomsbury group and even
Joyce. Its free play is assured by the initial fragmentation of the raw
material, which allows a relative independence between foreground
and background, a kind of coexistence between the radically different and even distinct materials of the narrative moment in question. When these are suddenly rearranged in such a way as to stand
in a relationship of textual generation to one another, there is a
shock like that of Althusserian overdetermination: so the members
of the village family whose trial precedes Jim's own hearing have
nothing whatsoever to do with his plight, yet their dog serves as the
narrative bridge to the meeting with Marlow (Jim imagines that the
remark "Look at that wretched cur" refers to him: p. 43). In
such structural readjustment what was secondary and inessential in
one moment becomes the center and the dominant, the figure
against the ground, in the next. It is well known how the
Bloomsbury writers, especially Forster and Woolf, made of this
difficult aesthetic principle—difficult because it is the planned opposite of the throw-away; the detail must at first not only seem but
actually be utterly insignificant—a whole effect of pathos and even,
perhaps, an ethic: secondary characters who are really the heroes of
the narrative, apparent main characters who suddenly die, and so
forth. In Conrad, however, not only is this principle more openly a
generative one (thus, the central figure of Marlow himself is con-

jured up by Jim's gaze around the courtroom: p. 20)[21]; it is also linguistically diversified by the use of modalities, as we will later see in *Nostromo,* where not merely the secondary placement of the detail but also, especially, its mode—as example, optative, conditional, or whatever—operates the initial "accidentalization" on which the textual reversal is predicated.

From the perspective of language, however, this self-generation of the text translates itself as the boiling emergence and disappearance of so many transitory centers, now no longer points of view so much as sources of language: each new detail, each new perspective on the anecdote, brings into being, as the very center of its whirlpool, another new speaker, himself for the moment the transitory center of a narrative interest which will quickly sweep him away again. Thus it becomes a little clearer how what is archaic in Conrad could overleap the now classical Jamesian moment and become post-modernist. If the multiple narrative shifts in Conrad are to be seen as textbook exercises in point of view, then we must add something which changes everything: they are point of view conceived as being inseparable from speech, from the materiality of language.[22] In this historical and dialectical reversal, Conrad's yarn-spinning becomes the epitome of a thinking which has discovered the symbolic; James, on the other hand, if he manifests, along with other modernisms, a powerful practice of the symbolic and of linguistic invention, is still theoretically locked into nonsymbolic, essentially "expressive" categories. For him, point of view is still a psychological matter, a matter of consciousness; but the discovery of the symbolic in its widest sense (all the way from Saussure to semiotics, or from Wittgenstein to Whorf on the one hand and Derrida on the other) is the sheerest repudiation of just such notions as "consciousness" and "psychology."

III

Yet Conrad is also a late nineteenth-century novelist, and that in a rather different way than has yet been touched on. The affiliations of this particular Conrad are less with Henry James than they are

21. An interesting analogy is presented by that moment in the trial scene in Camus' *L'Etranger* in which Meursault's gaze conjures up the ideal witness in the person of the young journalist Albert Camus himself.

22. On the dialectic between speech and writing in Conrad, see Edward Said, "Conrad: The Presentation of Narrative," *Novel,* 7 (Winter, 1974), 116–132.

with Proust, and from this perspective his debt to Flaubert becomes equally modified, the relevant texts now being those that practice that hallucinatory imagery in which the positivist theory of perception was anticipated and legitimized *avant la lettre*. What must be stressed here is the intimate dialectical relationship between this properly positivist ideology of the sense datum and the accompanying notion of "consciousness"—a scientific or pseudoscientific theory which is ideological to the degree to which it projects a whole conception of subject-object relations, a whole vision of "human nature" which cannot but be a whole politics and philosophy of history as well—as well as a whole aesthetic movement ordinarily thought to be in opposition to it (and in fact profoundly antipositivist in spirit), namely impressionism. I will argue, on the one hand, that both positivism as ideological production and impressionism as aesthetic production are first to be understood in terms of the concrete situation to which they are both responses: that of rationalization and reification in late nineteenth-century capitalism. On the other, I want to show that Conrad may best be situated historically if we understand his practice of style as a literary and textual equivalent of the impressionist strategy in painting (hence his kinship with the greatest of all literary impressionists, Proust). But these assertions will be useful only to the degree to which we understand that the impressionistic strategy, although the dominant one for classical modernism, is only one of those structurally available to the modernists (the much rarer expressionism is another): to understand stylistic production this way is to free ourselves from the monotony of the formal history projected by the ideology of modernism itself (each new style is a break with the past, the history of styles is simply the sum total of all of these radical changes and innovations), and to substitute for it the possibility of reading a given style as a projected solution, on the aesthetic or imaginary level, to a genuinely contradictory situation in the concrete world of everyday social life.

To read Conrad's "will to style" as a socially symbolic act involves the practice of *mediation*, an operation that we have already characterized (in Chapter 1) as the invention of an analytic terminology or code which can be applied equally to two or more structurally distinct objects or sectors of being. As we there argued, it is not necessary that these analyses be homologous, that is, that each of the objects in question be seen as doing the same thing, having the same structure or emitting the same message. What is crucial is that, by being able to use the same language about each of these quite distinct objects or levels of an object, we can restore, at least methodologically, the lost unity of social life, and demonstrate that widely distant elements of the social totality are ultimately part of the same global historical process.

In the present case, this means the invention of a description of Conrad's stylistic practice (and of that of impressionist painting) which is adequate in its own terms and does justice to the autonomy or semi-autonomy of aesthetic language, but which at the same time, by articulating the description of a quite different type of reality—in the event, the organization and experience of daily life during the imperialist heyday of industrial capitalism—allows us to think these two distinct realities together in a meaningful way (causality, long the scarecrow used to frighten people away from social mediations of this kind, being only one of the possible meanings, only one of the possible relations that can obtain between such distinct terms).

It has no doubt already become clear to the reader that the mediatory code I have found most useful here is that variously termed rationalization by Weber and reification by Lukács. Yet the reader should also be reminded that Marxism knows a number of other such mediatory codes, the most obvious ones being social class, mode of production, the alienation of labor, commodification, the various ideologies of Otherness (sex or race), and political domination. The strategic selection of reification as a code for the reading and interpretation of Conrad's style does not constitute the choice of one kind of Marxism (let us say, a Lukácsean one) over others, but is instead an option open to all intelligent Marxisms and part of the richness of the Marxian system itself.

This said, it remains to show how the language of reification and rationalization, whose applicability to the increasing standardization of capitalist daily life has already been argued, can be useful for an account of style, either literary or pictorial. We must indeed at once place some distance between our own use of the concept and that to be found in Lukács' various later accounts of modernism,[23]

23. For example, "Healthy or Sick Art?" and "Narrate or Describe?" in Georg Lukács, *Writer and Critic,* trans. A. D. Kahn (New York: Grosset & Dunlap, 1970), as well as the more measured *Realism in Our Time.*

in which the term reification is simple shorthand for value judgment and for the repudiation by association of the various modern styles. Yet Lukács was not wrong to make the connection between modernism and the reification of daily life: his mistake was to have done so ahistorically and to have made his analysis the occasion for an ethical judgment rather than a historical perception. As we shall see shortly, even the terms of the judgment—progressive or reactionary—are not wrong, provided they lead to an ever greater sense of the complexity and dialectical ambivalence of history, rather than to its dogmatic simplification.

We have suggested that the rationalization process is first and foremost to be described as the analytical dismantling of the various traditional or "natural" [*naturwüchsige*] unities (social groups, institutions, human relationships, forms of authority, activities of a cultural and ideological as well as of a productive nature) into their component parts with a view to their "Taylorization," that is, their reorganization into more efficient systems which function according to an instrumental, or binary, means/ends logic. We have also touched on the loss inherent in this process, the wholesale dissolution of traditional institutions and social relations beginning in the heartland of capitalism (see Thomas More on enclosure) and ultimately extending to the last vestiges of precapitalist social relations in the most seemingly insignificant backwaters of the globe—which our first text designates as the village of Patusan, while the later novel tries more consequently to think this process in terms of the whole region of Costaguana. It should be stressed that the destructive effects of capitalism, both irreversible and fatal to the older social forms, are not particularly due to conscious planning on the part of the businessmen, who are neither personally wicked nor, in the earlier stages of this process at least, self-conscious efficiency experts. Rather the process is objective, and is impersonally achieved, or at least set in motion, by the penetration of a money economy and the consequent need to reorganize local institutions on a cash basis (that feature of the process nostalgically yet progressively underscored by Balzac in his pictures of a country aristocracy undermined by market relations).

What we have not yet pointed out, however, and what is crucial for the mediatory analysis we want to undertake of the relations between reification and style, is the existence of a third term: one that is neither the old institution or *Gemeinschaft*[24] nor the new mechanical and instrumental system which replaces it, but is constituted by the by-products and secondary formations thrown off in the course of the transition. The chemical analogy, indeed, suggests that there are few enough molecular transformations which are not accompanied by secondary waste materials of one kind or another. The terminology of fragmentation suggests an alternate formulation, in which the systematic analysis and segmentation of the older unities is accompanied by the increasing autonomization, or at least semi-autonomy, of the newly emergent constituent parts. Thus, to pursue our previous illustration of the division of labor at work within the psyche (Adam Smith and Schiller are no doubt the first great theorists of this historical event), the "rational," quantifying functions of the mind become privileged in such a way as to take structural precedence over older functions, a new form of unequal development being thereby perpetuated in which "technological advances" in the former (for example, the reproduction and development of particular kinds of scientific mentalities) go hand in hand with the systematic underdevelopment of archaic mental powers (the repression of the aesthetic in the industrializing United States and the related repression of the culinary senses, of what might be called the gastronomical libido, in Britain and the United States are obvious examples). What we must now underscore is the way in which each of these regions of the mind tends to go its own way, become semi-autonomous, and follow its own type of historical development. Thus the autonomization of the quantifying functions permits an immense leap in the production of new kinds of formalization and is the precondition for the coming into existence of hitherto unimaginable levels of abstraction. More important in the present context, the same is true of what we have been

24. The ideology ascribed to Conrad in Avrom Fleischman, *Conrad's Politics* (Baltimore: Johns Hopkins University Press, 1967), p. 48: "skeptical of the exclusive rightness of any ideology or class but unstinting in the hope that they may complement each other in a unified whole—the organic community of the nation," is from the Marxist perspective a most ambiguous one indeed. It will become clear below that we cannot accept Raymond Williams' analogous reading of *Nostromo* either: "What has happened is the disappearance of a *social* value" (Williams, *The English Novel from Dickens to Lawrence* [London: Chatto & Windus, 1970], p. 150). The paradox of *Nostromo* is that we are given to witness a *fall* without there having ever been any Eden to begin with.

terming the noninstrumental or archaic functions of the psyche, most notably here the senses themselves, and in particular the sense of sight.

The scandalous idea that the senses have a history is, as Marx once remarked, one of the touchstones of our own historicity;[25] if, in spite of our thoughts about history, we still feel that the Greeks, or better still, that primitive peoples, were very much like ourselves and in particular lived their bodies and their senses in the same way, then we have surely not made much progress in thinking historically. In the case of sight, it ought to be possible to understand how the deperceptualization of the sciences—the break with such perceptual pseudosciences as alchemy, for example, the Cartesian distinction between primary and secondary senses, and the geometrization of science more generally, which substitutes ideal quantities for physically perceivable objects of study—is accompanied by a release in perceptual energies. The very activity of sense perception has nowhere to go in a world in which science deals with ideal quantities, and comes to have little enough exchange value in a money economy dominated by considerations of calculation, measurement, profit, and the like. This unused surplus capacity of sense perception can only reorganize itself into a new and semi-autonomous activity, one which produces its own specific objects, new objects that are themselves the result of a process of abstraction and reification, such that older concrete unities are now sundered into measurable dimensions on one side, say, and pure color (or the experience of purely abstract color) on the other. To such a process, the Althusserian term *overdetermination* may be properly applied, insofar as an objective fragmentation of the so-called outside world is matched and accompanied by a fragmentation of the psyche which reinforces its effects. Such fragmentation, reification, but also production, of new semi-autonomous objects and activities, is clearly the objective precondition for the emergence of genres such as landscape, in which the viewing of an otherwise (or at least a traditionally) meaningless object—nature without people—comes to seem a self-justifying activity. An even more pertinent example is a style like Impressionism, which discards even the operative fiction of some interest in the constituted objects of the natural world, and

25. See Chapter 1, note 41.

offers the exercise of perception and the perceptual recombination of sense data as an end in itself.

This, then, is my justification in characterizing Conrad's stylistic production as an *aestheticizing strategy:* the term is not meant as moral or political castigation, but is rather to be taken literally, as the designation of a strategy which for whatever reason seeks to recode or rewrite the world and its own data in terms of perception as a semi-autonomous activity. We have already witnessed this process at work in a key place, namely in the sentence that articulated the infrastructure of ship and text—the boiler room—in the language of the sense of hearing, thereby secretly unraveling the very designation of an infrastructure by absorbing it into the final term of the tripartite passage, into the realm of the image, thereby transforming it into an art-commodity which one consumes by way of its own dynamic, that is, by "perceiving" it as image and as sense datum.

At its most intense, indeed, what we will call Conrad's sensorium virtually remakes its objects, refracting them through the totalized medium of a single sense, and more than that, of a single "lighting" or coloration of that sense. The possibility of this kind of sensory abstraction is, to be sure, at first given in the object—the unearthliness of the sea—but then returns upon that object to remake it anew as something never dreamed on heaven or earth. Anyone who doubts the Utopian vocation of Conrad's style at these extreme moments of intensity has only to reread passages such as the following description of the oncoming storm in *Typhoon:*

> At its setting the sun had a diminished diameter and an expiring brown, rayless glow, as if millions of centuries elapsing since the morning had brought it near its end. A dense bank of cloud became visible to the northward; it had a sinister dark olive tint, and lay low and motionless upon the sea, resembling a solid obstacle in the path of the ship. She went floundering towards it like an exhausted creature driven to its death. . . . The far-off blackness ahead of the ship was like another night seen through the starry night of the earth—the starless night of the immensities beyond the created universe, revealed in its appalling stillness through a low fissure in the glittering sphere of which the earth is the kernel.[26]

26. Conrad, *Nigger,* pp. 168, 171.

Such passages virtually fashion a new space and a new perspective, a new sense of depth, out of sheer color, in that perhaps less like Western Impressionism than certain of its Slavic equivalents, in particular the work of the Ukrainian painter Kuindzhi. The operative presence of motifs from the late nineteenth-century positivist or Wellsian metaphysic of entropy (the diminished sun, the approaching end of the universe, the night of the cosmos beyond the night of the earth) is nonideological insofar as the conventional relationship between narrative and ideology is here reversed. In such "purer" descriptive passages, the function of the literary representation is not to underscore and perpetuate an ideological system; rather, the latter is cited to authorize and reinforce a new representational space. This reversal then draws ideology inside out like a glove, awakening an alien space beyond it, founding a new and strange heaven and earth upon its inverted lining. In that stealthy struggle between ideology and representation, each secretly trying to use and appropriate the other for its own designs and purposes, the ideological allegory of the ship as the civilized world on its way to doom is subverted by the unfamiliar sensorium, which, like some new planet in the night sky, suggests senses and forms of libidinal gratification as unimaginable to us as the possession of additional senses, or the presence of nonearthly colors in the spectrum.

Indeed, this strategy of aestheticization is at work precisely in that construction of point of view which Conrad seemed to share with James; yet it works to undermine the characteristic strategies of the Jamesian aesthetic in ways that better than any we have identified so far allow us to gauge the historic distance between these two kinds of texts. The secondary model which organizes Jamesian point of view is the metaphor and the ideal of theatrical representation. As in the development of perspective (itself the end product of a theatrical metaphor), the structural corollary of the point of view of the spectator is the unity of organization of the theatrical space and the theatrical scene; hence the obsessive repetition throughout the nineteenth-century novel of theatrical terms like "scene," "spectacle," and "tableau," which urge on the reader a theater-goer's position with respect to the content of the narrative. Such terms are also abundant in Conrad, yet they are reappropriated by the perceptual vocation of his style, which undermines the unity of the theatrical metaphor just as surely as would the attention of a deaf or foreign or schizophrenic visitor who had eyes only for the color combinations of this or that theatrical production. Conrad displaces the theatrical metaphor by transforming it into a matter of sense perception, into a virtually filmic experience: "all this happened in much less time than it takes to tell, since I am trying to interpret for you into slow speech the instantaneous effect of visual perceptions" (*Lord Jim*, 30); yet this is an ambition novelists before Flaubert at best conceived intermittently, and even then mediated by the theatrical category of the momentary tableau in which the novelist from time to time "surprised" his characters. The preface to the *Nigger of the "Narcissus,"* however, ("My task, which I am trying to achieve is, by the power of the written word to make you hear, to make you feel—it is, before all, to make you *see*. That—and no more, and it is everything"), is not a defense of the dramatic, nor even of Jamesian "rendering"; it is the declaration of independence of the image as such.[27]

So far, we have tended to separate our presentation of the subject and the object of rationalization, thereby suggesting that one can distinguish between the autonomization of sight, the new ideology of the image, on the one hand, and the objective fragmentation of the outside world, or of the objects of perception, on the other. But these two phenomena are rigorously identical: in order to be read or seen *qua* image, to be grasped as a symbolic act which is image-production, or, following Sartre's account, derealization,[28] such

---

27. See for an exegesis of this Preface, Ian Watt, *Conrad in the Nineteenth Century*, pp. 76–88.

28. "There can thus be a causality of the imaginary. Nothingness can, without ceasing to be nothingness, produce real effects. In that case, why not generalize the derealizing attitude? . . . [Genet] wants to draw the real into the imaginary and to drown it there. The dreamer must contaminate others by his dream, he must make them fall into it: if he is to act upon Others, he must do so like a virus, like an agent of derealization. . . . Time is inverted: the blow of the hammer is not given in-order-to-put-up-the-merry-go-round, but the fair, the future earnings on which the owner is counting, the merry-go-round, all exist only in order to bring about the blow of the hammer; the future and the past are given at the same time in order to produce the present. This regressive time and the progressive time which Genet continues to live suddenly interfere, Genet lives in eternity. Meanwhile, the booths, the houses, the ground, everything becomes a setting: in an outdoor theater, as soon as the actors appear the trees are cardboard, the sky changes into painted canvas. In being transformed into a gesture, the act all at once drags the enormous mass of being along with itself into the unreal" (J.-P. Sartre, *Saint Genet*, trans. Bernard Frechtman [New York: New American Library, 1963], pp. 368–369, 375–376).

transformations of the world into images must always be marked as the reunification of data which were originally chaotic or fragmentary. Both terms of the act, the initial raw material and the final glossy reunified and perceptual product, must be present within the image:

> There was, as I walked along, the clear sunshine, a brilliance too passionate to be consoling, the streets full of jumbled bits of color like a damaged kaleidoscope: yellow, green, blue, dazzling white, the brown nudity of an undraped shoulder, a bullock-cart with a red canopy, a company of native infantry in a drab body with dark heads marching in dusty laced boots, a native policeman in a sombre uniform of scanty cut and belted in patent leather. [96]

In one sense, the "damaged kaleidoscope" of this image is the miniaturization of the larger process of text-production at the level of the plot; or the other way round, the latter may be seen as the projection on the level of plot of this molecular, microscopic production of style at the level of the individual sentences. What it is important to stress is that the relationship between these two levels is not some mere static homology; they must rather be understood as two independent branches of the same general process. The larger fragmentation and reconstitution of events will be dealt with in later sections of this chapter; as for the present experience, which is something like the dissociation of meaning and intellection from the immediate and sensory, Nietzsche is no doubt the first to have lived fully what Barthes generalizes as the dominant feature of the experience of the modern *par excellence*:

> The pure and simple "representation" of the "real," the naked account of "what is" (or what has been), thus proves to resist meaning; such resistance reconfirms the great mythic opposition between the *vécu* [the experiential, or "lived experience"] (or the living) and the intelligible; we have only to recall how, in the ideology of our time, the obsessional evocation of the "concrete" (in what we rhetorically demand of the human sciences, of literature, of social practices) is always staged as an aggressive arm against meaning, as though, by some *de jure* exclusion, what lives is structurally incapable of carrying a meaning—and vice versa.[29]

29. Roland Barthes, "L'Effet de réel," *Communications*, No. 11 (1968), p. 87.

The problem with such a description is the same as the one we have with later Lukács: and indeed each "diagnosis" is the other's inversion and dialectical mirror-image. Both, indeed, read the cultural experience of the image (or any of the other forms taken by the dissociation of sense-datum and meaning in contemporary aesthetic discourse) as the mere reflection of modern "infrastructural" reality; only where the Barthes-Nietzsche position stresses the lucidity with which the contemporary writer lives and comes to terms with this particular situation (about which it is not clear whether they see it in historical terms, as is the case with the analogous split between life and essence, *Leben* and *Wesen*, in Lukács' *Theory of the Novel*, or rather interpret it in existential fashion as the very bedrock of existence), the Lukács of the essays on realism castigates this modern aesthetic discourse as the reinforcement of the experience thereby expressed (reification), proposing instead a voluntaristic substitution of a kind of aesthetic discourse(progressive or critical realism) whose merit presumably lies in the fact that it does *not* reflect or express the phenomenology of daily life under capitalism.

It is clear that the work of art cannot itself be asked to change the world or to transform itself into political praxis; on the other hand, it would be desirable to develop a keener sense of the complexity and ambiguity of that process loosely termed reflection or expression. To think dialectically about such a process means to invent a thought which goes "beyond good and evil" not by abolishing these qualifications or judgments but by understanding their interrelationship. Briefly, we can suggest that, as Nietzsche taught us, the judgmental habit of ethical thinking, of ranging everything in the antagonistic categories of good and evil (or their other binary equivalents), is not merely an error but is objectively rooted in the inevitable and inescapable centeredness of every individual consciousness or individual subject: what is good is what belongs to me, what is bad is what belongs to the Other (or any dialectical variation on this nondialectical opposition: for example, Nietzsche showed that Christian charity—what is good is what is associated with the Other—is a simple structural variant of the first opposition). The Nietzschean solution to this constitutional ethical habit of the individual subject—the Eternal Return—is for most of us both intolerable in its rigor and unconvincingly ingenious in the prestidigitation with which it desperately squares its circle. What is less well understood is that the dialectic also addresses itself to this same issue, and proposes a rather different stance (this time, outside the subject in the transindividual, or in other words in History) from which to transcend the double bind of the merely ethical. The modernism debate is an excellent occasion for demonstrating this vocation of dialectical thinking and the originality with which it historicizes ethical categories, categories of the individual subject.

Clearly, notions such as "progressive" and "regressive" are simply ethical categories projected onto political and historical phenomena:[30] in classical Marxism (but also in Hegel), these categories are maintained but fused into a wholly new order of thinking by the concept of historical inevitability. Thus, in the *Communist Manifesto*, Marx showed that the historically revolutionary role of the bourgeoisie (which "during its rule of scarce one hundred years has created more massive and more colossal productive forces than have all preceding generations together"[31]) is at one with a whole catalogue of desolations that range from the destruction of older social forms to the degradation of the values and activities of individuals and their transformation into sheer exchange value. To think dialectically is to invent a space from which to think these two identical yet antagonistic features together all at once: in that, dialectical thinking is related to tragic thought, or better still, it is the latter's collective and "comic" inversion.

In the present context of cultural analysis, I would propose to identify these twin negative and positive features of a given phenomenon—what in the realm of political forces Marxism traditionally terms reactionary and progressive—by the terms "ideological" and "Utopian," it being understood that the word

---

30. See, for a persuasive attempt to read the novel as a critique of imperialism, Stephen Zelnick, "Conrad's *Lord Jim:* Meditations on the Other Hemisphere," *Minnesota Review* No. 11 (Fall, 1978), pp. 73–89. I am indebted to Zelnick's paper, presented at the First Summer Institute of the Marxist Literary Group in St. Cloud, Minnesota, July–August 1977, for stimulating the formulations of the present chapter. I will explain in the Conclusion why it seems to me that any effort of Marxist criticism to articulate the "progressive" content of a classical work—as Zelnick's article does—needs to be accompanied by a reminder of what is essentially "reactionary" about it, as so much in Conrad unquestionably is. (As a more general principle, this may be applied to Fleishman and even to some of Raymond Williams' interpretations; see above, note 24.)

31. Marx and Engels, *Communist Manifesto*, in *On revolution*, ed. Padover, p. 83.

"ideology" is here being used in its most restricted and pejorative sense (it can have others), while the term "Utopian" is intended in Ernst Bloch's fashion to resonate a Marxist perspective on the future rather than the pre-Marxian one denounced by Engels and Marx in so-called Utopian socialism.[32]

That modernism is itself an ideological expression of capitalism, and in particular, of the latter's reification of daily life, may be granted a local validity. It has at least been possible to show that the objective preconditions of Conrad's modernism are to be found in the increasing fragmentation both of the rationalized external world and of the colonized psyche alike. And surely, there is a sense in which such faithful "expression" of the underlying logic of the daily life of capitalism programs us to it and helps to make us increasingly at home in what would otherwise—for a time traveler from another social formation—be a distressingly alienating reality. Viewed in this way, then, modernism can be seen as a late stage in the bourgeois cultural revolution, as a final and extremely specialized phase of that immense process of superstructural transformation whereby the inhabitants of older social formations are culturally and psychologically retrained for life in the market system.

Yet modernism can at one and the same time be read as a Utopian compensation for everything reification brings with it. We stressed the semi-autonomy of the fragmented senses, the new autonomy and intrinsic logic of their henceforth abstract objects such as color or pure sound; but it is precisely this new semi-autonomy and the presence of these waste products of capitalist rationalization that open up a life space in which the opposite and the negation of such rationalization can be, at least imaginatively, experienced. The increasing abstraction of visual art thus proves not only to express the abstraction of daily life and to presuppose fragmentation and reification; it also constitutes a Utopian compensation for everything lost in the process of the development of capitalism—the place of quality in an increasingly quantified world, the place of the archaic and of feeling amid the desacralization of the market sys-

32. See below, Conclusion. I have hoped, here and elsewhere, that the quite unintended and inapplicable resonance of Mannheim's use of this formula will have faded by now from most readers' minds.

tem, the place of sheer color and intensity within the grayness of measurable extension and geometrical abstraction. The perceptual is in this sense a historically new experience, which has no equivalent in older kinds of social life. Meanwhile this vocation of the perceptual, its Utopian mission as the libidinal transformation of an increasingly dessicated and repressive reality, undergoes a final political mutation in the countercultural movements of the 1960s (at which point the ambiguity of the impulse also becomes more pronounced, and the reminder of the accompanying "ideological" value of the perceptual as the expression of psychic fragmentation is once more politically timely). Our present concern is to respect the ambivalent value of Conrad's impressionism, that ambiguity at the very heart of his will to style which alone makes it a complex and interesting historical act, and ensures it a vitality outside the cultural museum. Seen as ideology and Utopia all at once, Conrad's stylistic practice can be grasped as a symbolic act which, seizing on the Real in all of its reified resistance, at one and the same time projects a unique sensorium of its own, a libidinal resonance no doubt historically determinate, yet whose ultimate ambiguity lies in its attempt to stand beyond history.

In arguing for this particular historical and historicizing "reading" of Conrad's style, we have perhaps implied that he is himself unaware of the symbolic social value of his verbal practice. If so, this is an error which we must now correct, for it is certain that— whatever the thoughts and awarenesses of the biographical Conrad—a reflexivity, a self-consciousness of the nature of this symbolic process, is inscribed in the text itself, and most strikingly in *Lord Jim*. This is, indeed, the meaning of the character of Stein, inserted strategically, as one of Jim's series of father figures, between the great bravura unfolding of the *Patna* story and the later romantic adventure in Patusan, where Stein has influence and interests, and where he is able to install the stigmatized Jim, thereby giving him a final chance with destiny.

Stein is thus a pivotal figure from the narrative point of view; but I would argue that this particular plot function is itself merely a figure of a quite different value, and a way of framing the character of Stein in such a way as to make that second or emblematic value momentarily visible to us. The story of Stein, indeed, is the story of the passing of the heroic age of capitalist expansion; it marks the end of the era when individual entrepreneurs were giants, and the setting in place of the worldwide institutions of capitalism in its monopoly stage. Conrad will tell this particular story again; indeed, I will shortly try to show that it is the informing center of *Nostromo* as well. For the moment, however, it is enough to invoke characteristic late nineteenth-century terms like individualism and heroism to understand why such a situation should have fascinated Conrad (who brought his own particular historical "uneven development" and his background as a Pole and a Russian subject to this exploration of the British business empire).

What is of interest to us is, however, not only the symptomatic break in Stein's career—the high adventure of heroic colonialism succeeded by the sedate vocation of the ever more prosperous merchant—but also and in particular the compensatory formation that accompanies such a change of life. For Stein becomes a butterfly collector, that is to say, essentially a collector of images; and the serene melancholy of the collector's passion is surely here to be taken as the same gesture of renunciation, the same withdrawal from life and repudiation of the world that, in *The Hidden God*, Lucien Goldmann has shown to be the symbolic meaning of the invention of Jansenism by that whole class-fraction which was the seventeenth-century *noblesse de robe*:

> I respected the intense, almost passionate absorption with which he looked at a butterfly, as though on the bronze sheen of these frail wings, in the white tracings, in the gorgeous markings, he could see other things, an image of something as perishable and defying destruction as these delicate and lifeless tissues displaying a splendor unmarred by death. [126]

For us, however, the thematics of "death" and the rhetoric of mortality is here but a disguise for the sharper pain of exclusion by history, just as the passion for butterfly collecting must be read as the fable and the allegory of the ideology of the image, and of Conrad's own passionate choice of impressionism—the vocation to arrest the living raw material of life, and by wrenching it from the historical situation in which alone its change is meaningful, to preserve it, beyond time, in the imaginary.

Yet ultimately, it seems to me, Conrad's text, if not the biographical Conrad himself, is aware even of this, the very origins of its own stylistic passion. To suggest this awareness, and to conclude this particular theme of our argument, before we deal with *Lord Jim* on the narrative level, we will anticipate our discussion of that later book in which the historical content and narrative framework of the earlier novel is so decisively enlarged. The question of impressionism is, indeed, the only context in which properly to appreciate a modification, perhaps even a decisive evolution in *Nostromo,* of what we have called Conrad's sensorium. We have hitherto spoken of the senses as the medium through which reality became image, the terms into which the broken data and reified fragments of a quantified world were libidinally transcoded and Utopianly transfigured. Now for the first time the senses become foregrounded as a theme in their own right, as content rather than as form. Nor is it an accident that in *Nostromo*—a text, incidentally, from which the underpinning of a Marlow figure, the story-telling infrastructure, has been removed—the earlier commitment to the visual ("above all, to make you *see*") has given way to the primacy of that "most abstract of all the senses," as Adorno called the auditory.

Nostromo is a textual apparatus for registering auditory perceptions of a peculiarly pure type: so the British railway executive arrives "too late to hear the magnificent and inaudible strain sung by the sunset amongst the high peaks of the Sierra":

> In the transparent air of the high altitudes everything seemed very near, steeped in a clear stillness as in an imponderable liquid; and with his ear ready to catch the first sound of the expected *diligencia* the engineer-in-chief, at the door of a hut of rough stones, had contemplated the changing hues on the enormous side of the mountain, thinking that in this sight, as in a piece of inspired music, there could be found together the utmost delicacy of shaded expression and a stupendous magnificence of effect. [45]

If such rhetorical efforts seem unacceptable to the dispassionate reader, this is scarcely a matter of Conrad's talent, but rather directly attributable to the inner drama of this sentence, in which the fully developed and now passively inherited apparatus of a purely visual impressionism is contested and undermined by the new ideal of an auditory image, which ruins its stylistic antagonist while remaining itself ("a piece of inspired music") an unrealized dead letter.

Even more striking is the interference of this level of the style in climactic narrative moments of the text. I am thinking, for instance, of Charles Gould's proposal, in the classical Tuscan landscape, at the moment he receives the news of his father's death:

> And then they stopped. Everywhere there were long shadows lying on the hills, on the roads, on the enclosed fields of olive trees; the shadows of poplars, of wide chestnuts, of farm buildings, of stone walls; and in mid-air the sound of a bell, thin and alert, was like the throbbing pulse of the sunset glow. [63]

For the future Mrs. Gould (Conrad's only interesting woman character), the marriage proposal—the prospect of a new and very different life in Costaguana—opens up a hole in time and a void at the center of reality which we will shortly see to have been the central analytical preoccupation of *Lord Jim:* yet the last thread that connects her to this world in momentary eclipse, like that ultimate thread which holds Decoud in life in his island solitude ("in the daytime he could look at the silence like a still cord stretched to breaking point, with his life, his vain life, suspended to it like a weight": p. 410), is the thread of hearing:

> The only thing he wanted to know now, he said, was whether she did love him enough—whether she would have the courage to go with him so far away? . . . She did. She would. And immediately the future hostess of all the Europeans in Sulaco had the physical experience of the earth falling away from under her. It vanished completely even to the very sound of the bell. When her feet touched the ground again, the bell was still ringing in the valley; she put her hands up to her hair, breathing quickly, and glanced up and down the stony lane. It was reassuringly empty. Meantime, Charles, stepping with one foot into a dry and dusty ditch, picked up the open parasol, which had bounded away from them with a martial sound of drum taps. [64]

Yet such passages are at best testimony for a modification of Conrad's thematics; they are inconclusive until we appreciate the degree to which, in this work, the entire sensory apparatus has been foregrounded, and the very experience of perception itself heightened to the point at which it touches its own outer limit and causes its own outer edge in the nonperceivable to rise before us.[33] Something of this momentum is already apparent in the above passages, in which silence as well as sound becomes an exercise in auditory perception; yet not simple failure to perceive, not mere deafness or blindness to the outside world, not the nonexercise of the senses nor the mere non-sensory preoccupation with something else (but with what? with abstract thinking? with calculation?)—none of these forms of privation is adequate to constitute the figure of that contrary of perception against the background of which alone perception can be vivid and upon which it can inscribe its intensities. The realm of nonperception must be a heightened form of perception in its own right, a realm of heightened yet blank intensity:

> The Isabels were somewhere at hand. "On your left as you look forward, Señor," said Nostromo, suddenly. When his voice ceased, the enormous stillness, without light or sound, seemed to affect Decoud's senses like a powerful drug. He didn't even know at times whether he were asleep or awake. Like a man lost in slumber, he heard nothing, he saw nothing. Even his hand held before his face did not exist for his eyes. The change from the agitation, the passions and the dangers, from the sights and sounds of the shore, was so complete that it would have resembled death had it not been for the survival of his thoughts. In this foretaste of eternal peace they floated vivid and light, like unearthly clear dreams of earthly things that may haunt the souls freed by death from the misty atmosphere of regrets and hopes. Decoud shook himself, shuddered a bit, though the air that drifted past him was warm. He had the strangest sensation of his soul having been returned into his body from the circumambient darkness in which land, sea, sky, the mountains, and the rocks were as if they had not been. [220]

These magical pages in which the Golfo Placido shrouded in fog opens up a space beyond the world itself mark the attainment by Conrad's impressionism of its own outer limit, the working through of the dialectic of sensory registers to the point at which the latter virtually abolish themselves. For the aesthetic of perception knows

33. Hillis Miller's earlier existential reading of Conrad depends on taking "darkness" as an inner-worldly phenomenon (*Poets of Reality,* pp. 27ff.), rather than, as here, as the limits of "world-ness" and perception.

the same inner dynamic of frame and totality that we have so far touched on only in connection with narrative realism and the framing or containment strategies of a narrative modernism: the senses must be tuned against one another, they are themselves the element in which they move, not a dimension of material being but rather an evanescent mirage of structure, a fading effect, a strategy of containment that must contain itself at the same time that it performs its ideological function of the displacement of reading attention toward the image. Nor is it an accident that in this episode alone in that great historical drama which is *Nostromo* we have again to do with the principal geographical frame or border of the earlier novels, that unique place outside of place that endows them with a totalizing realism in spite of themselves, namely the sea. But where in the earlier novels the sea was the enabling device that allowed something at one and the same time realistic and modernistic to come into being, it is here the term limit which spells the end and the fulfillment of Conrad's impressionism and opens up the chance to register history itself.

IV

We have, however, not yet reached the moment of *Nostromo,* and must now patiently retrace our steps and return to the earlier text in order to reconstruct the other slope of *Lord Jim,* the dimension (incommensurable with the molecular one of sentence production) of narrative proper, with its basic categories, the place of all those unavoidable false problems which are named character, event, plot, narrative meaning, and the like. Having, to use Hjelmslev's distinction,[34] examined the content of form—Conrad's style as a symbolic act and as ideology—we must now turn to the form of content.

First impressions, however, raise interpretive temptations: in particular the idea, encouraged by the text itself, that the novel is fundamentally "about" the problem of heroism, and indeed, even before we get as far as that, that the novel "has" a hero and is "about" Jim himself. These temptations our earlier chapter on the ideological nature of the category of a narrative "character" has

---

34. Louis Hjelmslev, *Prolegomena to a Theory of Language,* trans. F. J. Whitfield (Madison: University of Wisconsin Press, 1961), chap. 13.

perhaps supplied us with the means to withstand. Indeed, we there wondered whether it would not be desirable to consider the possibility that the literary "character" is no more substantive than the Lacanian ego, and that it is to be seen rather as an "effect of system" than as a full representational identity in its own right. The idea was to explore the systems, the network of preconscious *pensée sauvage,* in terms of which a given "character" had meaning, whether that meaning took on the form of an antinomy, as will be found to be the case here in Conrad, or on the other hand was the bearer, as in Balzac, of a more stable quasi-allegorical content: the hypothesis of a character system presupposes another one, namely that the subject, in the immediacy of his or her consciousness, has no meaning, but that when a given subject is endowed with meaning (as, for example, when it becomes a representation for another subject or when another subject becomes part of the cast of characters of our own private fantasies), then that particular meaning can be traced back to the system that generates it, and of which we have taken Greimas' semantic or semiotic rectangle as one of the most useful emblems.

In the present instance, it is certain that to dissolve the verisimilitude of the character of Jim into the mere effect or pole of some larger signifying system would at once discredit and dispatch into critical dilettantism the whole thematics of heroism and individual guilt and expiation about which we have already complained. On the other hand, it would seem that a book so completely organized around the investigation of a single individual destiny, a single unique yet also more largely consequent and socially significant life experience ("he was one of us"), risks being shattered by such a refusal to take it on its own organizational terms.

How does one go about rewriting and rereading this narrative in such a way that "Jim" comes to be the name for an empty slot in a system which then, far more than the "lifelike" character, proves to have been the absent center of the narrative? Such a process can often conveniently begin in typology, provided it gets out of it at the appropriate moment. The reiterated but enigmatic "one of us" suggests that the binary terms of Jim's system are probably not to be sought for in the direction of Marlow and his listeners, but rather elsewhere: for example, in Jim's own reflections on types of people and types of vocation during his enforced idleness in port after his accident:

> While waiting, he associated naturally with the men of his calling in the port. These were of two kinds. Some, very few and seen there but seldom, led mysterious lives, had preserved an undefaced energy with the temper of buccaneers and the eyes of dreamers. They appeared to live in a crazy maze of plans, hopes, dangers, enterprises, ahead of civilization, in the dark places of the sea; and their death was the only event of their fantastic existence that seemed to have a reasonable certitude of achievement. The majority were men who, like himself, thrown there by some accident, had remained as officers of country ships. They had now a horror of the home service, with its harder conditions, severer view of duty, and the hazard of stormy oceans. They were attuned to the eternal peace of Eastern sky and sea. They loved short passages, good deck-chairs, large native crews, and the distinction of being white. . . . In all they said—in their actions, in their looks, in their persons—could be detected the soft spot, the place of decay, the determination to lounge safely through existence. [8–9]

That Jim must initially test himself against these two categories, that neither is adequate to house him, suggests that the character system, if one is at work here, is far from complete and lacks certain key features or semes. Jim is presumably not one of the deck-chair captains, who from another point of view, are the non-narrative terms, the "characters" who have no story and no destiny; but though he may well, like the first group, have the eyes of a dreamer, the characterization of these Europeans is still, at least at this stage, too comic-satiric to suit him either, and ultimately finds a first generic fulfillment in the episode of the guano empire ("all at once, on the blank page, under the very point of the pen, the two figures of Chester and his antique partner, very distinct and complete, would dodge into view with stride and gestures, as if reproduced in the field of some optical toy. I would watch them for a while. No! They were too phantasmal and extravagant to enter into anyone's fate": p. 106): such dreamers will, however, return in a more baleful guise in the second half of the novel.

But in half a paragraph, Jim has a new berth (chief mate on the *Patna*) and in another half a page, in its passengers-to-be, confronts a new type of human being and a new category of human existence:

They streamed aboard over three gangways, they streamed in urged
by faith and the hope of paradise, they streamed in with a continuous
tramp and shuffle of bare feet, without a word, a murmur, or a look
back; and when clear of confining rails spread on all sides over the
deck, flowed forward and aft, overflowed down the yawning hatch-
ways, filled the inner recesses of the ship—like water filling a cistern,
like water flowing into crevices and crannies, like water rising silently
even with the rim. Eight hundred men and women with faith and
hopes, with affections and memories, they had collected there, coming
from north and south and from the outskirts of the East, after tread-
ing the jungle paths, descending the rivers, coasting in praus along the
shallows, crossing in small canoes from island to island, passing
through suffering, meeting strange sights, beset by strange fears, up-
held by one desire. They came from solitary huts in the wilderness,
from populous campongs, from villages by the sea. At the call of an
idea they had left their forests, their clearings, the protection of their
rulers, their prosperity, their poverty, the surroundings of their youth,
and the graves of their fathers. . . .

"Look at dese cattle," said the German skipper to his new chief
mate. [9–10]

The crude irony underscores the most obvious feature that distinguishes the pilgrims from the Europeans anatomized on the preceding page: their lack of "individualism." Yet even on this most superficial level, the initial stirrings of a differential system are at
work; we return from these anonymous masses to the equally faceless "deck-chair captains" of the previous page, themselves each
utterly lacking in individuality, yet living their indistinction one by
one, in the isolation of their bourgeois comfort, rather than, as here,
collectively.

Meanwhile, telltale expressions like "the call of an idea" not only
warn of semic echoes with the other category of European seamen,
those of the mysterious lives and "the eyes of dreamers," but also
suggest that from our now distant vantage point in late twentieth-
century consumer society we need a semantic reconstruction of
these terms themselves—terms such as "idea", and later, in *Nostromo,* "sentimentalism"—which are too charged not to carry with
them a whole historical ideology that must be drawn, massy and
dripping, up into the light before the text can be considered to have
been read. Conrad's discourse—an overlay of psychoanalytically
charged terms and ideological, public slogans—must be regarded as

a foreign language that we have to learn in the absence of any dictionary or grammar, ourselves reconstructing its syntax and assembling hypotheses about the meanings of this or that item of vocabulary for which we ourselves have no contemporary equivalent.

Before trying to reconstruct the semantics of this key passage, however, we must also argue something else: namely that what is merely a narrative device or pretext (Jim's crisis requires him to have put lives in danger, but it can scarcely matter which ones; these Mecca-bound pilgrims might just as easily have been replaced by Indian emigrants to South Africa, say, or by a group of families of overseas Chinese) has a substantive meaning in its own right, which is constitutive for the text. This is, it seems to me, the kind of situation in which the Althusserian notion of "overdetermination" is useful: we cannot argue the importance of this particular evocation of the pilgrims from its necessity in the mechanism of the plot, yet we can propose a secondary line of determination such that, even as narrative pretext, this content imposes itself and becomes unavoidable. Its necessity is, in other words, not to be found on the level of narrative construction, but outside, in the objective logic of the content, in the unavailability of any other "illustration" to fill this particular empty slot. So it is significant that from our enumeration of other possibilities passengers of European stock were excluded (for one thing, the Europeans would not have remained calm while the officers abandoned ship); the other Asian possibilities are also inappropriate, since both would represent commerce and business motives rather than the religious pilgrimage here described, and itself reinforced (or once again, "overdetermined," if you like) by the attitude of the nonpilgrim Malay pilots, who keep their stations and continue to guide the abandoned ship for no reason other than sheer *faith* ("It never came into his mind then that the white men were about to leave the ship through fear of death. He did not believe it now. There might have been secret reasons": p. 61).[35] Here too, in this secondary loop of the plot,

---

35. Obviously, the thematic selection of Islam is no historical accident; it is ironic that this mirage of plenitude attributed to the historical and cultural Other should also be the instrument—"Orientalism"—by which that same Other is systematically marginalized (see Edward W. Said, *Orientalism* [New York: Pantheon, 1978]). It is noteworthy that the passage in question already exists virtually word-for word in the

equally necessary for the construction of Jim's central ordeal—but was it not Valéry who observed that what is merely necessary in art is the place of the flaw and the soft pocket of bad writing?—the apparently secondary content of blind faith comes as a "motivation of the device" and a reappropriation of the plot mechanism in the service of some quite different thematic and semantic system.

So at length we find ourselves interrogating, as though it were the fundamental concern of this sea story and adventure tale, the clearly secondary and marginal phenomenon of religion and religious belief. We do not generally associate Conrad with the nineteenth-century ideologeme of aesthetic religion. The key moments in its development might be quickly sketched in as those of Chateaubriand, its inventor, in *Le Génie du christianisme* (1802), Flaubert's archeological passion for dead religions, his appropriation of that whole ideology of perception, sense-data, and hallucination mentioned above for the evocation of religious visions, as in *La Tentation de Saint Antoine* (1874) or *Trois Contes* (1877)—not to speak of the contemporaneous fascination with belief of the positivists, most notably Renan—and finally such late variants as Malraux's books on painting and sculpture after World War II, books in which the retreat from Marxism to a Gaullist nationalism seems to impose an intellectual detour through a meditation on all the dead religions, all the divers embodiments of the Absolute, in the human past. Into this geneology of an ideological fascination now relatively foreign to us (and it should be noted that the religious revival of the late nineteenth century and, in particular, phenomena like neo-Catholicism are quite different from this aestheticizing contemplation of religion from without), we must assuredly insert its most intellectually illustrious and productive

---

oldest sketch Conrad wrote of his novel-to-be; see "Tuan Jim", in Conrad, *Lord Jim*, ed. Thomas Moser (New York: Norton, 1968), pp. 283–291. This reading of the semantic content of one of the two "communities" who meet on the *Patna* (the other, dominant one is that of the British imperial bureaucracy, as we shall see in a moment) does not exclude the investment of other types of content in what is essentially an allegorical scheme: in particular, Gustav Morf's identification of the *Patna* with Poland, and his interpretation of Jim's guilt as a figure for Conrad's own obscure sense of having abandoned family, language, and nation, surely constitute one of the more dramatic interpretive gestures in recent criticism (Gustav Morf, *The Polish Heritage of Joseph Conrad* [London: Sampson Low, Marston, 1930], pp. 149–166).

monument: the studies undertaken by Conrad's virtual contemporary, Max Weber, of the dynamics and function of religion, not only in *The Protestant Ethic,* but above all in the elaborate, posthumously published *Sociology of Religion.* Indeed, Weber's wry characterization of himself as "religiously unmusical" may serve as the motto for the curious intellectual stance of all of these nonbelievers, who combine the allure of a religiously fellow-traveling agnosticism with the secret longings of the impotent in matters of belief. In the British tradition, the institutional position of Anglicanism and the historical shock of Darwinism's implicit challenge to it lend the thematics of religious belief a somewhat different symbolic and political meaning than they held in the floodtide of bourgeois city life on the continent; still, Conrad was not really British, and it may be a useful estrangement to place him for a moment in a different context than those (English intellectuals of the Ford/Garnett type, a romantic Polish intelligentsia, the world of the merchant marine) in which he is normally grasped.

The name of Weber makes it clear that we cannot begin to sense the real ideological function of religious aestheticism unless we place it within that larger intellectual and ideological preoccupation which is the study and interrogation of value, and which, even more than with Weber, is associated with the name of the latter's master, Nietzsche.[36] From this standpoint, Nietzsche's "transvaluation of all values" and Weber's misnamed and misunderstood ideal of a "value-free science" must both be seen as attempts to project an intellectual space from which one can study inner-worldly value as such, the whole chaotic variety of reasons and motives the citizens of a secular society have for pursuing the activities they set themselves. These ideals are implicit or explicit attempts to parry the powerful Marxian position, which sees intellectual activity as being historically situated and class-based: the Marxian objection makes it clear that the vocation to study value cannot simply embody one more inner-worldly value (the passion for knowledge? the pursuit of sheer disinterested science?) without at once itself becoming ideological, or, in the Nietzschean formula, one more embodiment of the will to power. Framed in these terms, then, the problem (it

36. See Eugène Fleischmann, "De Nietzsche à Weber," *Archives européennes de sociologie,* 5 (1964), 190–238.

will later, with Max Scheler and Karl Mannheim, flatten itself out into that "subdiscipline" conventionally labeled the "sociology of knowledge") is insoluble; but what is interesting about it for us are its preconditions, namely, the objective historical developments without which such a "problem" could never have been articulated in the first place.

These are clearly, first and foremost, the secularization of life under capitalism and the breaking up (or, in the current euphemism, the "modernization") of the older tradition-oriented systems of castes and inherited professions, as the combined result of the French Revolution and the spread of the market system. Now indeed, for the first time in any general and irreversible way, the realm of values becomes problematical, with the result that it can, for the first time, be isolated as a realm in itself and contemplated as a separate object of study. To say that value becomes a semi-autonomous object is to observe the way in which, in the new middle-class culture, for the first time people (but mainly men) must weigh the various activities against each other and choose their professions. What we call private life or the new subjectivity of individualism is objectively simply this distance which permits them to hold their professional activities at arm's length; hence the originality, in the realm of the novel, of the "Quel métier prendre?" of a Stendhal, whose works explore, as it were, the atomic weights of the various professions and political regimes as alternate life forms.

In Weber's scheme of things, all social institutions describe a fatal trajectory from the traditional to the rationalized, passing through a crucial transitional stage which is the moment—the vanishing mediation—of so-called charisma. The activities of older societies are for the most part inherited (the blacksmith's father and grandfather were blacksmiths), and the question about value— about the reason for pursuing this or that life task, in this or that fashion—is short-circuited by the classic reply of all traditional societies: Because it was always done that way, because that is the way we have always lived. The problem of value cannot therefore arise in this environment; or, to put it another way, in the world of the traditional village, or even of tribal culture, each activity is symbolically unique, so that the level of abstraction upon which they could be compared with one another is never attained: there is no least-common-denominator available to compare iron-welding or the preparation of curare with basket-weaving or the making of bread or pots. To use the Marxian terminology, in such societies we can only contemplate an incomparable variety of qualitatively different forms of concrete work or productive activity, because the common denominator of all of these forms of activity—equivalent labor-power—has not yet been made visible by the objective process of abstraction at work within society.

For Weber, the charismatic moment amounts to a kind of myth of meaning, a myth of the value of this or that activity, which is briefly sustained by the personal power and authority of the charismatic figure, generally a prophet. But this moment tends to give way at once to a system in which all activities are ruthlessly rationalized and restructured in forms we have already described. The moment of rationalization, then, is Weber's equivalent of Marx's notion of the universalization of equivalent labor-power, or the commodification of all labor; yet if we see the latter subterranean infrastructural process as the objective precondition for the former developments in the relations of production and throughout the superstructure there need be no particular inconsistency between the two accounts.

What we are here concerned to stress is the paradox of the very notion of value itself, which becomes visible as abstraction and as a strange afterimage on the retina, only at the moment in which it has ceased to exist as such. The characteristic form of rationalization is indeed the reorganization of operations in terms of the binary system of means and ends; indeed, the means/ends opposition, although it seems to retain the term and to make a specific place for value, has the objective result of abolishing value as such, bracketing the "end" or drawing it back into the system of pure means in such a way that the end is merely the empty aim of realizing these particular means. This secret one-dimensionality of the apparent means/ends opposition is usefully brought out by the Frankfurt School's alternate formulation, namely the concept of instrumentalization,[37] which makes it clear that rationalization involves the transformation of everything into sheer means (hence the tra-

37. See in particular Max Horkheimer, *Eclipse of Reason* (New York: Seabury, 1947), chap. 1 ("Means and Ends"), pp. 3–57; as well as Horkheimer and Adorno, *Dialectic of Enlightenment,* and the prolongation of these themes in the critique of positivism by Adorno, Habermas, and others (see *The Positivist Dispute in German Sociology,* trans. G. Adey and D. Frisby [New York: Harper & Row, 1976]).

ditional formula of a Marxist humanism, that capitalism is a wholly rationalized and indeed rational system of means in the service of irrational ends).[38]

Thus, the study of value, the very idea of value, comes into being at the moment of its own disappearance and of the virtual obliteration of all value by a universal process of instrumentalization: which is to say that—as again in the emblematic case of Nietzsche—the study of value is at one with nihilism, or the experience of its absence. What is paradoxical about such an experience is obviously that it is contemporaneous with one of the most active periods in human history, with all the mechanical animation of late Victorian city life, with all the smoke and conveyance inherent in new living conditions and in the rapid development of business and industry, with the experimental triumphs of positivistic science and its conquest of the university system, with all the bustling parliamentary and bureaucratic activity of the new middle-class regimes, the spread of the press, the diffusion of literacy and the rise of mass culture, the ready accessibility of the newly mass-produced commodities of an increasingly consumer-oriented civilization. We must ponder the anomaly that it is only in the most completely humanized environment, the one most fully and obviously the end product of human labor, production, and transformation, that life becomes meaningless, and that existential despair first appears as such in direct proportion to the elimination of nature, the non- or antihuman, to the increasing rollback of everything that threatens human life and the prospect of a well-nigh limitless control over the external universe. The most interesting artists and thinkers of such a period are those who cling to the experience of meaninglessness itself as to some ultimate reality, some ultimate bedrock of exis-

38. This description can be tested against that older and more elaborate anatomy of praxis furnished by the Aristotelian system of the four causes (material, effective, formal, and final), which clearly still maintains the place of concrete value. But the Aristotelian system is itself a transitional concept which reflects a transitional moment in the development of modern production, and this not merely because, as has often been pointed out, it essentially theorizes an artisinal or handicraft culture, but also because it systematically excludes whole areas of activity (in particular, agricultural production and warfare) from the concept of work it is meant to govern. Like so much in classical Greek culture, therefore, it cannot represent a positive solution or embody a concrete social or political or economic ideal for us. Still, it has the keenest diagnostic value, as a standard against which to measure the appalling rate and degree of dehumanization in modern society. See Jean-Pierre Vernant, "Travail et nature dans la Grèce ancienne," and "Aspects psychologiques du travail," in *Mythe et pensée chez les grecs* (Paris: Maspéro, 1965).

tence of which they do not wish to be cheated by illusions or "philosophies of as-if": "Lieber will noch der Mensch *das Nichts* wollen," cried Nietzsche, "als *nicht* wollen." Rather nihilism than ennui, rather an orchestral pessimism and a metaphysical vision of cosmic entropy than too stark and unpleasant a sense of the systematic exclusion of "value" by the new logic of capitalist social organization.

These are clearly the absolutes with which Conrad's own private pessimism has its "family resemblance" (although in the next section we will find it necessary to distinguish proto-existentialism as a metaphysic—pessimism, nihilism, the meaninglessness of existence, the absurd—from the rigorous analytical dissolution of acts and events by existentialism as a technical philosophy). It is also the perspective in which to grasp the ideological meaning of aesthetic religion: the melancholy of disbelief, the nostalgia of the nineteenth-century intellectual for the "wholeness" of a faith that is no longer possible, is itself a kind of ideological fable designed to transform into a matter of individual existence what is in reality a relationship between collective systems and social forms. Religion has the symbolic value of wholeness, no doubt: but it is the wholeness of the older organic society or *Gesellschaft* that it conveys, and not that—in any case surely a mirage—of some fully unified monad. Religion, to the henceforth "religiously unmusical" subjects of the market system, is the unity of older social life perceived from the outside: hence its structural affinity with the image as such and hallucination. Religion is the superstructural projection of a mode of production, the latter's only surviving trace in the form of linguistic and visual artifacts, thought systems, myths and narratives, which look as though they had something to do with the forms in which our own consciousness is at home, and yet which remain rigorously closed it. Because we can no longer think the figures of the sacred from within, we transform their external forms into aesthetic objects, but also monuments, pyramids, altars, presumed to have an inside, yet housing powers that will forever remain a mystery to us.[39]

---

39. This dialectic of inside and outside—Rabelais' Silenus box—is principally, as we have suggested in earlier chapters, what is stigmatized in the now canonical attacks on interpretation and on the hermeneutic model (as, e.g., in Derrida, *Of Grammatology*, pp. 30–65).

So religion, in this particular sense, takes its place in that complex of ideological themes and terms with which the nineteenth century sought to explore the new world of universal instrumentalization and to express its bewilderment at what that world excluded as much as at what it contained: other motifs, some of which appear in the evocation of the pilgrims quoted above, are the "idea" or the "ideal" (generally art or love) as that which allows one to transcend the intolerable double bind of means and ends; the somewhat lower but also more overtly social concept of the "philanthropic," as we observed it at work in the previous chapter—a conception of a form of social action which would not be that of mere "interest," or would, in other words, transcend the antivalue of the purely instrumental; Conrad's term "sentimentalism", finally, which comes to designate activities that cannot be reduced to interested motives and must therefore be credited to the account of some unbusinesslike and whimsically nonserious caprice (the Gidean *acte gratuit* will be a final, more heroic avatar of this still fairly leisure-class attribute).

Now we may reinvest the language of *Lord Jim* with something like its original ideological and semantic content, and make an effort to disengage the "system" that generates the typology of characters we have begun to articulate, and beyond that, assigns the narrative its ultimate terminus and dynamics. I believe that this system may best be grasped in terms of the major themes of the dilemma just outlined, and in particular of the opposition between activity and value. It is an opposition not unlike that which underlies Lukács' *Theory of the Novel,* where it takes the form of a dissociation between *Leben,* life, sheer contingent, inner-worldly experience, and *Wesen,* essence, meaning, immanent wholeness.[40] The inner dynamism of such oppositions springs from their incommensurability, their ec-centricity as a weighing of two incomparable phenomena: on the one hand, genuine degraded but existent inner-worldly experience, and on the other, sheer ideal, nostalgia, an imagined wholeness that is part of the existent real only insofar as it is dreamed there and projected by this particular real world, but has no other substance. In Conrad, however, as we have seen, owing to the coexistence of capitalism and precapitalist social

40. Lukács, *Theory of the Novel,* esp. pp. 40–55.

forms on the imperialist periphery, the term value is still able to have genuine social and historical substance; it marks communities and ways of life which still, for another moment yet, exist, and have not been reduced to the icons and melancholy images of the mainstream of religious aestheticism.

The point about this binary opposition, however, is not its logical accuracy as a thought concerned to compare only comparable entities and oppose only terms of the appropriate category, but, on the contrary, its existence as a symptom; the opposition between activity and value is not so much a logical contradiction, as rather an antinomy for the mind, a dilemma, an aporia, which itself expresses—in the form of an ideological closure—a concrete social contradiction.[41] Its existence as skewed thought, then, as a double bind and a conceptual scandal, is what accounts for the restless life of the system, its desperate attempts to square its own circles and to produce new terms out of itself which ultimately "solve" the dilemma at hand. Thus, in an initial move which Greimas' semantic rectangle allows us to register, each term generates its logical negation or "contradictory"; the nucleus of our ideological system thus contains the four terms of activity and value, and not-activity and not-value, articulated as in the diagram.

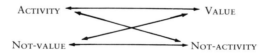

So far, clearly, these are semes or conceptual features, and not in any sense the slots of narrative characters or indeed other narrative categories. The place of characters and of a character system is opened up only at the point at which the mind seeks further release from its ideological closure by projecting combinations of these various semes: to work through the various possible combinations is then concretely to imagine the life forms, or the characterological types, that can embody and manifest such contradictions, which otherwise remain abstract and repressed. Thus, to follow our rectangle around clockwise beginning on the righthand side, it does not seem particularly farfetched to suggest that the synthesis of

41. See Chap. 1, pp. 46–49 and 82–83, and Chap. 3, pp. 166–168.

value and not-activity can be embodied only by the pilgrims, who are a breathing and living presence which does not exteriorize itself in any particular activity, in acts, struggles, "goal-oriented behavior": even the pilgrimage is simply the emanation of their being, as of an element, water draining the great watertables of Malaysia, "rising silently even with the rim."

Moving to the lower horizontal opposition, between not-activity and not-value—a synthesis suggestively designated as the neutral term in Greimas' version of this model—we see that the very terms of the judgment are virtually explicit in Conrad's contemptuous account of the "deck-chair sailors" who have no ideal but that of their own comfort, and whose energies, insofar as they have any, are wholly dedicated to avoiding activity as much as possible. These are indeed the "neuters" of Conrad's universe, the faceless anonymity against which passions become identifiable in all their own specificity.

As for the next possible synthesis, which would unite activity with not-value, the evocation of Nietzsche has perhaps made it more familiar to us than Conrad's text, at this stage in our reading of it, would authorize: "There are people who would rather will *nothingness* than want nothing at all." What is meant here is clearly not the merely eccentric figures of South Sea port "originals" (of which Jim himself for a moment becomes one), so much as nihilism itself, that formidable combination of energy and, more than utter lack of scruple, a passion for nothingness. To test our hypothesis would be to expect the text at length to generate such a figure, which, indeed, it does in Jim's Nemesis, the character of Gentleman Brown (about whom we will have more to say in a later section).

Finally, we come to what Greimas calls the "complex term," the ideal synthesis of the two major terms of the contradiction and thus the latter's unimaginable and impossible resolution and *Aufhebung;* the union of activity and value, of the energies of Western capitalism and the organic immanence of the religion of precapitalist societies, can only block out the place of Jim himself. But not the existential Jim, the antihero, of the first part of the novel: rather, the ideal Jim, the "Lord Jim" of the second half, the wish-fulfilling romance, which is marked as a degraded narrative precisely by its claim to have "resolved" the contradiction and generated the impossible hero, who, remaining problematical in the *Patna* section of the book as the Lukács of *The Theory of the Novel* told us the hero of a genuine novel must do, now solicits that lowering of our reality principle necessary to accredit this final burst of legend.[42]

The completed character system may therefore be schematically presented as follows:

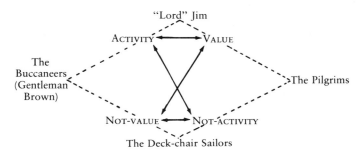

Such a schema not only articulates the generation of the characters, insofar as it represents a contradiction to be "solved," or an antinomy to be effaced or overcome; it also suggests the ideological service which the production of this narrative is ultimately intended to perform—in other words, the resolution of this particular determinate contradiction—or, more precisely, following Lévi-Strauss's seminal characterization of mythic narrative, the imaginary resolution of this particular determinate real contradiction. Such models—sometimes loosely formulated in terms of analogies with the "deep structures" and surface manifestations of linguistics—find their proper use in the staging of the fundamental problems of the narrative text—the antinomies or ideological closure it is called upon to imagine away—and in the evaluation of the narrative solution, or sequence of provisional solutions, invoked for this purpose. They are, however, less able to bridge the gap between an ideologi-

42. There has been considerable debate as to the "meaning" of the ending of *Lord Jim,* and in particular as to whether Jim can be said, by his death, to have "redeemed" himself; the exalted tone of the ending suggests a positive response which a sober reading of the narrative makes it rather difficult to accept. Surely this "undecidability" of the ending confirms the present analysis, and offers a virtual textbook illustration of an "imaginary resolution of a real contradiction," it being understood that an imaginary resolution is no resolution at all. All of Conrad's artfulness is in this concluding section mustered for a kind of prestidigitation designed to prevent the embarrassing question from being posed in the first place.

cal deep structure and the sentence-by-sentence life of the narrative text, as a perpetual generation and dissolution of events, a process for which we must now propose a rather different kind of lens.

V

Lord Jim is, however, a privileged text in this respect—a kind of reflexive or meta-text—in that its narrative construes the "event" as the analysis and dissolution of events in some more common everyday naive sense. The "event" in *Lord Jim* is the analysis and dissolution of the event. The originality of the text goes well beyond the conventional redoubling of plot and fable (Aristotle), *discours* and *histoire* (Benveniste), the conventional distinction between the exposition and "rendering" of narrative events and those events as sheer data, raw material, anecdotal precondition. Certainly, the slow unfolding of the "real story" of the *Patna* has all the excitement of a detective story and not a little of that form's peculiarly specialized and redoubled structure: but we have understood very little about this narrative unless we have come to realize that even that "real story" itself is for Conrad hollow and empty, and that there is a void at the heart of events and acts in this work which goes well beyond simple anecdotal mystification.

Consider for instance the following moment of crisis in the Patusan narrative: on arrival, Jim finds himself virtually but unofficially emprisoned by an old adversary of Stein and his allies. He passes his time in a closed courtyard, amusing himself by repairing the Rajah's broken clock. Suddenly, in panic, for the first time conceiving his plight and imminent danger, he climbs the stockade and makes his way across the mud flats to freedom. What interests us is the inner structure of this event, which is indubitably an act on Jim's part:

> The higher firm ground was about six feet in front of him. . . . He reached and grabbed desperately with his hands, and only succeeded in gathering a horrible cold shiny heap of slime against his breast—up to his very chin. It seemed to him he was burying himself alive, and then he struck out madly, scattering the mud with his fists. It fell on his head, on his face, over his eyes, into his mouth. He told me that he remembered suddenly the courtyard, as you remember a place where you had been very happy years ago. He longed—so he said—to be back there again, mending the clock. Mending the clock—that was the idea. He made efforts, tremendous sobbing, gasping efforts, ef-

forts that seemed to burst his eyeballs in their sockets and make him blind, and culminating in one mighty supreme effort in the darkness to crack the earth asunder, to throw it off his limbs—and he felt himself creeping feebly up the bank. He lay full length on the firm ground and saw the light, the sky. Then as a sort of happy thought the notion came to him that he would go to sleep. He will have it that he *did* actually go to sleep; that he slept—perhaps for a minute, perhaps for twenty seconds, or only for one second, but he recollects distinctly the violent convulsive start of awakening. [155–156] [At which point, then, Jim leaps to his feet again and continues his escape, racing through the village to safety.]

Now a passage of this kind can be taken, as its contemporaries surely would have taken it, as a psychological curiosity; we can almost hear them admiring this knowledge of the "human heart," this exploration of the intricacies of human reactions. We have already mentioned the "psychological" framework which limits Jamesian point of view. Now we must go even further and grasp "psychology" as a particular episteme that includes within itself, alongside the appropriate blueprints of normal mental machinery, a fascination with the data of the abnormal and psychopathological as well, one that envelops Dostoyevsky and Krafft-Ebing, and for which this particular "notation" of Conrad—extreme stress under crisis coupled with sleepiness—becomes an "insight" and a valuable note for the file.

But such a passage can also be read quite differently, and this is the moment to register the peculiar affinities of Conrad's work with certain of the themes of Sartrean existentialism, of which the obsession with treason and betrayal and the fascination with torture (compare the Monygham sections of *Nostromo* with analogous sequences in *Morts sans sépulture*) are only the most superficial.[43] Such themes evidently find their source in the common patrimony of Nietzschean nihilism and may in both cases be seen as a rather more consequent effort to imagine what kind of things are really possible if God is dead. The structural affinities between these two

43. The motif of treason, in particular, often expresses the classical anxiety of intellectuals at their "free-floating" status and their lack of organic links with one or the other of the fundamental social classes: this reflexive meaning is explicit in Sartre, but implicit only in writers like Conrad or Borges (on the meaning of treason in this last, see Jean Franco, "Borges," *Social Text*, No. 4 [Fall, 1980]).

otherwise very different bodies of work must be ultimately sought in the nature of the concrete social situation they address. The juxtaposition of Conrad's work with existentialism, however, needs a further initial clarification: I have indeed already implied the need to distinguish between a properly existential "metaphysic"—in other words, a set of propositions about the "meaning of life," even where the latter is declared in fact to be "the absurd"—and that more properly existential analytic, found principally in Heidegger and Sartre, which, an offshoot and a development of certain phenomenological explorations, lays out a whole anatomy of lived time, action, choice, emotion, and the like. The former, the metaphysic, is an ideology; the latter can be used ideologically, but is not necessarily in itself ideological. The distinction is one between showing that there is never any irreducible temporal present or presence at the heart of a project, and concluding, from the demonstration that action is itself hollow and unreal. Both "existentialisms" are present in Conrad's work; but it is the latter, the existential analytic, that we will be concerned with in the present section.

It should be clear that I am neither suggesting an influence of Conrad on Sartre, nor, inversely, making a case for Conrad as Sartre's precursor in this or that area. What we can argue at most is that there are objective preconditions for working out a particular thought system or thematics, and that the superficial similarity of two quite different works from different moments and spaces of the recent European past ought to direct our attention first to the similarity of the social situations and historical conditions in which, as symbolic gestures, they are meaningful. We ought therefore to make a first step by trying to understand the historical conditions of possibility of the existential analytic—a project that, whatever it tells us about Conrad, would be the start of a more concrete historical regrounding of Sartre's work than has been done so far (see Lukács' book on existentialism, with its clumsy mediations, for an object lesson in how not to do this particular job).[44] But the methodological resistance to a symptomal or sociological regrounding of technical philosophy is far greater than to similar operations in the areas of culture and ideology; that technical philosophy has histori-

---

44. Georg Lukács, *Existentialisme ou marxisme* (Paris: Nagel, 1948).

cal preconditions is a view of the history of philosophy which has never adequately been worked out, indeed which the cruder Marxian efforts (like that of Lukács just mentioned) have tended to discredit.

Yet it seems clear that we are already in a position to construct a historical and social subtext able to naturalize or make more plausible the otherwise peculiar experience of moments of action like Jim's escape from the courtyard, in which the act itself suddenly yawns and discloses at its heart a void which is at one with the temporary extinction of the subject. (Compare, in *Nostromo*, Mrs. Gould's brief loss of consciousness in the proposal scene, and Decoud's unconsciousness after writing the letter: "he swayed over the table as if struck by a bullet"—p. 210; not to speak of his suicide: "the stiffness of the fingers relaxes, and the lover of Antonia Avellanos rolled overboard without having heard the cord of silence snap in the solitude of the Placid Gulf, whose glittering surface remained untroubled by the fall of his body"—p. 411.)

What we are witnessing in such passages is essentially the emergence of the once hegemonic but now antiquated modernist experience of temporality: to interrogate the objective conditions of possibility of representations like these is to ask what the social and historical preconditions are for an experience of time "as a still cord stretched to the breaking point," an experience in which "natural" or *naturwüchsige* temporality, at first bracketed as a purely formal "unity of apperception" (Kant), then as though by way of some inexplicable muscular relaxation in the prospective and retrospective projections that bind future and past to this present of time, is suddenly seen to shatter like glass into random instants. To construct the subtext of that technical Sartrean and Heideggerian interrogation of time (the former essentially considering its active form in the project and the choice, the latter its passive dimension as the suffering of mortal finitude), we must identify and reestablish the mediation of a concrete experience of temporal activity which—the specific precondition required for the development of this or that technical philosophical investigation—may then itself be studied as a social and historical phenomenon in its own right. The point is thus less the "truth" of the philosophical description—our condemnation to be free, the discontinuity of time, ultimately even, if one likes, the absurdity of natural or organic life and of being itself—which every modern individual is surely prepared to accept as such: it is rather the situation which suddenly allows the veil to be ripped away from this intolerable ontological bedrock, and imposes it on consciousness as the ultimate lucidity ("I want to see how much I can bear," Weber wrote of a similarly unpleasant vocation for truth). As for the relationship of Marxism to such descriptions, it would surely be preferable not to substitute edifying sermons for them: that life is meaningless is not a proposition that need be inconsistent with Marxism, whose affirmation is the quite different one that History is meaningful, however absurd organic life may happen to be. The real issue is not the propositions of existentialism, but rather their charge of affect: in future societies people will still grow old and die, but the Pascalian wager of Marxism lies elsewhere, namely in the idea that death in a fragmented and individualized society is far more frightening and anxiety-laden than in a genuine community, in which dying is something that happens to the group more intensely than it happens to the individual subject. The hypothesis is that time will be no less structurally empty, or to use a current version, presence will be no less of a structural and ontological illusion, in a future communal social life, but rather that this particular "fundamental revelation of the nothingness of existence" will have lost its sharpness and pain and be of less consequence.

At any rate, this abstract structure of temporality clearly cannot emerge until the older traditional activities, projects, rituals through which time was experienced, and from which it was indistinguishable, have broken down. We are discussing a process of abstraction whereby, among many other things, a supreme abstract form slowly appears which is called that of Time itself, and which then holds out the mirage of some pure and immediate experience of itself. But as Kant showed (and in a different sense Hume before him), such temporality is not an object of experience but only a pure form, so that the failure to replace its nature as an abstraction—the reality of Bergson's physical or clock time—with some plenitude of experience—the mirage of Bergson's full or lived time—is scarcely surprising, even though it may have disastrous consequences for the individual subject.

My argument is, then, that the questions raised in Jim's apparent quest for self-knowledge—whether he was a coward and why, and the related Sartrean problem of whether cowardice is thus something that characterizes his very being, or whether it would be possible in some analogous situation, to choose otherwise—these ethical questions which turn around the nature of freedom are in fact (as in *Being and Nothingness*) something like a structural pretext for the quite different examination of what an act and what a temporal instant really are: when does the act happen, how much preparation is necessary, how far do you have to go in it before it suddenly "takes" and becomes irrevocable, is it then infinitely divisible like the sprint-lengths of the hare, or of Zeno's arrow, and if not, then (the other face of Zeno's paradox) how could that single hard ultimate indivisible atom which is the instant of action ever come into being in the first place?

It has not been sufficiently observed that the very situation which will become symbolically invested and privileged for Jim—jumping into a lifeboat, fleeing the doomed *Patna*—is one to which, in its empty form, he has already been sensitized. The episode is not, therefore, an example of a moral illustration, that "simple form" or molecular genre which Jolles calls the *casum*,[45] a vehicle for the debate and exercise of all of those ethical questions which we have here regarded as diversionary rather than irrelevant. Jim's trauma is, on the contrary, quite literally that and is constructed on the basis of an initial *repetition*. There was indeed an earlier scene that contained the elements of this one: lifeboat, people in distress, hesitation at the abyss of the instant and on the brink of the leap to freedom. The point is that in that earlier scene Jim *failed* to jump:

> Jim felt his shoulder gripped firmly. "Too late, youngster." The captain of the ship laid a restraining hand on that boy, who seemed on the point of leaping overboard, and Jim looked up with the pain of conscious defeat in his eyes. The captain smiled sympathetically. "Better luck next time. This will teach you to be smart." [6]

So the cutter returns without Jim with its rescued survivors, and an alter ego wins the glory and the satisfaction of celebrating his own heroism ("Jim thought it a pitiful display of vanity"). No wonder, then, that at the climactic moment of decision in the *Patna* crisis—

---

45. André Jolles, *Einfache Formen* (Halle: Niemeyer, 1929), pp. 171–199.

the cutter dancing ready below, people in imminent danger, Jim poised "as if I had been on the top of a tower" (68)— "instinctively" Jim corrects his earlier mistake and this time "does the right thing." The longing for the second chance, for the return of a situation in which you can prove yourself, this time triumphantly, is, when it declares itself in Jim's agony after the *Patna* episode and his trial, merely the repetition of a repetition: the real second chance, in the event the only one, is the *Patna* crisis itself, in which Jim is now given the unexpected opportunity to complete his long-suspended act, and to land in the cutter over which he was poised so many years before.

It is of course now exactly the wrong decision; my point is, however, that this "irony," if we must call it that, is incommensurable either with the various "stable ironies" of satire and comedy, or with those other more disturbingly "unstable" ones of Jamesian or Flaubertian point of view.[46] If irony is the right word, then we must distinguish between those ironies, which remain locked in the categories of the individual subject (either more objective ethical judgments, or more solipsistic "psychological" experiences within the monad) and this one, which is transindividual and more properly historical in character, but by some ideological misunderstanding projected back onto individual experience. This kind of irony is that of the "lessons of history," from which one is said to learn, for example, that they teach no lessons; it is the irony of reequipping oneself better to wage the previous war, for which one was so grievously unprepared, with the result that one is equally unprepared, but in a new way, to fight the following one. Such irony is, if you like, a negative version of the Hegelian "ruse of reason," and one which in this form is relatively cyclical and has no content (the latter would begin to emerge only when in a determinate historical situation we ask why the French general staff learned the lessons of 1870 so well that they had to unlearn them in 1914, and so on). The value of *Nostromo*, however, will lie for us in its attempt to pose this question all over again, yet this time with concrete content, a remarkable and form-transfiguring effort at lifting this entire problematic of the empty act up to the level of collective experience. For,

46. The distinction is Wayne Booth's, in *The Rhetoric of Irony* (Chicago: University of Chicago Press, 1974).

as we shall see shortly, *Nostromo* is, like *Lord Jim*, the interrogation of a hole in time, an act whose innermost instant falls away—proving thus at once irrevocable and impossible, a source of scandal and an aporia for contemplation. But the contemplation of *Nostromo* is a meditation on History.

That of *Lord Jim* remains stubbornly deflected onto the problematic of the individual act, and puts over and over again to itself questions that cannot be answered. The analytical interrogation of Jim's climactic moment indeed shows that nothing was there: " 'I had jumped . . .' he checked himself, averted his gaze. . . . 'It seems,' he added" (68). There is no present tense of the act, we are forever always before or after it, in past or future tenses, at the stage of the project or those of the consequences. The existential investigation has been rigorously prosecuted, but ends up in neither truth nor metaphysics, but in philosophical paradox.

At least for Jim himself. For however impossible the problem of the act may be at the level of the individual subject, it is evident that the social at once washes back across it, to transform it utterly. Here the focus on the existential problematic alters, or rather it becomes clear that there were always two problematics: the technical philosophical one, what we have called the existential analytic—Roquentin's "discovery" of being in *La Nausée*, with all the unavoidable results for himself as an individual subject—and that quite different matter which is the relationship of the social institution—the bourgeoisie of Bouville—and its structures of legitimation to this shattering discovery, and to the scandal of the asocial individual. Conrad pretends to tell us the story of an individual's struggle with his own fear and courage; but he knows very well that the real issues are elsewhere, in the social example Jim cannot but set, and the demoralizing effect of Jim's discovery of Sartrean freedom on the ideological myths that allow a governing class to function and to assert its unity and legitimacy: thus Brierly, Jim's judge, whose own suicide thereby becomes a social gesture and a class abdication rather than that existential discovery of nothingness that it has so often been interpreted to be:

> "We aren't an organized body of men, and the only thing that holds
> us together is just the name for that kind of decency. Such an affair
> destroys one's confidence. A man may go pretty near through his

whole sea-life without any call to show a stiff upper lip. But when the call comes. . . ." [42].

Nor is Marlow's reading any different, when at the inconspicuous turn of some elaborate sentence he blurts out his astonishment at his own interest in "an occurrence which, after all, concerned me no more than as a member of an obscure body of men held together by a community of inglorious toil and by fidelity to a certain standard of conduct" (31). But the body of men thus held together in the ideological cohesion of class values which cannot without peril be called into question is not merely the confraternity of the sea; it is the ruling class of the British Empire, the heroic bureaucracy of imperial capitalism which takes that lesser, but sometimes even more heroic, bureaucracy of the officers of the merchant fleet as a figure for itself.[47] Here, more even than in the practice of a Flaubertian verbal aesthetic, Conrad's work finally becomes contiguous to the elaborate presentation and self-questioning of the British aristocratic bureaucracy in Ford's *Parade's End,* and uses much the same anecdotal form of social *scandal* to deconceal social institutions otherwise imperceptible to the naked eye. In both works, therefore, the existential "extreme situation" (the *Patna*'s bulkhead, World War I) is less a laboratory experiment designed to expose the inner articulation of the act and of the instant than the precondition for the revelation of the texture of ideology.

VI

But if this is what *Lord Jim* is really all about, then it only remains to ask why nobody thinks so, least of all Conrad himself; it remains to raise the last but exceedingly troublesome formality of

47. "Jim has been taught a code, a set of laws about sailing, and these are not only technical but in their essence moral—definitions of responsibility and of duty which are at once specific practical rules and general social laws. He is part of a hierarchy—the officers of the ship—in which those laws are manifest or are supposed to be manifest. His moral conflict is not the product of isolation, of the lack of a society and of shared beliefs. It is that earlier kind of conflict, historically earlier, in which a man's strength is tested under pressure; in which others break the agreed rules and he goes along with this to his subsequent shame; in which, that is to say, what is really being looked at is *conduct,* within an agreed scheme of values. The ship in Conrad has this special quality, which was no longer ordinarily available to most novelists. It is a knowable community of a transparent kind" (Williams, *The English Novel,* p. 141).

the reality of the appearance, the structural origins of a misreading which is at once error and objective reality. Our reading of this novel has been based on—and has perhaps tended to confirm—a model of modernism according to which the latter is grasped as canceled realism, as a negation of "realistic content" which, like a Hegelian *Aufhebung,* continues to bear that content, crossed out and lifted up all at once, within itself. In short, it is evidently wrong to imagine, as Lukács sometimes seems to do, that modernism is some mere ideological distraction, a way of systematically displacing the reader's attention from history and society to pure form, metaphysics, and experiences of the individual monad; it is all those things, but they are not so easy to achieve as one might think. The modernist project is more adequately understood as the intent, following Norman Holland's convenient expression,[48] to "manage" historical and social, deeply political impulses, that is to say, to defuse them, to prepare substitute gratifications for them, and the like. But we must add that such impulses cannot be managed until they are aroused; this is the delicate part of the modernist project, the place at which it must be realistic in order in another moment to recontain that realism which it has awakened.

The burden of our reading of *Lord Jim* has been to restore the whole socially concrete subtext of late nineteenth-century rationalization and reification of which this novel is so powerfully, and on so many different formal levels, the expression and the Utopian compensation alike. Now we must turn to the mechanisms that ensure a structural displacement of such content, and that provide for a built-in substitute interpretive system whereby readers may, if they so desire—and we do all so desire, to avoid knowing about history!—rewrite the text in more inoffensive ways. The two strategies of containment which are constructed for this purpose are clearly both on some level ideologies, and they might well be examined as such. In the present instance, however, they are narrative projections of ideology, narrative strategies that have as their common aim the rewriting of a narrative whose dynamics might otherwise elude categories of the ethical and of the individual subject. Yet, as we have seen, the contents of *Lord Jim* are themselves heterogeneous, and are drawn from the seemingly unrelated dimen-

48. Holland, *Dynamics,* pp. 289–301.

sions of the microscopic (reified time, desacralized action) and the macroscopic (history and praxis). It is therefore appropriate that not one, but two distinct strategies of containment should be evolved in order to manage these two distinct sources of scandal and of ideological challenge.

The two strategies in question will therefore take forms we will characterize as metaphysical and melodramatic respectively; they aim to recontain the content of the events of Jim's narrative by locating "responsible parties" and assigning guilt. We have indeed already discussed the first of these strategies, the metaphysical, which projects a proto-existential metaphysic by singling out Nature, and in particular the sea—what crushes human life—as that ultimate villain against whom Jim must do anthropomorphic battle to prove himself. Nature in this personalized sense is fundamental if Jim's quest is to remain a matter of courage and fear, rather than that quite different thing we have shown it to be in the preceding section. This is not to say that people do not drown or that the sea is not frightening, but rather that any genuine existentialism would have to unravel itself and if nature is genuinely meaningless, would, in order to be consequent with itself, have painstakingly to undo all those anthropomorphic impressions of some "true horror behind the appalling face of things," "something invisible, a directing spirit of perdition that dwelt within, like a malevolent soul in a detestable body" (19).

But Jim is not destroyed at sea, and to prove oneself in this sense always seems to require a human adversary (see the analogous displacements back from nature to human agency in *The End of the Tether* and *Typhoon*). Thus, if the second part of the novel is to retrieve or ideologically to "resolve" what the first part so implacably laid out in the form of a dilemma, we must have recourse to the rather different strategy of melodrama, where the malevolent agency of Nature is replaced by that of man, in the person of Gentleman Brown.

The problem is the "motivation" of this device: how to imagine and to cause readers to accredit a motive for this remorseless pursuit of Jim at the very moment of his triumph? But as we showed in Chapter 4, such a motivation is available everywhere in late nineteenth-century ideology, devised initially as a psychological explanation of the revolt of mobs, but also for the revolutionary

vocation of disaffected intellectuals, and then more largely applied
to the presentation of daily life generally, and to the discrediting of
the political impulse in particular: this is, of course, the concept of
ressentiment, of which Conrad is by way of being the epic poet.
There is not a single work of his (although here too *Nostromo* is
uniquely privileged and almost an exception) in which the typical,
gratuitously malevolent bearer of this diseased passion does not lie
in wait for the innocent and unsuspecting.[49] Indeed, the great political novels, *Under Western Eyes* and *The Secret Agent*—as powerful counterrevolutionary tracts in their own ways as the masterpieces of Dostoyevsky or Orwell—emit the message of *ressentiment*
(and its role as the true source of all revolutionary vocation) so
obsessively that they betray their own inner dynamic: the concept
of *ressentiment* being, as I have observed earlier, itself the product
of the feeling in question.

This is not to say that Gentleman Brown is not a powerful figure,
although even his single-minded nihilistic power depends on a
rather complicated character system, whereby it is the lesser
homme de ressentiment, Cornelius, who draws off everything that
is grotesque about this passion to himself, thus leaving a purer
vision of evil and energy for Jim's worthier and more absolute
adversary:

> The others were merely vulgar and greedy brutes, but he seemed
> moved by some complex intention. He would rob a man as if only to
> demonstrate his poor opinion of the the creature. [214–
> 215]   There was in the broken, violent speech of that man, unveil-
> ing before me his thoughts with the very hand of Death upon his
> throat, an undisguised ruthlessness of purpose, a strange vengeful
> attitude towards his own past, and a blind belief in the righteousness
> of his will against all mankind, something of that feeling which could
> induce the leader of a horde of wandering cut-throats to call himself
> proudly the Scourge of God. [225]   I had to bear the sunken
> glare of his fierce crow-footed eyes, . . . reflecting how much certain
> forms of evil are akin to madness, derived from intense egoism, in-

49. I must therefore feel that Fleischman's assertion—"in the entire body of Conrad's work, in fact, the only examples of radical evil are Gentleman Brown in *Lord
Jim* and the weird trio of *Victory*" (*Conrad's Politics,* p. 28)—is singularly inexact.
On the other hand, it is clear that to recognize the obsessive motif of *ressentiment*
would unavoidably place the ideology of "organicism" that accompanies it in a new
and less favorable light.

flamed by resistance, tearing the soul to pieces, and giving factitious vigor to the body. [209]

In such powerful rhetoric, we can sense something of the violent displacement that must be done to narrative and to its *actants* to produce what we may call the effect of melodrama, and to conjure up the mythic feeling of the villain—so archaic and historically ugly a feeling, which has its genealogy deep in immemorial lynchings and pogroms, in the expulsion of the scapegoat and the ritual curse. It is mind-cleansing to juxtapose with this self-perpetuating vision of evil the great Brechtian lines on the mask of the Japanese demon, with its swollen veins and hideous grimace

> all betokening
> What an exhausting effort it takes
> To be evil.

VII

As we have already suggested, *Nostromo* is a dialectical intensification and transformation of the narrative apparatus of *Lord Jim,* and it is well, in conclusion, having shown all the things which Conrad preferred not to see, to show what he could see in a demanding and ambitious effort of the social and historical imagination. The point is less a matter of Conrad's personal development between 1900 and 1904 than it is a demonstration of structural transformations, and the way in which analogous materials are utterly metamorphosed when they are wrenched from the realm and categories of the individual subject to the new perspective of those of collective destiny.

As for the basic masking device, the fundamental "strategy of containment"—what in *Nostromo* performs the function of the sea in Conrad's other novels, motivating and legitimizing the boundary which seals off all of the social totality this narrative model can deal with—it would seem plausible to search for this framing mechanism horizontally rather than vertically, in the situation of English-speaking or at least foreign characters foregrounded against an indeterminate background of the Latin American "substance" (to use the Hegelian term). Today, when the Third World, and in particular Latin America, speaks in its own literary and political voice, we are better placed to appreciate everything which is offensive and caricatural about Conrad's representation of the politics and the people of Costaguana.[50] Indeed, the ideological interference here is threefold and layered. At the most general level, we have the classic "Anglo" picture of a Latin "race," lazy, shiftless, and the like, to which political order and economic progress must be "brought" from the outside. This attitude is more complex than simple racism in that it is invested with considerable fantasy-attraction and provides material for the practice of the idyll (think, say, of Lawrence's *Plumed Serpent*) at the same time that it accredits the good opinion the industrial West has of itself. Whatever the ambiguities of this perspective, however, it is certainly a thought of the "Other," and it is inconceivable that a Latin American novelist could without a Hegelian "Unhappy Consciousness" focus his material in this way, even if the facts and the anecdotes remained the same.

On a second level, there are, of course, Conrad's political reflections and attitudes proper; and he makes it possible for the reader to overlook the identification of his positive figures among the locals—the so-called Blancos—with the aristocratic party, and that of the evil Monteros with the mestizos: the most explicit statement about Monterist politics is its definition as "Caesarism: the imperial rule based on the direct popular vote" (335). But *Nostromo* is not a political novel in the sense in which it would allow these two political ideals to fight it out on their own terms (the ultimate model of that kind of political art remains, as Hegel showed us, *Antigone*); rather, Conrad's own political attitudes are presupposed, and rhetorically reinforced by ethical and melodramatic markers (the Blancos are good, the Monteristas evil).

Such markers then predictably lead us to the third and deepest ideological level, which is none other than, once again, the theory of *ressentiment;* and the Montero brothers are described, and their motives explained, in terms that are the commonplaces of all the

---

50. See Jean Franco, "The Limits of the Liberal Imagination," in *Point of contact/Punto di contacto* No. 1 (1979), pp. 4–16. Eagleton's remark, on the use of foreign material in Conrad such that "alien experience is allowed radically to question civilised structures which in turn gain fresh validation from the encounter" (Terry Eagleton, *Exiles and Emigrés* [New York; Schocken, 1970], p. 31) might well be further extended here.

great counterrevolutionary nineteenth-century historians. But the resonance of this motif in *Nostromo* is quite different from its effects on the structure of *Lord Jim,* where it transformed a modernist text into the precursor of a mass cultural one (a best-selling subgenre). We will assume, in any case, that the theory and vision of *ressentiment* will necessarily form the outer limit of any political or historical reflection conceived by Conrad: if this is so, then *Nostromo* is structurally organized to minimize its effects, for here *ressentiment* is itself recontained and thrust into the frame or border of the text proper, with the result that Conrad's principal and foregrounded narrative—the story of all the major (European or North American) characters, as it is played out against the mere backdrop or pretext of this particular banana republic—can develop and produce itself without reappropriation by what we have called the strategy of melodrama. When now we add that the metaphysical strategy, the proto-existential evocation of a baleful Nature, is also missing, we may well begin to anticipate a formal transformation of Conrad's narrative line of the greatest interest in illuminating the determinant relationship between ideology and the production of form.

We must stress the analogies with the narrative structure of *Lord Jim* in order to make the differences more visible and striking. The sense of textualization we felt in the first half of *Lord Jim* is less pronounced, since the *hommes-récits* or storytelling epicenters are here withdrawn and the text must function in a third-person voice which is but an uneasy compromise between old and new. Conrad is here premodern in that he has not been able to discover the transpersonal standpoint of, say, Joycean narrative, or even that of Flaubert. Yet the associational, aleatory movement of the text from detail to detail is no less intricate than in *Lord Jim,* and obeys, as we promised, the same fundamental principle of the slow analytic rotation around that central act about which we may fear that interrogated too closely, like the onion that was the symbol of being in the Upanishads, from which layer upon layer was carefully removed, it will prove to bear nothingness at its heart.

This event is at first taken by reader (and text alike) to be the Monterist revolution. A classic textualizing displacement first offers the donkey flight of the hapless Blanco dictator as a mere secondary detail, "told" rather than "shown," and evoked in conversation as a passing example of some quite unrelated topic (23)—only some hundreds of pages later to reactualize this same "event" as an absent sense-datum, the implied cause of a crowd of spectators blocking off from view some object of curiosity in the distance (192). The hold of conventional notions of presence, both physical and narrative, leads us to assume that it is only at this second point in the novel that the event in question "really" happens at last. Yet it would surely be more adequate to suggest that in that sense it never really happens at all, for the initial discursive reference to it—not as scene but as fact or background—dispenses Conrad from having to "render" it in all its lived presence later on. This central event is therefore present/absent in the most classic Derridean fashion, present only in its initial absence, absent when it is supposed to be most intensely present.

Yet this hole at the center of the narrative is itself but an external emblem of the greater one around which the gigantic system of events of the novel pivots as on some invisible axis. *Nostromo* is in other words not really a novel about political upheaval; the latter is itself only the pretext for that most fundamental event of all: the expedition of Decoud and Nostromo to the Great Isabel and the saving of the treasure, which is at one with the founding of the separatist Occidental Republic of Sulaco. On this level, there is no particular mystery about the overall coordinates of the plot (and no structural shift in those coordinates of the type we found in *Lord Jim*): the novel is a virtual textbook working-out of the structuralist dictum that all narrative enacts a passage from Nature to Culture. Indeed, the opening pages evoke the landscape of the gulf, a landscape without people; while the close (excluding the death of Nostromo) celebrates the achieved society of the new republic. In *Lord Jim,* the interrogation of the individual act and possibilities of action led to the projection of a degraded image of "legendary" heroism; here, on the contrary, a similar interrogation would seem to have been able to lift itself to the level of the collective and to generate a narrative production of society itself.

This is achieved, it would seem clear, not by the action of one individual, but by that of two: by a single act that, given its complex historical effectivity, could result only from the combined actions of two heroes, or better still, from their synthesis into some new collective *actant*. From the outset, then, we may suppose the presence of a semic system from which such combinations and syntheses draw their narrative meaning; on the most obvious level, clearly, on the level the most easily recuperable by some form of myth criticism, the new dual *actant* formed by the alliance of Nostromo and Decoud is simply that of body and mind, the man of action and the intellectual, the bearer of a personal, quasi-physical vanity and the lover of the ideal (both in the sense in which Decoud has an overriding *idée fixe*—the separatist republic—and that in which he is inspired" by his love for Antonia). But even admitting the investment of this type of content in the opposition/combination of Nostromo and Decoud, it is very difficult to see how this mythic reunion of body and mind would be enough, semically, to found Society; at best, it could result in a new and unified form of transfigured individual action, so that its supplementary "historical operativity" remains to be derived.

We can begin to do so, I think, by observing how the two figures of Decoud and Nostromo emerge from two different and unequal, largely unrelated groupings of characters and destinies slowly laid out for us by the movement of the text. Decoud, whose French culture and upbringing distance him from the purely "native" figures (as does his name), slowly emerges from the group of characters clustered around Charles Gould and the mine, and conveciently organized by Mrs. Gould's salon. Nostromo, on the other hand, steps forth from the much smaller grouping around old Viola and his Albergo; and our sense of the semiotic importance of this filiation is strengthened by the observation that from the point of view of the plot and its organizational necessities, the story of old Viola is strictly superfluous and must thus presumably obey a deeper necessity.

Yet thus contrasted, these two great lines of the book's character-groupings, that which descends from the mine owner Charles Gould and that which descends from the Italian immigrant and Garabaldino Viola, sort themselves out into an immediately identifiable opposition: they correspond to the two great forces of nineteenth-century history—industrial capitalism, expanding into its imperialist stage, and "popular" (that is, in the strictest sense, neither peasant nor proletarian) revolution of the classic 1848 type, of which the heroic figure of Garibaldi is both the Lenin and the Che, and the only leader of a successful revolution which founds an independent state. That the framed portrait of Garibaldi should preside over the founding of an independent Sulaco clearly opens up a basic space for the political meditation of this novel; for Sulaco was no more the realization of the ideals of 1848 than was the Piedmontese unification of Italy; while to Garibaldi's legendary patronage of the Viola plot, Holroyd, Charles Gould's even more shadowy San Francisco benefactor and capitalist underwriter, stands as a structural opposite and counterweight.

Conrad never went further politically than in this sympathetic portrayal of the nationalist-populist ideal; at the same time, it must be said that he contains and carefully qualifies this pole of his new historical vision, primarily by separating off one genuine Latin (but *European*) revolutionary impulse—the Italian, which is here exotic and foreign—from the indigenous Monterista variety. The phenomenon is akin to Freudian splitting, and we will observe something of this sort at work to complicate and qualify virtually all the terms of this emergent character system. The valorization of the positive term Viola/Garibaldi is in other words permitted only at the price of splitting off the bad double, the Montero brothers, with their "Caesarism," which itself becomes a bad mirror image of Garibaldian populist leadership. At the same time, the association of this supreme political value with the Nostromo motif of the body, vanity, pride, strength, individual action, suggests what will be borne out in a moment when we look at the other pole of the opposition, namely that populism is for Conrad the term for an immanence—some virtual identity of *Leben* and *Wesen,* of contingency and meaning—which is to that degree inaccessible to his own narrative machinery.

This will be clearer when we understand the degree to which Conrad understands capitalism as transcendence. The conventional rhetoric that links capitalism with the bringing of order—incidentally a very old argument for capitalism[51]—goes hand in hand with the sense that it is not a natural growth in countries like Sulaco, and that to the extent that it is artificial, it necessarily embodies an idea and an ideal which one must impose or which remains a moral imperative: something like the final

51. See Albert O. Hirschman, *The Passions and the Interests* (Princeton: Princeton University Press, 1977).

avatar of the "philanthropy" motif. The repeated period word, "sentimentalism"—the inexplicable caprice of people who do things for purely intellectual or philosophical or "altruistic" reasons—resonates this theme, which reaches a kind of climax in the celebration of the banker Holroyd's "imagination":

> To be a millionaire, and such a millionare as Holroyd, is like being eternally young. The audacity of youth reckons upon what it fancies an unlimited time at its disposal; but a millionaire has unlimited means in his hand—which is better. One's time on earth is an uncertain quantity, but about the long reach of millions there is no doubt. The introduction of a pure form of Christianity into this continent is a dream for a youthful enthusiast, and I have been trying to explain to you why Holroyd at fifty-eight is like a man on the threshold of life, and better, too. He's not a missionary, but the San Tome mine holds just that for him. I assure you, in sober truth, that he could not manage to keep this out of a strictly business conference upon the finances of Costaguana he had with Sir John a couple of years ago. Sir John mentioned it with amazement in a letter he wrote to me here, from San Francisco, when on his way home. Upon my word, doctor, things seem to be worth nothing by what they are in themselves. I begin to believe that the only solid thing about them is the spiritual value which everyone discovers in his own form of activity. [265–266]

To Holroyd as disembodied ideal and abstraction thus corresponds the visual image of Garibaldi on Viola's wall—as we have seen, the epitome of an impossible stylistic immanence. It is thus logical that this transcendent pole of the narrative's historical forces should at length embody itself in the concrete character of a man, Decoud, driven by an *idée fixe* and a political vision.

Now, moving from the ultimate opposition which codes the narrative to its concrete articulation in the characters and the local events of the text, we can begin to reconstruct a system analogous to that found operative in *Lord Jim*, but more complex. We will schematically suggest that the opposition of Decoud and Nostromo can be semically designated as that between the Ideal and the Self (this last taken to designate the impossible immanence either of the individual body or of the people): the consequence would then be that our other terms would mark out something like the place of an anti-ideal, or cynicism, and that of a selflessness or devotion:

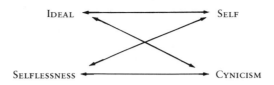

But with these new terms already the appropriate characters are given, for the women—Antonia as Decoud's political allegory and muse ("Antonia, gigantic and lovely like an allegorical statue, looking on with scornful eyes at his weakness": p. 409), and behind her Mrs. Gould—are evidently assigned the relatively ungrateful function of selfless devotion to the male actors; while the generation by the system of the new term of cynicism helps to account for the otherwise inexplicable emergence of a new character—Dr. Monygham—after the Decoud-Nostromo expedition, and the way in which this apparent narrative afterthought ends up dominating the final section of the novel, a disproportion which purists about organization and narrative unity would otherwise have to set down as a flaw. Monygham is almost literally generated by this text, produced, thrown up by it as a new permutation of its textual system: more than that, the neutral term which results from the combination of his cynical wisdom and experience with the selfless devotion of the women—the union of the two contradictories, a function assumed by Marlow in the earlier novel—is precisely the place of the Witness: the place of nonaction from which, across the system, the ideal action or complex term—union of Ideal and Self, of Decoud and Nostromo—can be narratively observed. (The process of "splitting" is also visible in this term at least to the degree that the bad or negative form of cynicism is simple mindlessness, a slot filled by that other important, but purely formal historical witness, Captain Mitchell.)

Now we can begin to sort out other dimensions of the novel. For one thing, the place of real history—the fallen history of Costaguana, of what we have hitherto termed the Latin American "substance," as externalized into Otherness by the Anglo vision—is given in the union of Self and Cynicism, the "nightmare of history" as one long uninterrupted and mindless succession of contingent events. The other semic combination, that of Ideal and Selflessness, the ideal union of Decoud and Antonia, presided over by the union of Gould and Mrs. Gould, can only be some imaginary vision of marriage as the ultimate private realm which lies over against the fallen public realm of history and whose semic valorization here may go some distance toward explaining the unreality, and the purely symbolic function, of Conrad's women.

Such a scheme would also seem to provide at least a starting point for a psychoanalytic interpretation of this writer, insofar as the term of History combines within it a son slain by a father figure (Nostromo) and a man tortured and left lame (Dr. Monygham). This semic space is therefore clearly that of castration, while its structural counterpart, which includes both Decoud and Mrs. Gould, and which is the place of love, marriage, and presumably also sexual experience, is dominated by the quite different affective experience of the fainting spell, or of extinction.

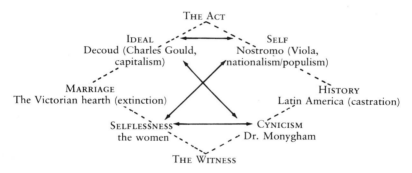

THE ACT

IDEAL
Decoud (Charles Gould, capitalism)

SELF
Nostromo (Viola, nationalism/populism)

MARRIAGE
The Victorian hearth (extinction)

HISTORY
Latin America (castration)

SELFLESSNESS
the women

CYNICISM
Dr. Monygham

THE WITNESS

Yet such a scheme explains everything but the essential, namely the dynamics of the ideal act itself, of the impossible synthesis or complex term, that foundation or new inauguration of society which will lift us out of fallen history (and perhaps incorporate much that is ideal about Victorian marriage as well).

As with *Lord Jim*, it is less a question of filling in the slot of this empty act than of being able to imagine it in the first place. The romance pages of *Lord Jim* supposed, however, that this effort of imagination was unproblematical, and thereby forfeited their status as a literary text; *Nostromo* will keep faith with this impossibility and insist to the end on everything problematical about the act that makes for genuine historical change. Indeed, the two great slogans of the book's closing pages both insist in their own way on the impossibility of envisioning such change, on the nature of genuine History, the historical Event which marks a decisive shift from one state of things (fallen nature) to another (genuine society), not as an event that can be narrated, but rather as an aporia around which the narrative must turn, never fully incorporating it into its own structure. This is clearly the sense of Nostromo's warning to himself: "Grow rich slowly!" Such a watchword offers all the paradoxes and puzzles of diachronic thinking: at what "point in time" do the minute accretions of coin, dropping one upon the other like the slow dripping of a faucet, suddenly become riches? How in the measurable world is time ultimately possible? How do things come into being, how can they possibly "happen"?

But the phrase that worries Mrs. Gould is no less scandalous and paradoxical for the mind, even though this particular aporia is rather of a synchronic type: namely the impossibility of getting into your mind what can be meant by "material interests." The whole drama of value and abstraction is concentrated in this antithetical phrase, in which the ideal sentimentalism of the capitalist dynamic is suddenly and brutally demystified. If it is "material," then it is immanent in our earlier sense, and at one with simple selfishness and egoism; if it can be isolated as an "interest," that is an abstractable value, then it is no longer material in that earlier sense but transcendent. But to be able to conceive of the specificity of capitalism would be to hold both these incommensurable and irreconcilable things in your mind at once, in the unity of a single impossible thought, whose meaningless name Mrs. Gould finds herself condemned over and over to murmur.

So the act happens—capitalism arrives in Sulaco—even though it is impossible. Nowhere is this more vivid than in that disjunction between the movement of history and its enactment by individual subjects which is *Nostromo*'s ultimate narrative message. For even on this level, it turns out that the act, the event, never happened: but in a very different way than in the framework of *Lord Jim*'s existential analytic. Here the central act, the heroic expedition of Decoud and Nostromo, which ought to have grounded their status as heroes, as ultimate legendary forms of the individual subject, is appropriated by collective history, in which it also exists, but in a very different way, as the founding of institutions. In classical Sartrean language, we can say that the historical act of Decoud and

Nostromo has been alienated and stolen from them even before they achieve it; or in more Hegelian terminology, their action can be characterized as that of structurally ephemeral mediation. They stand indeed in the Weberian place of the "vanishing mediator," of the prophetic or charismatic individual term whose historical but transindividual function, according to the "ruse of history," is merely to enable the coming into being after him of a new type of collectivity. Decoud's and Nostromo's is the moment of the action of the individual subject, but one which is at once reabsorbed by the very stability and transindividuality of the institutions it is necessary to found. History uses their individual passions and values as its unwitting instruments for the construction of a new institutional space in which they fail to recognize themselves or their actions and from which they can only, either slowly or violently, be effaced, remnants of another age—not, this time, the myth of origins and the golden age of the giants, but rather the moment of the mediatory transition to another social form, a form as degraded, as transindividual, as non-narratable, as the one that preceded it, although in it own quite different way. So this great historical novel finally achieves its end by unraveling its own means of expression, "rendering" History by its thoroughgoing demonstration of the impossibility of narrating this unthinkable dimension of collective reality, systematically undermining the individual categories of storytelling in order to project, beyond the stories it must continue to tell, the concept of a process beyond storytelling.

This is, I think, the concrete historical content of the dialectic between action and record which Edward Said's reading of *Nostromo* demonstrates: a search for events and their origins, which coming up short against a well-nigh Althusserian/Derridean realization of their status as "always-already-begun," suddenly finds itself deflected into autoreferentiality, and begins to foreground this textual and representational search as a process: "Instead of mimetically authoring a new world, *Nostromo* turns back to its beginning as a novel, to the fictional, illusory assumption of reality: in thus overturning the confident edifice that novels normally construct *Nostromo* reveals itself to be no more than a *record* of novelistic self-reflection."[52] But unlike much of later modernism, this move-

52. Said, *Beginnings*, p. 137.

ment of autoreferentiality is in Conrad neither gratuitous nor complacent. The resonance of his book springs from a kind of un-
planned harmony between this textual dynamic and its specific
historical content: the emergence of capitalism as just such an
always-already-begun dynamic, as the supreme and privileged mystery of a synchronic system which, once in place, discredits the
attempts of "linear" history or the habits of the diachronic mind to
conceive of its beginnings. *Nostromo* is thus ultimately, if you like,
no longer a political or historical novel, no longer a realistic representation of history; yet in the very movement in which it represses
such content and seeks to demonstrate the impossibility of such
representation, by a wondrous dialectical transfer the historical
"object" itself becomes inscribed in the very form.

After the peculiar heterogeneity of the moment of Conrad, a high
modernism is set in place which it is not the object of this book to
consider. The perfected poetic apparatus of high modernism represses History just as successfully as the perfected narrative apparatus of high realism did the random heterogeneity of the as yet
uncentered subject. At that point, however, the political, no longer
visible in the high modernist texts, any more than in the everyday
world of appearance of bourgeois life, and relentlessly driven underground by accumulated reification, has at last become a genuine
Unconscious.

6

CONCLUSION:
The Dialectic of
Utopia and Ideology

As in all previous history, whoever emerges as victor still participates in that triumph in which today's rulers march over the prostrate bodies of their victims. As is customary, the spoils are borne aloft in that triumphal parade. These are generally called the cultural heritage. The latter finds a rather distanced observer in the historical materialist. For such cultural riches, as he surveys them, everywhere betray an origin which he cannot but contemplate with horror. They owe their existence, not merely to the toil of the great creators who have produced them, but equally to the anonymous forced labor of the latters' contemporaries. There has never been a document of culture which was not at one and the same time a document of barbarism.

> —Walter Benjamin,
> "Theses on the Philosophy of History," VII

The conception of the political unconscious developed in the preceding pages has tended to distance itself, at certain strategic moments, from those implacably polemic and demystifying procedures traditionally associated with the Marxist practice of ideological analysis. It is now time to confront the latter directly and to spell out such modifications in more detail. The most influential lesson of Marx—the one which ranges him alongside Freud and Nietzsche as one of the great negative diagnosticians of contemporary culture and social life—has, of course, rightly been taken to be the lesson of false consciousness, of class bias and ideological programming, the lesson of the structural limits of the values and attitudes of particular social classes, or in other words of the constitutive relationship between the praxis of such groups and what they conceptualize as value or desire and project in the form of culture.

In a splendidly argued confrontation with Marxism, the anthropologist Marshall Sahlins has attempted to demonstrate that it is by its very philosophical structure locked into an approach to culture which must thus remain functional or instrumental in the broadest sense.[1] Given the Marxian orientation toward the reading or demystification of superstructures in terms of their base, or relations of production, even the most sophisticated Marxian analyses of cultural texts must, according to Sahlins, necessarily always presuppose a certain structural functionality about culture: the latter will always "ultimately" (if not far more immediately) be grasped as the instrument, witting or unwitting, of class domination, legitimation, and social mystification. Sahlins is untroubled by the paradox that Marx himself reserved his most brilliant polemic onslaughts for the classical form taken by an instrumental theory of culture in his own time, namely utilitarianism; nor does Sahlins seem aware that his own targets—economism, technological determinism, the primacy of the forces of production—are also those that have been subjected to powerful critiques by a range of contemporary Marxisms which regard them as deviations from the authentic Marxist spirit. It may, however, readily be admitted that what he calls the instrumentalization of culture is a temptation or tendency within all Marxisms, without, for all that, being a necessary and fatal consequence.

Before offering a perspective in which this particular problem becomes a false one, we must clarify the troubled position of the individual subject within it. We suggested in our opening chapter that most forms of contemporary criticism tend, as toward their ideal, toward a model of immanence: on the theoretical level that concerns us here, this is to say that the phenomenological ideal—that of some ideal unity of consciousness or thinking and experience or the "objective" fact—continues to dominate modern thought even where phenomenology as such is explicitly repudiated.[2] Even the Freudian model of the unconscious, which has

---

1. Marshall Sahlins, *Culture and Practical Reason* (Chicago: University of Chicago Press, 1976).

2. As far as literary criticism is concerned, it is often easier to denounce this mirage of immanence on the level of theory than to resist its hold on the level of

been exemplary in our own proposal of a properly political unconscious here, is everywhere subverted by the neo-Freudian nostalgia
for some ultimate moment of *cure,* in which the dynamics of the
unconscious proper rise to the light of day and of consciousness and
are somehow "integrated" in an active lucidity about ourselves and
the determinations of our desires and our behavior. But the cure in
that sense is a myth, as is the equivalent mirage within a Marxian
ideological analysis: namely, the vision of a moment in which the
individual subject would be somehow fully conscious of his or her
determination by class and would be able to square the circle of
ideological conditioning by sheer lucidity and the taking of thought.
But in the Marxian system, only a collective unity—whether that of
a particular class, the proletariat, or of its "organ of consciousness," the revolutionary party—can achieve this transparency; the
individual subject is always positioned within the social totality
(and this is the sense of Althusser's insistence on the *permanence* of
ideology).

What this impossibility of immanence means in practice is that
the dialectical reversal must always involve a painful "decentering"
of the consciousness of the individual subject, whom it confronts
with a determination (whether of the Freudian or the political unconscious) that must necessarily be felt as extrinsic or external to

---

pratical exegesis. An instructive and influential example of this contradiction may be
found in the contemporary reaction against an "old-fashioned" Lukácsean "content
analysis" (as documented in the important Cluny colloquium held by *La Nouvelle
Critique* in April, 1970, and published as *Littérature et idéologies*): the codification
of a whole new alternate method—which explores the inscription of ideology in an
ensemble of purely formal categories, such as representation, narrative closure, the
organization around the centered subject, or the illusion of presence—is generally
associated with the *Tel quel* and *Screen* groups, and also, in a different way, with the
work of Jacques Derrida (see in particular "Hors Livre," in *La Dissémination* [Paris:
Seuil, 1972], pp. 9–67). The unmasking of such categories and their ideological
consequences is then achieved in the name of newer aesthetic, psychoanalytic, and
moral values variously termed heterogeneity, dissemination, discontinuity, schizo-
phrenia, and *écriture,* that is, in the name of explicitly antiimmanent (but also antitranscendent) concepts. Yet the impulse behind the critical practice thereby theorized
is often precisely an immanent one, which brackets the historical situations in which
texts are effective and insists that ideological positions can be identified by the
identification of inner-textual or purely formal features. Such an approach is thereby
able to confine its work to individual printed texts, and projects the ahistorical view
that the formal features in question always and everywhere bear the same ideological
charge. Paradoxically, then, the extrinsic, "contextual" or situational references
repudiated by this system turn out to be precisely what is *heterogeneous* to it.

conscious experience. It would be a mistake to think that anyone ever really learns to live with this ideological "Copernican revolution," any more than the most lucid subjects of psychoanalysis ever really achieve the habit of lucidity and self-knowledge; the approach to the Real is at best fitful, the retreat from it into this or that form of intellectual comfort perpetual. But if this is so, it follows that we must bracket that whole dimension of the critique of the Marxist doctrine of determination by social being which springs from exasperation with this unpleasant reflexivity. In particular, it should be stressed that the process of totalization outlined in our opening chapter offers no way out of this the "labor and suffering of the negative," but must necessarily be accompanied by it, if the process is to be authentically realized.

Once this unavoidable experiential accompaniment of the dialectic is granted, however, the theoretical problem of interpretive alternatives to an instrumental or functional theory of culture may more adequately be raised. That such alternatives are at least abstractly conceivable may be demonstrated by Paul Ricoeur's seminal reflections on the dual nature of the hermeneutic process:

> At one pole, hermeneutics is understood as the manifestation and restoration of a meaning addressed to me in the manner of a message, a proclamation, or as is sometimes said, a kerygma; according to the other pole, it is understood as a demystification, as a reduction of illusion. . . . The situation in which language finds itself today comprises this double possibility, this double solicitation and urgency: on the one hand, to purify discourse of its excrescences, liquidate the idols, go from drunkenness to sobriety, realize our state of poverty once and for all; on the other hand, to use the most "nihilistic," destructive, iconoclastic movement so as to *let speak* what once, what each time, was *said,* when meaning appeared anew, when meaning was at its fullest. Hermeneutics seems to me to be animated by this double motivation: willingness to suspect, willingness to listen: vow of rigor, vow of obedience. In our time we have not finished doing away with *idols* and we have barely begun to listen to *symbols.*[3]

It is unnecessary to underscore the obvious, namely the origins of Ricoeur's thought and figures in the tradition of religious exegesis

3. Paul Ricoeur, *Freud and Philosophy,* trans. D. Savage (New Haven: Yale, 1970), p. 27.

and Christian historicism. The limits of Ricoeur's formulation are, however, not specifically theological ones, but are attributable to the persistence of categories of the individual subject: specifically, his conception of "positive" meaning as a kerygma or interpellation (retained in Althusser's theory of ideology[4]) is modeled on the act of communication between individual subjects, and cannot therefore be appropriated as such for any view of meaning as a collective process.

As far as the religious framework of Ricoeur's account is concerned, I have throughout the present work implied what I have suggested explicitly elsewhere, that any comparison of Marxism with religion is a two-way street, in which the former is not necessarily discredited by its association with the latter. On the contrary, such a comparison may also function to rewrite certain religious concepts—most notably Christian historicism and the "concept" of providence, but also the pretheological systems of primitive magic—as anticipatory foreshadowings of historical materialism within precapitalist social formations in which scientific thinking is unavailable as such. Marx's own notion of the so-called Asiatic mode of production (or "Oriental despotism") is the very locus for such reinterpretation of religious categories, as we will see below.

Meanwhile, the historically original form of the negative dialectic in Marxism—whether ideology is in it grasped as mere "false consciousness," or, more comprehensively, as structural limitation—should not be allowed to overshadow the presence in the Marxian tradition of a whole series of equivalents to Ricoeur's doctrine of meaning or positive hermeneutic. Ernst Bloch's ideal of hope or of the Utopian impulse; Mikhail Bakhtin's notion of the dialogical as a rupture of the one-dimensional text of bourgeois narrative, as a carnivalesque dispersal of the hegemonic order of a dominant culture; the Frankfurt School's conception of strong memory as the trace of gratification, of the revolutionary power of that *promesse de bonheur* most immediately inscribed in the aesthetic text: all these formulations hint at a variety of options for articulating a properly Marxian version of meaning beyond the purely ideological.

Yet we have also suggested, in our discussion of Northrop Frye's

---

4. See Louis Althusser, "Ideological State Apparatuses," in *Lenin and Philosophy*, trans. Ben Brewster, (New York: Monthly Review, 1971), pp. 170–177.

system in Chapter 1, that even within an ostensibly religious framework such varied options can be measured against the standard of the medieval system of four levels, which helped us to distinguish the resonance of the "moral" level—that of the individual soul, or of the libidinal Utopia of the individual body—from that ultimate and logically prior level traditionally termed the "anagogical," in which even such individual visions of Utopian transfiguration are rewritten in terms of the collective, of the destiny of the human race. Such a distinction allows us to spell out the priority, within the Marxist tradition, of a "positive hermeneutic" based on social class from those still limited by anarchist categories of the individual subject and individual experience. The concept of class is thus the space in which, if anywhere, a Marxian version of the hermeneutics of meaning, of some noninstrumental conception of culture, may be tested, particularly insofar as it is from this same concept of social class that the strongest form of a Marxian "negative hermeneutic"—of the class character and functionality of ideology as such—also derives.

Such a demonstration might be staged under a reversal of Walter Benjamin's great dictum that "there is no document of civilization which is not at one and the same time a document of barbarism," and would seek to argue the proposition that the effectively ideological is also, at the same time, necessarily Utopian. What is logically paradoxical about such a proposition can be understood, if not "resolved," by considering the conceptual limits imposed on our thinking and our language by categories that we have had frequent enough occasion to unmask in the preceding pages, namely those of the ethical code of good and evil, in which even our own terminology of "positive" and "negative" remains unavoidably imprisoned. We have suggested that the vocation of the dialectic lies in the transcendence of this opposition toward some collective logic "beyond good and evil," while noting that the language of the classics of dialectical thought has historically failed to overcome this opposition, which it can only neutralize by reflexive play across these categories. Nor is this particularly surprising, if we take dialectical thought to be the anticipation of the logic of a collectivity which has not yet come into being. In this sense, to project an imperative to thought in which the ideological would be grasped as somehow at one with the Utopian, and the Utopian at one with the ideological, is to formulate a question to which a collective dialectic is the only conceivable answer.

Yet at a lower and more practical level of cultural analysis this proposition is perhaps somewhat less paradoxical in its consequences, and may initially be argued in terms of a manipulatory theory of culture. Such theories, which are strongest in areas like the study of the media and mass culture in contemporary society, must otherwise rest on a peculiarly unconvincing notion of the psychology of the viewer, as some inert and passive material on which the manipulatory operation works. Yet it does not take much reflection to see that a process of compensatory exchange must be involved here, in which the henceforth manipulated viewer is offered specific gratifications in return for his or her consent to passivity. In other words, if the ideological function of mass culture is understood as a process whereby otherwise dangerous and protopolitical impulses are "managed" and defused, rechanneled and offered spurious objects, then some preliminary step must also be theorized in which these same impulses—the raw material upon which the process works—are initially awakened within the very text that seeks to still them. If the function of the mass cultural text is meanwhile seen rather as the production of false consciousness and the symbolic reaffirmation of this or that legitimizing strategy, even this process cannot be grasped as one of sheer violence (the theory of hegemony is explicitly distinguished from control by brute force) nor as one inscribing the appropriate attitudes upon a blank slate, but must necessarily involve a complex strategy of rhetorical persuasion in which substantial incentives are offered for ideological adherence. We will say that such incentives, as well as the impulses to be managed by the mass cultural text, are necessarily Utopian in nature. Ernst Bloch's luminous recovery of the Utopian impulses at work in that most degraded of all mass cultural texts, advertising slogans—visions of external life, of the transfigured body, of preternatural sexual gratification—may serve as the model for an analysis of the dependence of the crudest forms of manipulation on the oldest Utopian longings of humankind.[5] As for the influential Adorno-Horkheimer denunciation of the "culture industry," this

5. Ernst Bloch, *Das Prinzip Hoffnung* (Frankfurt: Suhrkamp, 1959), pp. 395–409.

same Utopian hermeneutic—implicit in their system as well—is in their *Dialectic of Enlightenment* obscured by an embattled commitment to high culture; yet it has not sufficiently been noticed that it has been displaced to the succeeding chapter of that work,[6] where a similar, yet even more difficult analysis is undertaken, in which one of the ugliest of all human passions, antisemitism, is shown to be profoundly Utopian in character, as a form of cultural envy which is at the same time a repressed recognition of the Utopian impulse.

Still, such analyses, methodologically suggestive though they are, do not go far enough along the lines proposed above. In particular, they depend on an initial separation between means and ends—between Utopian gratification and ideological manipulation—which might well serve as evidence for the opposite of what was to have been demonstrated, and might be invoked to deny the profound identity between these two dimensions of the cultural text. It is possible, indeed, that such a separation springs objectively from the peculiar structure of the mass cultural texts themselves; and that culture proper, by which we may understand the "organic" culture of older societies fully as much as the "high" culture of the present day,[7] may be expected to embody such identity in a rather different form.

We must therefore return to the "strong" form of the problem, and to the class terms in which we began by posing it. Its traditional Marxist formulation would then run as follows: how is it possible for a cultural text which fulfills a demonstrably ideological function, as a hegemonic work whose formal categories as well as its content secure the legitimation of this or that form of class domination—how is it possible for such a text to embody a properly Utopian impulse, or to resonate a universal value inconsistent with the narrower limits of class privilege which inform its more immediate ideological vocation? The dilemma is intensified when we deny ourselves, as we just have, the solution of a coexistence of

---

6. Max Horkheimer and Theodor W. Adorno, *Dialectic of Enlightenment*, trans. J. Cumming, (New York: Herder & Herder, 1972), pp. 168–208.

7. In "Reification and Utopia in Mass Culture" (*Social Text* No. 1, [1979] pp. 130–148), I suggest, however, that it may well be more adequate to study contemporary "high culture" (that is to say, modernism) as part of a larger cultural unity in which mass culture stands as its inseparable dialectical counterpole.

different functions, as when, for instance, it is suggested that the greatness of a given writer may be separated from his deplorable opinions, and is achieved in spite of them or even against them. Such a separation is possible only for a world-view—liberalism—in which the political and the ideological are mere secondary or "public" adjuncts to the content of a real "private" life, which alone is authentic and genuine. It is not possible for any world-view—whether conservative or radical and revolutionary—that takes politics seriously.

There can, I think, be only one consequent "solution" to the problem thus posed: it is the proposition that *all* class consciousness—or in other words, all ideology in the strongest sense, including the most exclusive forms of ruling-class consciousness just as much as that of oppositional or oppressed classes—is in its very nature Utopian. This proposition rests on a specific analysis of the dynamics of class consciousness which can only briefly be summarized here,[8] and whose informing idea grasps the emergence of class consciousness as such (what in Hegelian language is sometimes called the emergence of a class-for-itself, as opposed to the merely potential class-in-itself of the positioning of a social group within the economic structure) as a result of the struggle between groups or classes. According to this analysis, the prior moment of class consciousness is that of the oppressed classes (whose structural identity—whether a peasantry, slaves, serfs, or a genuine proletariat—evidently derives from the mode of production). On such a view, those who must work and produce surplus value for others will necessarily grasp their own solidarity—initially, in the unarticulated form of rage, helplessness, victimization, oppression by a common enemy—*before* the dominant or ruling class has any particular incentive for doing so. Indeed, it is the glimpse of such

8. See *Marxism and Form*, pp. 376–390; and the related reflections in "Class and Allegory in Contemporary Mass Culture: *Dog Day Afternoon* as a Political Film," *College English*, Vol. 38, No. 7 (March, 1977), reprinted in *Screen Education*, No. 30 (Spring, 1979). These formulations draw on Ralf Dahrendorf, *Class and Class Conflict in Industrial Society* (Palo Alto: Stanford University Press, 1959), pp. 280–289; on E. P. Thompson, *The Making of the English Working Classes* (New York: Vintage, 1966), Preface (but see also his "Eighteenth Century English Society: Class Struggle without Class?" *Social History*, 3 [May, 1978]; and *The Poverty of Theory* [London: Merlin, 1979], pp. 298ff.); and finally on Jean-Paul Sartre, *Critique of Dialectical Reason*, trans. by A. Sheridan-Smith (London: New Left Books, 1976), esp. pp. 363–404, on the "fused group."

290 / The Political Unconscious

sullen resistance, and the sense of the nascent political dangers of such potential unification of the laboring population, which generates the mirror image of class solidarity among the ruling groups (or the possessors of the means of production). This suggests, to use another Hegelian formula, that the *truth* of ruling-class consciousness (that is, of hegemonic ideology and cultural production) is to be found in working-class consciousness. It suggests, even more strongly, that the index of all class consciousness is to be found not in the latter's "contents" or ideological motifs, but first and foremost in the dawning sense of solidarity with other members of a particular group or class, whether the latter happen to be your fellow landowners, those who enjoy structural privileges linked to your own, or, on the contrary, fellow workers and producers, slaves, serfs, or peasants. Only an ethical politics, linked to those ethical categories we have often had occasion to criticize and to deconstruct in the preceding pages, will feel the need to "prove" that one of these forms of class consciousness is good or positive and the other reprehensible or wicked: on the grounds, for example, that working-class consciousness is potentially more universal than ruling-class consciousness, or that the latter is essentially linked to violence and repression. It is unnecessary to argue these quite correct propositions; ideological commitment is not first and foremost a matter of moral choice but of the taking of sides in a struggle between embattled groups. In a fragmented social life—that is, essentially in all class societies—the political thrust of the struggle of all groups against each other can never be immediately universal but must always necessarily be focused on the class enemy. Even in preclass society (what is called tribal or segmentary society, or in the Marxian tradition, primitive communism), collective consciousness is similarly organized around the perception of what threatens the survival of the group: indeed, the most powerful contemporary vision of "primitive communism," Colin Turnbull's description of pygmy society,[9] suggests that the culture of prepolitical society organizes itself around the external threat of the nonhuman or of nature, in the form of the rain forest, conceived as the overarching spirit of the world.

The preceding analysis entitles us to conclude that all class con-

9. Colin Turnbull, *The Forest People* (New York: Simon and Schuster, 1962).

sciousness of whatever type is Utopian insofar as it expresses the unity of a collectivity; yet it must be added that this proposition is an allegorical one. The achieved collectivity or organic group of whatever kind—oppressors fully as much as oppressed—is Utopian not in itself, but only insofar as all such collectivities are themselves *figures* for the ultimate concrete collective life of an achieved Utopian or classless society. Now we are in a better position to understand how even hegemonic or ruling-class culture and ideology are Utopian, not in spite of their instrumental function to secure and perpetuate class privilege and power, but rather precisely because that function is also in and of itself the affirmation of collective solidarity.

Such a view dictates an enlarged perspective for any Marxist analysis of culture, which can no longer be content with its demystifying vocation to unmask and to demonstrate the ways in which a cultural artifact fulfills a specific ideological mission, in legitimating a given power structure, in perpetuating and reproducing the latter, and in generating specific forms of false consciousness (or ideology in the narrower sense). It must not cease to practice this essentially negative hermeneutic function (which Marxism is virtually the only current critical method to assume today) but must also seek, through and beyond this demonstration of the instrumental function of a given cultural object, to project its simultaneously Utopian power as the symbolic affirmation of a specific historical and class form of collective unity.[10] This is a unified perspective and not the juxtaposition of two options or analytic alternatives: neither is satisfactory in itself. The Marxian "negative hermeneutic," indeed, practiced in isolation, fully justifies Sahlins' complaints about the "mechanical" or purely instrumental nature of certain Marxian

---

10. That this is no mere theoretical or literary-critical issue may be demonstrated by the renewal of interest in the nature and dynamics of fascism, and the urgency of grasping this phenomenon in some more adequate way than as the mere epiphenomenal "false consciousness" of a certain moment of monopoly capitalism. Such attempts, many of them grounded on Reich and seeking to measure the mass "libidinal investment" in fascism constitute the attempt, in our current terminology, to complete an "ideological" analysis of fascism by one which identifies its "Utopian" power and sources. See, for example, Jean-Pierre Faye, *Langages totalitaires* (Paris: Hermann, 1972); Maria Antonietta Macciochi, ed., *Eléments pour une analyse du fascisme*, 2 vols. (Paris: 10/18, 1976); as well as Ernst Bloch's *Erbschaft dieser Zeit* (1935; Frankfurt: Suhrkamp, 1973).

cultural analyses; while the Utopian or "positive hermeneutic," practiced in similar isolation as it is in Frye's doctrine of the collective origins of art, relaxes into the religious or the theological, the edifying and the moralistic, if it is not informed by a sense of the class dynamics of social life and cultural production.

A number of significant objections can be made to this proposal. It will be observed, for one thing, that it amounts to a generalization of Durkheim's theory of religion to cultural production as a whole; and that, if this observation is correct—and I think it is—serious reservations about the "adaptation" of what is essentially a bourgeois and conservative social philosophy must be raised both from a Marxist position and also, as we shall see shortly, from a post-structuralist one.

Durkheim's system—in which a number of currents, from Rousseau to Hegel and Feuerbach, converge—views religion as the symbolic affirmation of the unity of a given tribe, collectivity, or even social formation;[11] religion is thus in Durkheimian sociology the archaic or Utopian counterpart to the latter's analysis of social dissolution and *anomie* in modern society. Evolved in the emergent years of the Third Republic, then threatened in its secular institutions both by the Right and by working-class agitation, Durkheim's theory is clearly a conservative one; like other forms of positivism, it seeks to project a functional defense of the bourgeois parliamentary state. Indeed, to theorize religion as an "eternal" drive by which social divisions are suspended or overcome, to propose religious and ritual practices as a symbolic way of affirming social unity in a society which is objectively class divided, is clearly an ideological operation and an attempt to conjure such divisions away by an appeal to some higher (and imaginary) principle of collective and social unity. To stress the purely *symbolic* character of such unification, however, is to place this theory in a perspective in which religious practices and cultural production—the nostalgia for the collective and the Utopian—are harnessed to ideological ends.

We must, however, ask whether even such a theory as Durkheim's can be said to elude Marshall Sahlins' critique of instru-

---

11. Emile Durkheim, *Les Formes élémentaires de la vie religieuse* (Paris: PUF, 1968), pp. 593–638.

mental conceptions of culture as we have outlined it at the beginning of this chapter. There would, in other words, seem to persist an instrumental or functional view of culture and religion even here, since the symbolic affirmation of the unity of society is understood as playing a vital role in the health, survival and reproduction of the social formation in question. In fact, few enough aesthetic systems proper—apart from those of religious inspiration—have been able to dispense with some hypothesis as to the ultimate social functionality of art; only Heidegger's great vision of the work of art as the momentary glimpse of Being itself comes to mind as a purely secular and nonfunctional model of culture; and even in the case of Heidegger, a theological reading of the late texts is certainly possible, as is a political and social one in which the *polis* (the temple) and the peasant community (the pair of peasant shoes, and the "Feldweg") are invoked in the service of an essentially protofascist celebration of the social order.[12]

I would argue that the problem of a functional or instrumental conception of culture is basically transcended and annulled in the Utopian perspective which is ours here. In a classless society, Rousseau's conception of the festival as the moment in which society celebrates itself and its own unity, Durkheim's analogous conception of the unifying "function" of religion, and our own view of culture as the expression of a properly Utopian or collective impulse are no longer basely functional or instrumental in Sahlins' sense. This is to say, if one likes, that Durkheim's view of religion (which we have expanded to include cultural activity generally) as a symbolic affirmation of human relationships, along with Heidegger's conception of the work of art as a symbolic enactment of the relationship of human beings to the nonhuman, to Nature and to Being, are in this society false and ideological; but they will know their truth and come into their own at the end of what Marx calls prehistory. At that moment, then, the problem of the opposition of the ideological to the Utopian, or the functional-instrumental to the collective, will have become a false one.

In the problematic of post-structuralism, however, the Durkheimian formulations must be the object of a rather different

---

12. See, on Heidegger's relationship to Nazism, M. A. Palmier, ed., *Les Ecrits politiques de Heidegger* (Paris: L'Herne, 1968).

critique, in their reliance on categories of the individual subject.[13] It is clear, indeed, that not merely Durkheim's notion of collective "consciousness," but also the notion of "class consciousness," as it is central in a certain Marxist tradition, rests on an unrigorous and figurative assimilation of the consciousness of the individual subject to the dynamics of groups. The Althusserian and post-structuralist critique of these and other versions of the notion of a "subject of history" may readily be admitted. The alternatives presented by the Althusserians, however—the notion of the individual subject or of social class as an "effect of structure," or that of classes as the *Träger* or *bearers* of an ensemble of structures[14] (a conceptual abstraction analogous to Greimas' notion of the *actant* of narrative as opposed to its surface categories of the narrative "character")— have a purely negative or second-degree critical function, and offer no new conceptual categories. What is wanted here—and it is one of the most urgent tasks for Marxist theory today—is a whole new logic of collective dynamics, with categories that escape the taint of some mere application of terms drawn from individual experience (in that sense, even the concept of praxis remains a suspect one). Suggestive work has been done in this area; I think, for example, of the perhaps ultimately unsatisfactory but still largely undiscussed machinery of Sartre's *Critique of Dialectical Reason*.[15] But the problem has rarely been focused in an adequate way. Until this task is completed, it seems possible to continue to use a Durkheimian or Lukácsean vocabulary of collective consciousness or of the subject of history "under erasure," provided we understand that any such discussion refers, not to the concepts designated by such terms, but to the as yet untheorized object— the collective—to which they make imperfect allusion.

As for the idea that the Durkheimian problematic is alien to Marxism, it should be observed that in Marx's own mature work

13. This is the moment to restore the incriminating sentence strategically omitted from the Durkheim passage which serves as a motto to the present work: "Only a subject which includes all individual subjects would be capable of embracing such an object [society as a totality]" (*Formes élémentaires*, p. 630).

14. See, for example, Nicos Poulantzas, *Political Power and Social Classes*, trans. T. O'Hagan (London: New Left Books, 1973), p. 62.

15. A fuller preliminary discussion of this machinery may be found in *Marxism and Form*, esp. pp. 244–257.

there exists an equivalent to Durkheim's notion of religion, namely the rather Hegelian conception of the Asiatic mode of production formulated in the *Grundrisse:*

> In most of the *Asiatic* land-forms, the *comprehensive unity* standing above all these little communities appears as the higher *proprietor* or as the *sole* proprietor. . . . Because the *unity* is the real proprietor and the real presupposition of communal property . . . the relation of the individual to the *natural* conditions of labor and of repro-duction . . . appears mediated for him through a cession by the total unity—a unity realized in the form of the despot, the father of many communities—to the individual, through the mediation of the particu-lar commune.[16]

It is evident that in such a conception of social unity expressed in the "body of the despot," the problem of the ideological function of religion must be raised more urgently than at any other nexus of the Marxian theory of modes of production, and in a far more concrete and historical way than in Durkheim's ahistorical theory of reli-gion. The literature on this much debated but properly Marxian concept is enormous;[17] and the most consequent contemporary crit-ics of Durkheim from a Marxist standpoint have also been among

16. Karl Marx, *Grundrisse,* trans. Martin Nicolaus (Harmondsworth: Penguin, 1973), pp. 472–473. A pathbreaking effort to rewrite the concept of "Oriental despotism" in terms of a cultural production that would be specific to it may be found in Gilles Deleuze and Félix Guattari, *Anti-Oedipus,* trans. Robert Hurley, Mark Seem, and Helen R. Lane (New York: Viking, 1977), pp. 192–222 (the "barbarism" section of chap. 3, "Savages, Barbarians, and Civilized"). Maurice Godelier has been the most consistent in extending this concept to the study of primitive society (in *Horizon: trajets marxistes en anthropologie* [Paris: Maspéro, 1973]), an extension which has drawn a good deal of theoretical criticism of the type to be found in note 17, below. The cultural fantasies which cluster around the notion of "Oriental despotism" in the political unconscious would seem to correspond to that henceforth archaic moment of a "world empire" displaced by the new organiza-tion of a properly capitalist world system (see Immanuel Wallerstein, *The Modern World System* [New York: Academic, 1974], esp. pp. 16–18, 32–33, 60–62).

17. See in particular Jean Chesneaux, ed., *Sur le "mode de production asiatique"* (Paris: Editions sociales, 1969); Perry Anderson, "The 'Asiatic Mode of Produc-tion,'" in *Lineages of the Absolute State* (London: New Left Books, 1974), pp. 462–549; and Barry Hindess and Paul Hirst, *Pre-Capitalist Modes of Production* (London: Routledge & Kegan Paul, 1975), chap. 4. (The second and third of these titles develop powerful critiques of the concept.)

those concerned to expunge the "pseudoconcept" of the Asiatic mode of production from the Marxist problematic and the Marxist tradition.[18] Yet we have perhaps said enough to show that the *problem* of the symbolic enactment of collective unity is inscribed in that problematic by Marx himself at this point, whatever solution may ultimately be devised for it.

Such is then the general theoretical framework in which I would wish to argue the methodological proposition outlined here: that a Marxist negative hermeneutic, a Marxist practice of ideological analysis proper, must in the practical work of reading and interpretation be exercised *simultaneously* with a Marxist positive hermeneutic, or a decipherment of the Utopian impulses of these same still ideological cultural texts. If the Mannheimian overtones of this dual perspective—ideology and Utopia—remain active enough to offer communicational noise and conceptual interference, then alternative formulations may be proposed, in which an *instrumental* analysis is coordinated with a *collective-associational* or *communal* reading of culture, or in which a *functional* method for describing cultural texts is articulated with an *anticipatory* one.

I would not want to conclude, however, without observing that the issues and dilemmas such a proposal seeks to address greatly transcend the limited field of literary or even cultural criticism. One hesitates to defend the privileged position of cultural criticism in a self-serving way. Still, it is a historical fact that the "structuralist" or textual revolution—as, mainly through Althusserianism, it has transformed a whole range of other disciplines, from political science to anthropology, and from economics to legal and juridical studies—takes as its model a kind of decipherment of which literary and textual criticism is in many ways the strong form. This "revolution," essentially antiempiricist, drives the wedge of the concept of a "text" into the traditional disciplines by extrapolating the notion of "discourse" or "writing" onto objects previously thought to be "realities" or objects in the real world, such as the various levels or

18. Speaking of an analogous view of religion in contemporary Marxist anthropology, Hindess and Hirst observe: "Meillassoux clearly interprets the collective hunt as performing the function of a collective ritual serving to reinforce collective sentiments. Such positions may have a place within a Durkheimian problematic of forms of ritual and social cohesion but it has nothing whatever to do with Marxism" (Hindess and Hirst, *Pre-Capitalist Modes,* p. 55). One is tempted to add: in that case, too bad for Marxism!

instances of a social formation: political power, social class, institutions, and events themselves. When properly used, the concept of the "text" does not, as in garden-variety semiotic practice today, "reduce" these realities to small and manageable written documents of one kind or another, but rather liberates us from the empirical object—whether institution, event, or individual work—by displacing our attention to its *constitution* as an object and its *relationship* to the other objects thus constituted.

The specific problems addressed by literary and cultural interpretation today may thus be expected to present suggestive analogies with the methodological problems of the other social sciences (it being understood that for Marxism, literary and cultural analysis *is* a social science). I would go even further and suggest that the solution outlined in this conclusion to those specifically cultural dilemmas has a good deal of relevance for other fields, where indeed analogous solutions are everywhere the order of the day. I will illustrate these analogies with brief reference to three such areas, namely the problem of the state, the constitution of radical legal studies, and the national question. We have already touched earlier on the first, in which a contemporary political science, particularly in the work of Nicos Poulantzas,[19] has sought to free the study of the state and of state power from the older Marxian view in which the state is little more than an instrument or vehicle of class domination. Such traditional reduction of the political corresponds clearly enough to what we have described above as the instrumental-functional view of ideology. As against this tradition, Poulantzas offers a view of the state as a semi-autonomous arena, which is not the vehicle of any one class but rather a space of class struggle generally. Such a view has evident political consequences, and reflects the immense expansion of the public sector in modern societies, as well as the dynamic of nonhegemonic forces such as pressure groups of unemployed or marginalized people and the more militant work of public-sector trade unions. This vision of the state or the public sector as a collectivity in its own right evidently corresponds to what we have called the Utopian reading or decipherment of the "text" of the state.

---

19. E.g., *Political Power and Social Classes*, chap. 4, "The Relative Autonomy of the Capitalist State."

In radical legal studies, as well as in related areas of the study of public policy such as health care and housing, the problem of the "text" is even more vivid. There is, in the area of the juridical as the Left conceives it today, an open antithesis between a school based on ideological interpretation—which seeks to unmask existing law as the instrument of class domination—and one working in a Utopian perspective—which on the contrary sees its work as the conception and projection of a radically new form of some properly socialist legality that cannot be achieved within the existing institutions, or that is in them merely "emergent." Here too, then, the coordination of the ideological with the Utopian would seem to have a theoretical urgency which is accompanied by very real political and strategic consequences.

Finally, I will take Tom Nairn's pathbreaking book on the national question, *The Break-up of Britain,* as an example of an analogous theoretical solution to that proposed here in an area which remains one of the fundamental ones of contemporary world politics but about which Nairn rightly observes that it stands as "Marxism's great historical failure," blocked precisely by a practice of the traditional Marxian negative hermeneutic for which the national question is a mere ideological epiphenomenon of the economic. "The task of a theory of nationalism . . . must be to embrace both horns of the dilemma. It must be to see the phenomenon as a whole, in a way that rises above these 'positive' and 'negative' sides. . . . [Such] distinctions do not imply the existence of two brands of nationalism, one healthy and one morbid. The point is that, as the most elementary comparative analysis will show, all nationalism is both healthy and morbid. Both progress and regress are inscribed in its genetic code from the start."[20] Nor is this insistence on the simultaneously ideological and Utopian character of the national phenomenon a merely theoretical issue. On the contrary, it is increasingly clear in today's world (if it had ever been in doubt) that a Left which cannot grasp the immense Utopian appeal of nationalism (any more than it can grasp that of religion or of fascism) can scarcely hope to "reappropriate" such collective energies and must effectively doom itself to political impotence.

20. Tom Nairn, *The Break-up of Britain* (London: New Left Books, 1977), pp. 332, 347–348.

But at this point, we must restore Benjamin's identification of culture and barbarism to its proper sequence, as the affirmation not merely of the Utopian dimension of ideological texts, but also and above all of the ideological dimension of all high culture. So it is that a Marxist hermeneutic—the decipherment by historical materialism of the cultural monuments and traces of the past—must come to terms with the certainty that all the works of class history as they have survived and been transmitted to people the various museums, canons and "traditions" of our own time, are all in one way or another profoundly ideological, have all had a vested interest in and a functional relationship to social formations based on violence and exploitation; and that, finally, the restoration of the meaning of the greatest cultural monuments cannot be separated from a passionate and partisan assessment of everything that is oppressive in them and that knows complicity with privilege and class domination, stained with the guilt not merely of culture in particular but of History itself as one long nightmare.

Yet Benjamin's slogan is a hard saying, and not only for liberal and apoliticizing critics of art and literature, for whom it spells the return of class realities and the painful recollection of the dark underside of even the most seemingly innocent and "life-enhancing" masterpieces of the canon. For a certain radicalism also, Benjamin's formulation comes as a rebuke and a warning against the facile reappropriation of the classics as humanistic expressions of this or that historically "progressive" force. It comes, finally, as an appropriate corrective to the doctrine of the political unconscious which has been developed in these pages, reasserting the undiminished power of ideological distortion that persists even within the restored Utopian meaning of cultural artifacts, and reminding us that within the symbolic power of art and culture the will to domination perseveres intact. It is only at this price—that of the simultaneous recognition of the ideological and Utopian functions of the artistic text—that a Marxist cultural study can hope to play its part in political praxis, which remains, of course, what Marxism is all about.

INDEX